CANADIAN AGRICULTURAL TRADE

CANADIAN AGRICULTURAL TRADE:
Disputes, Actions and Prospects

Edited by G. Lermer and
K.K. Klein

University of Calgary Press

ISBN 0-919813-90-9

University of Calgary Press
2500 University Drive N.W.
Calgary, Alberta, Canada T2N 1N4

Canadian Cataloguing in Publication Data

Main entry under title:

Canadian agricultural trade

Includes Bibliographical references
ISBN 0-919813-90-9

1. Produce trade - Canada - Case studies.
I. Lermer, George. II. Klein, K.K. (Kurt K.)
HD9014.C22C35 1990   382'.41'0971   C89-091628-4

Cover design by Rhae Ann Bromley.
Cover photo by R. Heinzen/*SUPERSTOCK*

Printed and bound in Canada

CONTENTS

ACKNOWLEDGEMENTS

The editors gratefully acknowledge the financial support of the Burns Foods Limited Endowment Fund toward the publication of this book and the conference at which many of the papers contained herein were first presented. The conference held at the Lethbridge Lodge—entitled Canadian Agriculture: Facing a New Trading Environment—was one of a series of conferences on public policy and management issues sponsored by the Faculty of Management at the University of Lethbridge.

The outstanding editorial assistance by Kate Chiste provided the necessary impetus for the publication of this manuscript.

G. Lermer
K.K. Klein

CHAPTER 1

PROBLEMS AND PROSPECTS OF CANADIAN AGRICULTURAL TRADE: AN INTRODUCTION

G. Lermer and K. K. Klein

The decade of the 1980s has been one in which the world's agricultural trading system has seriously deteriorated. Protectionism has intensified, with the result that both producers and consumers throughout the world are responding to inaccurate price signals that generally invite excess production and inadequate consumption. At the present time (late 1989) it is impossible to be optimistic about the possible victory of economic rationality over local political interests. Negotiations towards a more liberal trade regime are proceeding, but many governments seem immovably committed to agricultural protection. In the European Community (EC), provisions of the Common Agricultural Policy have resulted in such huge increases in wheat production that the countries in the EC have become the world's second largest exporter of wheat. This contrasts with their traditional position as major importers of wheat. In the United States, trade contingency law continues to hinder Canadian hog exports despite the signing of the Canada-U.S. Free Trade Agreement. In Canada, the federal government persists with the support of supply and import controlling agricultural marketing boards for poultry and dairy products.

In his presidential address to the 1987 annual meeting of the Canadian Agricultural Economics and Farm Management Society, Dr. Brian Oleson noted that "In the current environment the economic concept of gains from trade seems to have been forgotten... Major exporters are now conducting business which is reducing the economic wealth of their nation..." (p. 513). He further observed that the United States "seems content to follow a lose-lose strategy in which the concept of gains to trade is dropped for one of imposing misery on other exporters, particularly the EC" (p. 513). Oleson was referring to events of the mid-1980s, when the United States had engaged the European

1

Community in an agricultural trade war. The fallout from this trade war wreaked havoc not only on bystanders (such as Canada, Australia, New Zealand, and Argentina), but also on the very countries that were doing the fighting.

What is the cause of these apparently irrational economic policies? The high levels of domestic subsidies and restrictive import practices employed by the EC and Japan have stimulated major increases in production in those regions, with a consequent loss of markets for the traditional agricultural exporting countries: the U.S., Canada, Australia, New Zealand, Argentina, and others. The United States government decided in the mid-1980s to fight a trade war to try to regain their former market share. The 1985 Farm Bill in the U.S. was designed to lower international prices for grain products while at the same time maintaining the prices available to U.S. producers. These actions, supplemented by a system of export subsidies for particular grains, called the Export Enhancement Program (EEP), put a great deal of financial pressure on the EC, by making it more expensive to continue the Common Agricultural Policy. The main instrument used by the United States to achieve its objective was to raise the target price and lower the loan rate. Since the loan rate is the price at which the U.S. government buys grains for storage, it is a world trend-setting price.

The agricultural trade war between the U.S. and the EC has repercussions far beyond the boundaries of these two political units. The economic pressure of the trade war on other exporting countries has resulted in a major commitment by affected countries to negotiate agricultural reforms during the current (Uruguay) round of trade negotiations of the General Agreement on Tariffs and Trade (GATT).

In the next chapter, Chase Wilde, Klein and Richter discuss the international trade laws of the GATT, the world's major forum for negotiation and arbitration of international trade. The GATT arose as an interim measure and a by-product of a more encompassing mandate; its weakness in dealing with current trade disputes in agriculture can be traced to exclusions which have been permitted to support domestic agricultural programs. The authors argue that U.S. trade law, while following GATT terminology, does not always retain its spirit; Canadian trade law, they add, is more in keeping with the GATT.

Canada and the United States signed the Canada-U.S. Free Trade Agreement (FTA), which came into effect on 1 January 1989. The establishment of a free trade area in the North American continent raises a fundamental question about how GATT will respond to this bilateral agreement. The two countries hope that the bilateral agreement will represent a model for change in the GATT, and an inducement to countries (especially the EC and Japan) to negotiate downward some of their many trade barriers. Chase Wilde and associates review the provisions of the FTA relating to agriculture, and conclude that the most significant change from the GATT framework is the binding nature of decisions from the bi-national panel established to deal with countervail and anti-dumping cases.

The mechanism for resolving disputes in the U.S.-Canada Free Trade Agreement is so important that the third chapter is devoted entirely to this topic. For Canada, the dispute resolution mechanism is a major benefit of the FTA. It is the instrument that Canada hopes will discourage U.S. protection seekers from turning to the U.S. trade contingency law. Lermer reports that access to the U.S. anti-dump and countervail duties has, in the past decade, been made ever easier. Predictably, rent-seeking special interests exploited the new rules. The U.S. system damages Canada because access is easy, and because decisions are made by political appointees who often respond to political rather than economic criteria. The dispute resolution mechanism in the FTA, according to Lermer, raises the costs and the uncertainty for anyone seeking to use U.S. trade contingency instruments against Canadian producers. It should therefore discourage trade harassment. The FTA is as good a system as Canada could have anticipated negotiating at this time. Canada could not realistically have anticipated winning a complete exemption to the provisions of the U.S. trade law. In the meantime, negotiations will continue over a common approach to measuring and classifying subsidies.

The second section of this book contains six chapters covering countervailing duty and dumping cases for agricultural products. Two chapters review the U.S. countervail case that attacked subsidies to Canadian hog producers. Two other chapters examine Canada's countervail case against low quality beef subsidized by the European Community. A fifth chapter considers the suit initiated by eastern U.S. potato growers against dumping from Canada, and compares that case with the suit commenced in Canada by B.C. potato growers against dumping by western U.S. producers. The sixth chapter in this section describes the Canadian countervail duty case against U.S. corn subsidies.

Although all the reviewed cases focus on problems between the two neighboring countries in agricultural trade, the circumstances in each case are different. Chapter 9 probably has the most general application. Written by Lermer, this chapter deals directly with the 1985 U.S. Farm Bill which is at the heart of the conflict between the EC and the United States. This agricultural trade war is the source of the economic problems facing grain producers in Canada, Argentina and Australia. Several new elements of Canadian import contingency legislation were tested in the corn case, and it is no exaggeration to say that here the Canadian Import Tribunal broke important new ground with several bold and imaginative decisions.

In the case of low quality European beef, the Canadian Import Tribunal demonstrated some willingness to determine injury on the basis of political considerations rather than merely by measuring import shares and resultant price effects; the Tribunal's analysis gets a good grade in both studies of the beef case (Kerr and McGivern, and van Duren and Martin). The same cannot be said of its earlier finding in the potato case. There the authors (Carter, Stern and Schmitz) note that increased potato imports from Washington into British Columbia were due to lower costs of production in the U.S. and not to dumping in the traditional sense, whereby producers sell at a lower price abroad than at home and often below the full cost of production. But the fault does not lie with the Tribunal, which is forced to accept Revenue Canada's finding that dumping exists.

In the two offsetting potato cases, the United States International Trade Commission (ITC) appears in a better light than do the Canadian authorities. The ITC rejected the potato growers' claim that Canadian producers were dumping and that the alleged dumping had materially injured American producers. But in the hog countervail case, the U.S. ITC is severely criticized for the methods it used to calculate injury (Meilke and van Duren, Schmitz and Sigurdson). Interestingly, the U.S. Department of Commerce announced in mid-1988 that it was recommending that the duty on Canadian hogs be halved.

Several authors indicate that the recent flurry of agricultural trade disputes between Canada and the United States has been the result of not having a dispute settlement mechanism like the one created in the Free Trade Agreement. Other authors stress that there is something to be learned by studying these cases today, since in the new trade environment negotiators must determine equivalencies among various subsidy regimes. It is simple to observe subsidy programs and government intervention in agricultural markets, but it is difficult to measure increased production and exports induced by the subsidies; it is still more difficult to measure injury to domestic industries. All six case studies in the second section of this volume report on various degrees of failure on the part of Canadian and American trade officials to distinguish between the transfer and economic components of subsidies. The economic component distorts production and exports. In cases where trade officials fail to correctly determine the trade consequences from a subsidy program, the likelihood is low that equivalencies can be determined among different subsidy programs across industries.

Agricultural markets pose special problems for trade negotiators as well as for administrators and adjudicators of contingency trade laws. Some problems are products of the traditional environment of protection which agricultural special interests in all countries are quick to defend. Other problems are associated with the competitive nature of agricultural markets. In the absence of government interference, generally there are many producers selling virtually homogeneous products to many buyers. Spot and future markets are usually efficient processors of new information about potential changes in factors affecting supply and demand. Prices rise and fall continuously as new information becomes available on changes in demand or supply. Given the level of market risk and the speed of market adjustment, it may be natural for producers to seek political means for lowering risk. However, the competitive nature of international markets that generates risk also turns one government's interference into a "beggar-thy-neighbor" policy, and, accordingly, the international trading system deteriorates at everyone's expense.

All authors of the case studies in this book recognize that the designers of dumping and subsidy codes in the GATT seem to have had in mind a rigid market price for determining impacts of subsidies on domestic producers and exports. As Lermer explains in Chapter 9, domestic producers are usually myopic and import penetration follows a pattern. First, the market share of imports increases. Second, prices adjust downward because domestic producers maintain their previous level of production. The effect of subsidies is measured through the increased market penetration of subsidized exports, and the injury to domestic producers is measured by the subsequent drop in prices.

As far as a producer is concerned, government can duplicate the effect of a tariff through an equivalent subsidy. With tariffs, consumers pay higher prices to the domestic producers. With subsidies, transfers to domestic producers are paid out of general tax revenues. Economists prefer the latter policy over the former because it is more visible and it creates fewer distortions in the domestic economy. Tariffs are usually preferred to subsidies by politicians, however, because budgets and tax rates are monitored continuously by the electorate. Nonetheless, the major threat to politicians who are tempted to offer a subsidy to a domestic interest group is the likely reaction of trading partners. "Beggar-thy-neighbor" policies are as pernicious and self-serving for subsidies as they are for tariffs; but experience suggests that despite their futility, periodic waves of protectionism are inevitable. Institutionalized processes for maneuvering protectionist pressures into well-worn channels for negotiating trade disputes provide an important line of defence in trying to contain the spread of the destructive forces of protectionism. GATT's subsidies code and the trade contingency law of GATT signatories are containment systems, designed to dissuade member countries from substituting subsidies for other protectionist measures.

The weave of any institutional fabric can give way when a protectionist wave gains sufficient momentum. Just such a wave has, in the early 1980s, engulfed the United States' system of trade contingency law. Pietro Nivola (1986) reports that the U.S. International Trade Commission "took up almost twice as many investigations of unfair trade practices in 1984 as in 1980 . . . over three times as many anti-dumping investigations . . . and over four times as many countervailing duty cases" (p. 578). Moreover, "the proportion of affirmative opinions by the Commission climbed from 56 per cent to 66 per cent after anti-dumping hearings, and from only 5.5 per cent to 83 per cent in countervailing duty cases" (p. 578). The recent surge of protectionist sentiment in the United States has turned the U.S. trade contingency system into a more responsive mechanism for those producers seeking protection. This reality, more than any other consideration, has driven Canada to seek a bilateral free trade agreement with the United States.

The third section of the book contains four chapters on prospects for Canadian agricultural trade in a less distorted trading environment. The first chapter in this section looks at effects on different regions in Canada of complete elimination of subsidies and other distortions in agricultural trade around the world. The second chapter assesses the future prospects for exports of wheat, traditionally Canada's largest export commodity. A marketing strategy for Canadian beef exports to Japan is outlined in the third chapter. This is a subject of renewed interest to the Canadian beef industry due to the recent agreement by Japan to eliminate all import quotas on beef by 1991. The fourth chapter provides lessons that can be learned from the New Zealand experience of economic liberalization and deregulation.

MacGregor et al. analyze the expected impacts on Canadian agriculture of complete trade liberalization of agricultural products. They use a regional programming model of Canadian agriculture in a comparative static, partial equilibrium analysis. Their results indicate that little change would occur in the grain and oilseed sector. Higher market prices to producers would largely be offset by the loss of government payments. Beef producers in Canada would probably lose, since the increase in costs of feed grain would not be offset by higher market prices for cattle; the impact on the pork sector is expected to be similar. Decreases in revenues would also occur for dairy and poultry sectors with the dismantling of producer marketing boards. The analysis showed that aggregate agricultural incomes would fall in every province except Ontario. However, governments (and taxpayers) would save as subsidies and some product prices decrease.

Veeman and Veeman note that recent world trade in wheat has been characterized by structural changes in world markets. The structural changes are a result of changes in domestic agricultural policies, agricultural technology, and economic circumstances. It is expected that in the future the importance of industrialized importers of grain will decline, while that of centrally planned and developing countries will increase. The authors use a constant market share model to assess the performance of five major wheat exporters over the last 15 years, noting that most recently the EC and Argentina have exhibited increases in market share (suggesting an increase in their competitiveness), while Canada, Australia, and the U.S. appear to have suffered a decline in relative competitiveness. The authors assert that the most important issue for grain exporters is trade access to medium-and low-income markets, which are forecast to be the major source of future demand increases for grain.

Up until now the Canadian beef industry has failed to take advantage of the slow liberalization of the Japanese beef market that has taken place over the last few years. Kerr and Cullen review the Japanese market for beef, concluding that continued growth in demand for (especially high quality) beef can be expected, while it is unlikely that significant increases in domestic production will be forthcoming. In a detailed analysis of the Japanese quota and marketing system, the authors explain why Canadians could realistically expect to export more high quality beef to Japan. The authors propose a three-part marketing strategy for exporting Canadian beef to Japan: research on the required grade of cattle for the Japanese market, development of mechanisms for dealing with risks involved in the opening of marketing channels to Japan, and reform of Canadian exporting regulations to make it easier for exporters to satisfy Japanese requirements.

The last chapter in the book contains lessons that can be learned from the New Zealand experience of deregulating their economy. A change of government in 1984 brought a sudden economic liberalization in the agricultural sector. It might be expected that the New Zealand economy would have been thrown into severe trauma, but such was not the case. While farm output and income have been reduced somewhat, there has not been the mass exodus from the industry that was predicted, nor has there been a flood of mortgagee sales. Rayner attributes the New Zealand response to the entrepreneurial ability of domestic farmers to adapt to new conditions, the refinancing of some farm loans (made possible by the government), and the fortuitous occurrence of record prices for wool.

The New Zealand experience suggests that liberalizing reforms should be implemented quickly, adjustment costs being almost always overestimated in advance. Reforms should also be balanced across the various economic sectors, rather than forcing one sector (in the New Zealand case, agriculture) to bear the brunt of adjustment costs. And finally, reform-minded governments should avoid compensating segments of the economy which have lost economically as a result of policy reforms.

Most observers of the reform process acknowledge that it is unrealistic to hope for the elimination by all countries of all subsidies and non-tariff barriers to agricultural trade. Instead, the hope is to develop a practical means of measuring the trade distortion impacts of domestic subsidies and to find a single-valued measure of complex subsidy regimes, to allow authorities to compare degrees of subsidization. This would facilitate negotiation of producer subsidy equivalents among trading partners. This is the first step in creating a "level playing field" among agricultural trading partners, even though the entire "playing field" among agricultural trading partners is propped up by protectionist measures. The U.S., however, still holds to the ideal wherein all trade distortions in agricultural products would be removed. At the time of writing, the resolution of these arguments in the Uruguay Round of trade negotiations is still unclear. However, agreement was reached in early 1989 to limit all increases in subsidy levels while the negotiation process is underway.

REFERENCES

Oleson, Brian. (1987). "Presidential Address: World Grain Trade: An Economic Perspective of the Current Trade War." *Canadian Journal of Agricultural Economics, 31*, 501–514.

Nivola, Pietro S. (1986). "The New Protectionism: U.S. Trade Policy in Historical Perspective." *Political Science Quarterly, 101*, 577–600.

CHAPTER 2

BILATERAL NEGOTIATIONS IN THE CONTEXT OF GATT RULES

L. Chase Wilde, K.K. Klein and J. J. Richter

In January 1989 Canada and the United States signed their historic Free Trade Agreement (FTA), just over forty years since these two countries had cooperated in establishing the General Agreement on Tariffs and Trade (GATT). The FTA represented the culmination of a year and a half of difficult negotiations and over one hundred years of attempts to lower trade barriers between the two countries on a bilateral basis.

Canada and the U.S. remain a part of the GATT, which now has 95 members (as well as 30 other associates that apply similar trade rules). The GATT's major objective is to reduce barriers to trade around the world. Seven rounds of trade negotiations have been held since its inception; the GATT embarked on the eighth round in 1986 (the so-called Uruguay Round, thus entitled because the inaugural meeting was held in Punta del Este, Uruguay). The current round is scheduled to end in December 1990.

Since the GATT is a contractual agreement among the signatory nations, the bilateral trade agreement between Canada and the U.S. must fit within the legal framework of the GATT. However, one motivation for entering into negotiations for a bilateral FTA stems from the two countries' frustrations with the GATT. In this chapter, these motivations are explored with emphasis on the differences in trade laws of the two countries. The historical difficulties of the GATT in reducing trade barriers around the world are described in the next section. The following two sections focus on the trade law systems in the U.S. and Canada as well as on their differences in interpretation of free and fair trade. The paper concludes with an analysis of the impact on the GATT of the Canada-U.S. FTA, and the impact on the bilateral trade agreement of the GATT.

The Multilateral System

The GATT is the world's major trade institution. It is the recognized forum for multilateral discussions regarding rules for international exchange, and it offers an avenue for arbitration of trade disputes. Despite its key role in the international economy, the GATT arose as an interim measure, as a by-product of a more encompassing mandate. Herein lies the seed of its weaknesses in dealing with current trade, especially agricultural trade situations.

The GATT emerged after World War II at a time of international institution building. To ward off the chaos which had followed World War I, world leaders conceived of an international triad shown graphically in Figure 1: the International Monetary Fund (IMF), the International Bank of Reconstruction and Development (IBRD), and the International Trade Organization (ITO). The IMF was established to ease countries' liquidity and balance of payment problems. The focus of the IBRD was

FIGURE 1
INSTITUTIONAL TRIPOD FOR INTERNATIONAL RELATIONS

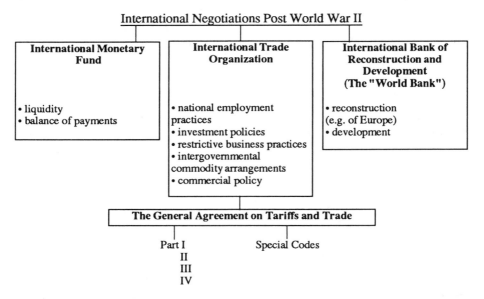

Source: Adapted from A.I. MacBean and P.N. Snowden, *International Institution in Trade and Finance*, New Allen: George Allen & Unwin, (1981); and J.C. Thomas lecture as the Eldon D. Foote Visiting Chair in International Business/Law, University of Alberta, October 27, 1987.

on lending funds to less developed countries. The ITO was designed to oversee various aspects of trade, including national employment practices, investment policies, restrictive business practices, intergovernmental commodity arrangements, and commercial policies. An ITO Charter was drawn up in 1947. However, when the U.S. Senate failed to ratify the Charter, a compromise was reached. Chapter Four of the ITO, which dealt with commercial policy, became the GATT.

What is the GATT? It is a contractual arrangement among member countries (Blackhurst, 1986). Belief in a commercial, rule-based trading system is at the heart of its operation. Members are obliged to give up a certain amount of discretion over their trade behavior in return for the benefits of order and predictability. But when actions of members belie or disregard the necessary disciplines, credibility and effectiveness of the multilateral system are reduced.

The GATT is based on three main Articles (Thomas, 1987). Article I of the GATT grants unconditional Most-Favored-Nation (MFN) status to all members, thus allowing all member states to share equally in any negotiated reduction of trade barriers. Article II of the GATT is intended to put continuous downward pressure on tariff levels. Article III calls for non-discrimination of domestic and foreign produced goods; its main purpose is to prevent re-emergence of discrimination once trade has occurred. Although in principle it is difficult to take issue with these precepts, in practice they have been harder to achieve. Table 1 provides an outline of GATT articles of particular interest to agriculture.

MFN status, simply known as nondiscrimination, is designed to ensure that all member countries are equally eligible for the benefits of lower levels of protection agreed upon by any of the members. This Article is an attempt to base trade on the principle of comparative advantage rather than on the presence of political or economic power (Anjaria, 1986; Blackhurst, 1986). But as powerful an ideology as MFN is and as necessary as it is to realizing theoretical benefits from trade, nondiscrimination is modified even within the GATT itself. For example, regional economic arrangements are allowed and encouraged, such as the European Community (EC) and the Canada-U.S. bilateral trade agreement. Furthermore, less developed countries are given special treatment through the Generalized System of Preferences. Finally, safeguard provisions allow temporary discrimination to protect a nation from short-term adjustment costs incurred from trade.

Tariff reductions and national treatment have contributed in some ways to problems found in today's trade environment. As tariffs were reduced and bound, nations found other, non-tariff means of protecting their interests. And while national treatment was a common principle, subsidies and other domestic measures which inhibit trade proliferated. There has been a significant shift from transparent trade impediments to ones which are so complex and whose effects are so intermingled that even the originating country would be hard pressed to sort out their actual impacts.

TABLE 1
OUTLINE OF SELECTED GATT ARTICLES AND CODES

GATT Rules	Coverage	Impact[1]
Part I[2]		
Article I	General Most Favored Nation Treatment	*Establishes nondiscrimination among contracting parties of any trade concessions. Selectively waived in 1971 to provide a generalized system of preferences for developing countries.
Article II	Schedules of Concessions	*Includes schedule of tariff bindings.
Part II[3]		
Article III	National Treatment on Internal Taxation and Regulation	*Applies principle of nondiscrimination to domestically-produced and foreign goods. Does not apply to foreign investment, or government procurement.
Article VI	Anti-dumping and Countervailing Duties	*Permits any signatory to levy a duty in the event that foreign subsidies or pricing practices injure domestic industry.
Article VII	Valuation for Customs Purposes	*Establishes broad guidelines for aligning national valuation practices.
Article XI	General Elimination of Quantitative Restrictions	*Prohibits use of import or export quotas; not applying to agricultural and fisheries products if domestic price support programs are in place. (Voluntary Export Restrictions are not recognized by the GATT, therefore are not prohibited.)
Article XII	Restrictions to Safeguard the Balance of Payments	*Waives obligation of Article XI to protest currency problems.
Article XIII	Nondiscriminatory Administration of Quantitative Restrictions	*Any allowable quantitative restriction must be applied equally to all contracting parties (softened somewhat by Article XIV).
Article XVI	Subsidies	*Distinguishes between domestic (allowable) subsidies and those intended to enhance exports (prohibited). Allows export subsidies for primary products only.
Article XVII	State Trading Enterprises	*Specifies that such organizations must comply with GATT obligations.
Article XIX	Emergency Action on Imports of Particular Products	*Allows extraordinary action (in violation of other Articles) to restrict imports on a temporary basis—the so-called escape clause.
Article XX	General Exceptions	*Allows protection against such public concerns as health and morals.

TABLE 1 (Continued)
OUTLINE OF SELECTED GATT ARTICLES AND CODES

GATT Rules	Coverage	Impact[1]
Article XXI	Security Exception	*Allows protection for security reasons.
Article XXII	Consultation	*Ensures the right to consult with contracting parties in the event of a dispute.
Article XXIII	Nullification or Impairment	*Permits retaliation if GATT rules are thought to be violated—the basis for dispute settlement.
Part III		
Article XXIV	Territorial Application-Frontier Traffic-Customs Unions and Free Trade Areas	*Permits negotiation of customs unions and free trade areas between a group of countries smaller than all signatories to the GATT, i.e., breaks with principle of MFN.
Article XXVII	Modification of Schedules	*Tariff bindings may be renegotiated. Employed, for example, when tariff classification changes alter tariff impacts.
Part IV[4]		

[1] Description of impacts are simplified and thus may omit some of the subtleties of rule application.
[2] The two Articles in Part I can be amended only with unanimous consent of the contracting parties (Parts II and IV can be amended with a two-thirds vote).
[3] Part II contains Articles III to XXIII. These Articles were signed with "provisional" application, meaning that signatories agreed to apply these rules "to the fullest extent not inconsistent with existing legislation," i.e., existing legislation was "grandfathered."
[4] Added in 1964 to deal with special concerns of developing countries.

Source: Adapted from the GATT, *The Text of the General Agreement on Tariffs and Trade*, Geneva, 1986; and Jock A. Finlayson, "Canada and the International Regulation of Trade Barriers: The General Agreement on Tariffs and Trade. In R.K. Paterson, *Canadian Regulation of International Trade and Investment*. Carswell, 1986.

Other problems inherent in the GATT undermine its ability to function. From the outset, its jurisdiction in trade-related matters was only partial. For example, services and investment were excluded, yet these areas have shown rapid growth in post-war trade. Even in the traded goods sector, the GATT coverage has been partial. In 1955, the U.S. sought and obtained a waiver which allows exclusion from import quota obligations in order to support its domestic farm programs (Hathaway, 1987, p. 82). Within a few years, the EC and other countries were to make good use of this exclusion. Grants of special status set precedents for more requests and, indeed, the list of special products excluded from negotiated commitments has grown over time (Blackhurst, 1986).

Another problem inherent in the GATT is found in the reliance on a fixed exchange rate system for effective tariff negotiations. Without a fixed exchange rate system, changes in exchange rates can counteract tariff reductions, thus lessening the benefits of agreed-upon reductions in protection. When the fixed exchange rate system broke down over the period 1971–73, efforts at the GATT were significantly weakened.

Lastly, as the membership of the GATT has enlarged, its original homogeneity has been diluted, making agreement more difficult. An obvious example of this trend was seen in the Tokyo Round with the emergence of the nine special codes[1] outside the GATT, to which only certain parties became signatories.

In summary, the concept of a commercial, rule-based trading system through the ITO has evolved into both more and less than was initially conceived. On the plus side, precedents have accumulated over the years which add a degree of certainty to the international trading environment. Furthermore, there is acute recognition today by many more countries than the original 23 members of the GATT that international rules are essential to continued economic benefits from international trade. However, the multilateral framework of the GATT today is overshadowed by bilateral and regional arrangements, and is weakened by the growing heterogeneity of trading partners and by its historical focus on tariffs to the exclusion of services, investment and non-tariff barriers.

The United States

The U.S. trade law system can be viewed from two perspectives. First, there is the internal structure which is dependent upon the constitutional division of powers in the U.S. government. Second, there are the external relationships between the U.S. and other sovereign states or regional entities. These internal and external legal structures in the U.S. govern, to a large extent, the operation of American trade law, and thus the types of decisions that can be expected from this system.

The Internal Structure

The constitutional separation of powers in the U.S. government, particularly between Congress and the executive branch, sets the stage for U.S. participation in international forums. Congress is dominant in U.S. trade policy, having been given under the Constitution the power to regulate interstate and foreign trade (Howell and Wolfe, 1985; Grey, 1982). Prior to the 1930s, tariffs were entirely a matter to be dealt with by Congress and were, therefore, openly subject to the domestic political pressures to which Congressmen are vulnerable. It was within this environment that the extremely protectionist Smoot-Hawley Tariff Act was legislated in 1930.

During the depression period that followed the imposition of the Smoot-Hawley tariffs, a new pattern emerged for negotiating changes in trade legislation. As part of the effort to rebuild the economy, President Roosevelt asked for and received from Congress delegated authority to negotiate tariff reductions (Howell and Wolfe, 1985). Two points are significant here: first, the delegation of authority to the executive branch was conditional upon tariff reductions being reciprocal (Howell and Wolfe) and, second, the power to negotiate was granted for a limited time period only (Grey, 1982). It is also worth noting that subsequently executive authority to effect change in U.S. trade legislation has been granted piecemeal by Congress and usually not without conditions attached.

Another aspect of the trade law procedures associated with constitutional separation of powers lies in the usual postures of the executive branch and the Congress toward protection. Congress is typically less enthusiastic about freer trade than is the President's office (Howell and Wolfe, 1985). Regional interests are represented in Congress in particular, whereas the executive must also deal with global issues.

This divergence in attitudes has particular relevance for U.S.-GATT interactions. For example, even during discussions on the ITO, U.S. negotiators were required to consider the wishes of Congress in any agreement. It was for this reason that in the ITO, and subsequently in the GATT, agriculture was given special treatment (Hathaway, 1987). The binding of tariffs was included as a principal element in the GATT largely in reaction to the Congressional Smoot-Hawley tariffs (Thomas, 1987). In a more current framework, it has been argued that trade negotiations themselves are considered desirable by the U.S. executive branch, for it is only during such talks that this branch of government is given authority to act on trade issues (Bhagwati et al., 1987). In the same vein, international negotiations can be effective in containing or even off-setting domestic interest group pressures for protection (Winters, 1987). This is as true for bilateral negotiations such as the Canada-U.S. talks as it is for multilateral ones.

The External Structure

The second perspective from which to view the U.S. trade law system relates to U.S. ideas on free and fair trade. Precepts of free and fair trade underly the purpose of the GATT. The U.S. supports free trade as a means of bringing about fair trade. However, because rules agreed upon at the international level must be translated into national rules to become operational, there are incentives for rent-seeking behavior in the adoption and exercise of national laws. How the U.S. incorporates GATT commitments into its own system of law affects economic opportunities and constraints within the U.S., and other countries as well.

Free trade here means "a single market ... without trade barriers, national discrimination, export subsidies, or other manifestations of mercantalism" (Howell and Wolfe, 1985, p. 3-2). Fair trade has the connotation of a trade relationship in which power between partners has been equalized; it also requires legislation to be ensured or secured. To achieve fair trade, trade remedies (or protective actions) are designed to counteract benefits received by others but not of their own making (Howell and Wolfe; Grey, 1982). Ideas of free and fair trade were incorporated into U.S. law long before the GATT came into being. As early as 1890, countervailing duties were applied to counteract unfair foreign subsidies for sugar, and in 1897 these were extended to any dutiable imports (Grey). Anti-dumping legislation, too, was enacted early in the century in the United States.

Individual state legislation of GATT guidelines has resulted in substantial differences in legal interpretations (Nam, 1987). An example of legislative license is provided by looking at how the concept of injury is interpreted from the GATT to U.S. law. In both the GATT and U.S. law, injury is associated with protective retaliation. Such retaliation may be invoked as a result of unfair trade practices such as subsidies or selling at less-than-fair-value. Retaliation may also occur as a temporary safeguard action when trade has been fair but still threatens a particular domestic industry. Choosing just one of these situations of injury, that involving subsidies and the requisite retaliation, countervailing duties (CVD), will suffice to point out legislative license.

GATT Articles VI and XVI plus the Subsidies Code negotiated during the Tokyo Round deal specifically with subsidies and CVD. The GATT rules specify that a CVD may be applied if material injury resulting from the application of a subsidy can be shown. Actually, both material injury and serious injury are recognized, the latter being a stronger form to be applied in temporary safeguard decisions as opposed to claims of unfair trade. A CVD is intended to neutralize the negative economic effects of an unfair subsidy.

Although U.S. legal terminology follows that of the GATT, the spirit of the GATT is not always retained (Hennig, 1987). Several differences between the two can be noted. The use of the qualifier "material" for injury in the GATT had been intended to raise the threshold of injury. However, following the Tokyo Round, the U.S. viewed all of its past and current claims of injury as falling into the "material" injury category (Grey, 1982). This view, while potentially correct, is disputable in practice. Furthermore, the GATT requires that causality between the subsidy and the injury be established, whereas U.S. action does not require this connection (Nam, 1987). Causality is a stronger test, since it is often more difficult to prove. U.S. law *requires* that "relief" action be taken; that is, a CVD must be imposed if material injury from a subsidy is found. The GATT merely allows for the possibility of such action (Grey). Finally, the Subsidies Code of the GATT recognizes that some subsidies are legitimate. For example, domestic subsidies used to achieve internal social or economic policy objectives (such as reducing unemployment or offsetting regional economic disadvantage) are allowed (Nam). Clearly, recent practice of the U.S. has tended to interpret allowable subsidies more narrowly, as illustrated by the changing U.S. rulings on Canadian stumpage fees.

It is apparent that the U.S. has relied increasingly on CVDs to settle trade disputes. Over the period 1980–85, 252 CVD cases were initiated by the U.S., compared with 12 by Canada, 18 by Australia and 7 by the EC (Finger and Nogues, 1987, p. 708). This is an average for the U.S. of 34 cases per year between 1980 and 1985. Between 1975 and 1979, U.S. cases averaged 21 per year; between 1970 and 1974, they averaged two per year; between 1930 and 1964, they averaged only one per year. The significance of these data is that national CVD legislation in particular, and contingency protection in general, are being used more and more as a form of protection rather than as a means to neutralize unfair trade. Unilateral action by way of formation and interpretation of law increases the possibility that trade will be determined at a political rather than at an economic level (Finger and Nogues; Rugman and Anderson, 1987). This politicizing of trade decisions occurs despite the ideology of free trade espoused and embraced by the GATT.

An associated aspect of the use of law as a form of protection is the increasing complexity of formal legalese. There is a tendency, particularly in the U.S., "to deal with international economic conflicts through adversarial litigation" (Hemmendinger, 1985, p. 2–2). The legal detail relied upon for U.S. decisions has a tendency to mask protection behind a guise of remedying unfair trade practices (Howell and Wolfe, 1985).

In summary, the impacts of the U.S. trade law system stem largely from two distinct sources: the constitutional division of powers in the U.S. government, and the interpretations of free and fair trade. Effective control over trade law is held by Congress. Thus, commitments made at the executive level must be either approved in principle at the outset of negotiation or ratified in particular at the end. Either way, Congress is responsible for legal enactment of any international agreement. Differences between these two branches of government have contributed to the nature of the

GATT, and to options available at the bilateral level (for example, the Canada-U.S. Free Trade Agreement). Meanwhile, there has been a tendency within the U.S. to move away from a goal of free trade to one of fair trade. Freer trade is a principal objective of the GATT, to be achieved through reciprocal reductions in trade barriers. Interpretation and implementation of GATT guidelines to achieve fair trade leads the trading system down a different path (World Bank, 1987). Fair trade arguments require judgements about what is fair. In such a view, the erection of trade barriers may be justified and even considered desirable if they are seen to increase "fairness." A focus on fairness in trade enhances the opportunity for interest group pressure, rent-seeking or merely opinion to be determining factors.

Canada

The trade law system in Canada is influenced strongly both by the General Agreement on Tariffs and Trade and by the U.S. legal environment. Again, any agreement reached at the multilateral level must be formally ratified at the national level to become operational. In the case of the Tokyo Round agreements, those articles and codes dealing with anti-dumping and countervail were incorporated into Canadian law through the 1984 Canadian Special Import Measures Act. On the bilateral side, there is little doubt that U.S. protectionist attitudes of recent years contributed to the willingness of the Canadian government to enter into negotiations with the United States. This section will look at Canada's relationship with and responses to both the multilateral trade law system (GATT) and the U.S. trade law system. The following section will discuss Canada's options under the new Free Trade Agreement with the United States.

Historically, Canada has placed a great deal of importance on multilateral trade negotiations. The importance of trade to the Canadian economy is relatively high. Canada earns approximately 30 per cent of gross domestic product abroad, while the same statistic for the U.S. is 10 per cent and for Japan 14 per cent (Paterson, 1986, p. 3). Canada views trade rules as being very important. The alternative to a trade environment ordered by rules is a trade environment ordered by power. One of the strengths of the GATT system of trade liberalization, from Canada's point of view, is thus the principle of MFN. All countries, small and large, have the same access to negotiated reductions in trade barriers. Since Canada is a relatively small world power, particularly with respect to her major trading partner, the U.S., there is good reason for Canada to support a multilateral trade system which is rule-based.

There is, however, another view of the nondiscrimination principle. Developing countries, in particular, argue that the GATT rules should favor them because they are currently not equal in an economic sense. That is, the GATT rules should allow for discrimination in the application of some rules where that discrimination helps to put trading partners on a more equal footing (Paterson, 1986). Although historically, Canada has joined other industrialized countries in resisting discriminatory application of trade remedies such as countervail, in some contexts unequal treatment may be important to Canada (Cohn, 1985). For example, Canada already takes advantage of certain discriminatory rights allowed by the GATT, such as retaining Commonwealth Preferential tariffs. (The question of equal versus unequal treatment will be discussed again later in a bilateral context.)

The GATT system is one of minimal control which relies on compliance and conciliation. As such, the GATT has not been effective in garnering genuine adherents. This weakness of the multilateral system has been recognized by Canada as well as by other traders. Attempts to strengthen compliance with GATT rules have been piecemeal. For example, problems exist with the dispute settlement mechanism (Paterson, 1986). GATT's somewhat hazy definition of what constitutes a subsidy and what is meant by "material injury," even with the addition of the Anti-dumping and Subsidy Codes, has actually fostered international disagreement (Nam, 1987). Each country tends to interpret the guidelines differently. If Canada is to benefit from a multilateral system for, say, solutions to claims of unfair trade practices, a clearer definition of subsidy (Warly and Barichello, 1986) and, perhaps more importantly, acceptance of a strong injury test (Paterson) would be necessary changes at the least.

Given the volume of trade between Canada and the U.S., American interpretation of GATT rules becomes very important. As has been seen, the U.S. tends to see its commitment under the GATT in a legalistic framework, more oriented to litigation than to settlement (Winham, 1985). Such a legalistic approach is effective, but can promote more protection rather than less. Canada, as a small, open economy, needs less. There is potential, at least, for problems stemming from GATT's deficiences in power and enforcement of rules to be exacerbated in the Canadian economic context as opposed to one of less U.S.-dependent economies.

The Canadian response to the international trade law environment has been to move its own trade law system closer to that of the United States. It has been said that "comparative advantage is often made rather than born" (Thomas, 1985, p. 220). The exigencies of world trade encourage nations and even groups within nations to adopt, if possible, rules which are to their benefit. The adoption of the Special Import Measures Act (SIMA) represents a "loss of innocence" for Canada in the international trade environment (Potter, 1986). It is a symbol of recognition that trade law can be used to inhibit, as well as to neutralize the behavior of, other countries. As mentioned, reliance on legalism introduces the opportunity for use of power, not only among countries but also within;[2] here the focus is given to the former.

SIMA embraces a legalistic orientation in dealing with trade disputes. For example, the Act provides for a two-step process of examining a claim for "import relief" as found in the United States. In the U.S., a claimant must go to the Department of Commerce for determination that dumping or a subsidy exists, and to the International Trade Commission for a determination of injury. In Canada, the Department of

Revenue, Customs and Excise determines the fact of dumping or subsidy and the Canadian Import Tribunal determines causation. Similar rules exist in both countries with respect to such details as preliminary and final investigations, authorization to initiate action, and bases for valuation. In both countries it is required by law that duties be imposed if findings are positive.

The Canadian perception is that Canadian law is more in the spirit of the GATT than is that of the U.S., since it applies the stronger requirement of a causal link between the unfair trade practice and injury rather than merely a test for injury (Warley and Barichello, 1986). However, Canada has also used GATT rules not only to protect the interests of Canadian producers from unfair trade practices but also to change international trade flows (Finger and Nogues, 1987). Over the period 1980–85, Canada applied safeguards, CVDs and anti-dumping duties 235 times. This is a substantial number even when compared with the 786 cases by the U.S. Further, it is misleading to suppose that Canada automatically suffers from American use of law (Horlick, 1987). It is true that the U.S. initiates most of the world's CVD cases; during 1980–85, the U.S. initiated 87 per cent of all CVDs that originated in a group composed of the U.S., Canada, Australia and the EC (Finger and Nogues, p. 708). Developing countries tend to be the big losers in such actions. But when dumping complaints are considered, Canada is a much stronger player. In cases against each other, the U.S. brought seven anti-dumping and eight countervail cases against Canada during 1980–84 while Canada brought 20 anti-dumping and no countervail cases against the U.S. in the same period (Horlick, p.49).

Looking beyond the numbers, the economic impacts of U.S. legal action against Canada have been mixed. For example, the countervail on hogs resulted in an impetus for Canadian value added in the pork industry, though not without some short-term pain in the Canadian hog industry in general. And the lumber countervail, which resulted in a cost being imposed on Canadian producers, was still to the benefit of the Canadian public due to the collection of an export tax.[3]

In summary, trade law in Canada reflects agreements undertaken at various rounds of the GATT and also reflects the litigious attitudes prevailing in the United States. The rule-based trade environment offered by the GATT has both advantages and disadvantages for Canada. The advantages are related in part to MFN and the associated equivalence of rules. However, the GATT lacks the power of law and enforcement. Potential Canadian trade problems are worsened by the legalistic interpretation of GATT commitments by the United States. Current Canadian legislation dealing with unfair trade practices recognizes a "coming of age" of Canadian law with respect to its power to protect from as well as to facilitate trade. This recognition has implications for the way Canada treats foreign trade practices and even, perhaps, domestic development opportunities.

The Canada-U.S. Free Trade Agreement

How does this international trade law environment relate to the Canada-U.S. Free Trade Agreement? Both Canada and the U.S. have continuing commitments under the GATT and both are likely to continue to support the multilateral trade system, but with a new emphasis. It is anticipated that the bilateral deal will represent to the world trading system a model for change in the GATT while at the same time offering to Canada and the U.S. an alternative should substantive change within the GATT not occur (Warley and Barichello, 1986).

In light of the foregoing, a Canadian bilateral trade agreement with the U.S. appears as a culmination of events. There have been many attempts at a free trade or reciprocal trade arrangement between Canada and the United States. For Canada at least, three general economic factors helped to launch an effective period of negotiation. First, political impetus was provided by the failure of Prime Minister Trudeau's third option of decreasing reliance on the U.S. market and increasing trade with European countries and Japan. Second, the GATT system was perceived to be increasingly weak in dealing with the exigencies of today's trade environment. Finally, Canada's proximity to the U.S., where the trade law system appears to offer protection as well as facilitate competition, gave a needed push in the direction of a bilateral trade agreement.

It should be noted that a bilateral agreement between GATT signatories contravenes to a degree the Most Favored Nation principle. There are two ways Canada and the United States could reconcile the Free Trade Agreement with GATT rules. If the agreement was sector-based, as is the Auto Pact, a waiver would have to be obtained from other GATT signatories. If substantially all bilateral trade is covered in a bilateral arrangement,[4] general acceptance is automatically granted (Paterson, 1986). The latter route was taken in the 1987 agreement.

Two perspectives are taken in this analysis of the relationships between the Canada-U.S. FTA and the GATT. The first involves the impact of the GATT on the FTA; the other looks at effects the FTA may have for the GATT.

Impacts of the GATT on the Canada-U.S. FTA

The preamble of the FTA text states clearly that the Agreement

takes various GATT commitments, bilateral arrangements and ad hoc understandings and transforms them into a treaty-based relationship between Canada and the United States which should govern the trade and economic relationship for the foreseeable future. (*Canada U.S. Free Trade Agreement*, p. 1)

Even the decision to take the "comprehensive" route rather than the "sectoral" route in the Agreement is a reflection of GATT Article XXIV.

Since the majority of goods traded between the two countries are already tariff free (Paterson, 1986), non-tariff barriers are a major concern. However, what tariffs remain are to be eliminated either immediately upon the Agreement taking force or on a five or ten year sliding scale depending on the product (FTA, p. 43). Previous rounds of tariff reductions at the GATT have also staged reductions in tariffs; many of the non-tariff barriers expressly considered in the FTA, such as border measures other than tariffs, national treatment, technical standards, and government procurement, come basically from the GATT (FTA, various chapters; Raworth, 1987).

With respect to national treatment, which ensures that no internal measures will be taken to discriminate between domestic and foreign products, Chapter Five of the FTA goes a little further than the GATT. An explicit provision is included which subjects provinces and states to the practice of national treatment (FTA, p. 66).

Chapter Six of the FTA deals with technical standards and follows the Standards Code negotiated during the Tokyo Round of the GATT. Canada and the U.S. already have very similar product standards and standards systems (Cohen, 1985). In fact, the GATT Standards Code has been considered a vehicle for the U.S. to export its norms elsewhere (Cohen, p. 274). Many regulations (e.g., packaging, labelling and information) have been deemed "minor irritants" (Cohen, pp. 245, 273), a conclusion supported by the fact that these have not been points of contention in the FTA.

One potential problem area for Canada is related to the litigious attitude in the United States. With respect to consumer protection, the United States has much more rigorous product liability laws than does Canada. Thus, Canadian exporters are subject to an implicit cost and American exporters to an implicit benefit with respect to liability risks (Cohen, 1985). Differences of treatment with respect to this aspect of goods trade was not part of the FTA, implying unequal effects on exporters in the two countries.

Following the precedent set in the GATT, agriculture is given special treatment in the FTA. The most obvious derogation of the FTA with respect to agriculture is for products sold under quotas—such as poultry, eggs, and dairy, for Canada and sugar for the United States. As with allowable exceptions under the GATT, quota programs for these products have been specifically retained in the bilateral arrangement (FTA, Ch. 7), though these are still negotiable under the GATT. Other provisions affecting Canada go somewhat beyond what was achieved through the GATT. For example, most tariffs will eventually be eliminated between the two countries, and export subsidies on goods traded between the two countries are prohibited.

The general exceptions for trade in goods follow GATT procedures (FTA, pp. 173–4). Article XX of GATT, which provides exceptions for issues such as health and safety, is adopted, as long as its implementation is not actually disguising an unfair trade practice. Questions can arise about trade in agricultural products where the distinction between protection and safety is somewhat debatable. However, since health and safety standards are currently very similar in the two countries, problems here are likely to be minimal. In any event, the dispute settlement mechanism provides a forum for debate. A second form of exception applies a grandfather clause to restrictions in trade of certain goods. For example, Canada retains its right to limit exports of logs and the U.S. retains its traditional restrictions on marine transportation. However, some of the more contentious issues here of interest to Canada (such as beer or west coast fish) are subject to GATT rulings first.

Emergency action is covered in Chapter Eleven of the FTA. This section relates to trade actions under Article XIX of the GATT and Section 201 of U.S. trade law. Safeguards are considered necessary to counteract temporary injury caused by implementation of the Agreement. Such actions between the two countries are to be phased out over a ten-year transition period. Should disputes arise during this period, an attempt is to be made to use a bilateral, and binding, form of arbitration rather than the GATT mechanism. As with the GATT, compensation involving another traded product will be allowed. The U.S. has also agreed to an explicit warning mechanism if its escape clause is triggered.

An interesting facet of the FTA is that it specifies a threshold below which escape action may not be taken (FTA, p. 168). Thus the Agreement goes beyond the GATT in stipulating that temporary safeguards may be applied if the partner country were an "important" cause of serious injury to the other. This level of test goes beyond those found in the GATT. Presumably this will provide greater certainty to Canada with respect to the use of voluntary export restraints by the United States. This threshold is measured as the ratio of imports to total imports of each commodity classification in each country.

A dispute settlement mechanism is established to deal with cases of anti-dumping and countervail (FTA, Ch. 19). Arbitration of disputes is to be carried out by a panel of five people: two representatives from each country and one "neutral" member. The most significant change from the GATT framework is that all decisions of the process are binding on both parties. If nothing else, this provides the U.S. executive with ammunition to deal with a more protectionist Congress, assuming that the historical patterns continue with respect to free trade ideology. Furthermore, any changes to trade legislation in either country are subject to consultation with the other. In the event of a dispute, a change may be brought before the bilateral panel. The outcome of the bilateral agreement, then, is likely to bring Canadian and American trade law even closer together in the future.

Impacts of the Canada-U.S. FTA on the GATT

One of the purposes for the U.S. having entered into bilateral negotiations with Canada was to influence changes in the GATT, particularly in the Uruguay Round. Three areas in which this may be the case are considered briefly here: agriculture, services and investment.

As previously noted, agriculture has been a particularly thorny sector to negotiate in the GATT. This is largely because of protectionist measures undertaken by all countries in support of their own agricultural industry. Ironically, it was U.S. insistence on an exemption for domestic agricultural programs at the inception of GATT that has caused this problem (Hathaway, 1987). Although GATT treatment of agriculture appears little changed in the FTA, the bilateral agreement is likely to put North America in a somewhat stronger position during multilateral negotiations if only because Canada and the United States are major world exporters of agricultural products.

Another use of the FTA for GATT deliberations on agriculture is in the area of subsidy calculation, an all-important step in curbing protection in agriculture. In order to determine the timing for elimination of import licenses, the FTA contains a specific formula for calculating subsidy levels based on producer subsidy equivalents. Use of this formula will provide an opportunity to test and to refine this method of measuring protection.

The U.S. is keen to have trade in services and investment included in the Uruguay Round of the GATT. Other areas such as "intellectual property" are also important, but have received less attention in the FTA. Trade in services and investment has not, as yet, been treated in the GATT and thus any, even preliminary, bilateral negotiations may be useful in the multilateral forum. Part Four of the FTA, in particular Chapter Fourteen on Services and Chapter Sixteen on Investment, provides a good beginning for the multilateral negotiations.

Concluding Note

The trade law systems of Canada and the U.S. have developed along the lines of the GATT. Important differences, however, in the two countries' interpretations of trade laws have arisen over time, due mainly to attempts to protect each country's producers from outside competition.

The bilateral trade agreement negotiated between Canada and the United States is a reflection of political desire in the two countries to lower trade barriers between them and to put pressure on other nations (in particular EC members and Japan) to negotiate downward some of their many trade barriers. By including the historically protected sectors of agriculture, services and investment in the FTA, the two countries demonstrated their desire to resolve long-standing trade distortions among the major trading nations of the world.

NOTES

1. Anti-dumping, subsidies, customs valuation, government procurement, Import Licensing Procedures, Bovine Meat, Civil Aircraft, Dairy, technical barriers to trade.

2. Canadian trade law can also have domestic regional effects. At a 1983 international trade conference, concern was expressed that the SIMA bill then before Parliament favored the concerns of central Canada more than those of either the Western or Atlantic provinces (Curtis et al., 1985, xxiv).

3. Canada has also lost some recent battles with the EC in the GATT, for example, in provincial liquor practices and beef countervail tariffs.

4. GATT Article xxiv:8(b) "requires free trade partners to eliminate restrictions on substantially all the trade between them"; primarily tariffs and with allowance for certain exceptions (Rayworth, 351).

REFERENCES

Anjaria, S.J. (1986). "A New Round of Global Trade Negotiations." *Finance and Development 23* (2), 2–6.

Bhagwati, Jadish N., Anne O. Krueger and Richard H. Snape. (1987). "Introduction." *The World Bank Economic Review, 1*, 539–548.

Blackhurst, Richard. (1986, April). "The New Round of GATT Negotiation: Rejuvenating the Trading System." *EFTA Bulletin*, 3–9.

Canada. (1987, May). *Special Import Measures Act*. Ottawa: Minister of Supply and Services, Office Consolidation.

Canada. (1987). *The Canada-U.S., Free Trade Agreement*. Ottawa: Department of External Affairs, The International Trade Communications Group.

Cohen, David. (1985). "The Intersection of Consumer Protection Law and International Trade: Implications for Canadian Regulators." *Canada and International Trade*. Ottawa: The Institute for Research on Public Policy, 235–310.

Cohn, Theodore. (1985). "Canadian and Mexican Trade Policies Toward the United States: A Perspective from Canada." In *Canada and International Trade*. Ottawa: Institute for Research on Public Policy, 3–62.

Curtis, John M., David Haglund and Roman Lepiesza. (1985). "Summary." *Canada and International Trade*. Ottawa: The Institute for Research on Public Policy, xix–lii.

Finger, J. Michael and Julio Nogues. (1987). "International Control of Subsidies and Countervailing Duties." *The World Bank Economic Review, 1*, 707–726.

GATT. *The Text of the General Agreement on Tariffs and Trade*, Geneva, July 1986.

Grey, Rodney de C. (1982). *United States Trade Policy Legislation: A Canadian View*. Ottawa: The Institute for Research on Public Policy.

Hathaway, Dale E. (1987). *Agriculture and the GATT: Rewriting the Rules*. Washington, D.C.: Institute for International Economics.

Hemmendinger, Noel. (1985). "Shifting Sands: an Examination of the Philosophical Basis for U.S. Trade Laws." In John J. Jackson, R.O. Cunningham and Claude G.B. Fontham (Eds.). *International Trade Policy: A Lawyer's Perspective*. New York: Matthew Bender, 2.1–2.10.

Hennig, Jutta. (1987, July/August). "E.C. Concerned Over Proposed U.S. Trade Bills." *Europe*, 14–16.

Horlick, Gary N. (1987). "Comments" In M.G. Smith, (Ed.). *Bridging the Gap: Trade Laws in the Canadian-U.S. Negotiations*. Toronto: C.D. Howe Institute Canadian-American Committee, 49–55.

Howell, Thos. R. and Alan Wm. Wolff. (1985). "The Role of Trade Law in the Making of Trade Policy." In John H. Jackson, R.O. Cunningham and Claude G.B. Fontham (Eds.). *International Trade Policy: A Lawyer's Perspective*. New York: Matthew Bender, 3.1–3.24.

Jackson, John H., Richard O. Cunningham and Claude O.B. Fontheim (Eds.). (1985). *International Trade Policy: The Lawyer's Perspective*. New York: Matthew Bender.

Nam Chong-Hyun. (1987, September). "Export-Promoting Subsidies, Countervailing Threats and the General Agreement on Tariffs and Trade." *The World Bank Economic Review, 1*, 727–743.

Paterson, R.K. (1986). *Canadian Regulation of International* Trade and Investment. Agincourt, Ontario: Carswell.

Potter, Simon V. (1986, October). *Recent Developments and Future Trends in Canadian Anti-Dumping and Countervail Practice or...Loss of Innocence.* Paper presented at the 4th International Trade Law Seminar, Ottawa.

Raworth, Philip. (1987). "Canada-U.S. Free Trade: A Legal Perspective". *Canadian Public Policy, 13*, 350–365.

Rugman, Allan M. (1986, July/August). "U.S. Protectionism and Canadian Trade Policy." *Journal of World Trade Law, 20*, 363–380.

Rugman, Alan M. and Andrew Anderson. (1987). "A Fishy Business: The Abuse of American Trade Law in the Atlantic Groundfish Case of 1985–1986." *Canadian Public Policy, 13*, 152–164.

Thomas, J.C. (1985). "Conflict Over the Extraterritorial Application of U.S. Antitrust Law: A Canadian Perspective." In *Canada and International Trade.* Institute for Research on Public Policy, 191–234.

Thomas, J.C. (1987, November). *A Canadian View of the U.S. Omnibus Trade Bill.* The Eldon D. Foote Visiting Chair in Public Lecture Series, International Business Law, University of Alberta, Edmonton.

Warley, T.K. and R.R. Barichello. (1986, September). "Agricultural Issues in a Comprehensive Canada-U.S.A. Trade Agreement: A Canadian Perspective." In part from *Policy Harmonization: The Effects of a Canadian-American Free Trade Area.* Toronto: C.D. Howe Institute.

Watson, William G. (1987). "Canada-U.S. Free Trade: Why Now?" *Canadian Public Policy, 13*, 337–349.

Winham, Gilbert. (1985, October). "The Institutional Structures for Managing Canada-U.S.A. Trade Relations." *Proceedings of the 3rd International Trade Law Seminar-1985.* Ottawa: Department of Justice.

Winters, L. Alan. (1987). "The Political Economy of the Agricultural Policy of Industrial Countries." *European Review of Agricultural Economics, 14*, 285–304.

World Bank. (1987). *World Development Report 1987.* Oxford: Oxford University Press.

CHAPTER 3

THE DISPUTE RESOLUTION MECHANISM IN THE FREE TRADE AGREEMENT

G. Lermer

Dating from the late 1970s, a rise in U.S. protectionism has caused Canadians to take an unparalleled interest in the arcane subject of international trade law and in particular the trade contingency laws that encompass anti-dumping duties, counter-vailing duties and emergency trade provisions. Because of the recent spate of U.S. anti-dumping and countervailing cases against Canadian industries such as pork, potash, shakes, shingles, fish and potatoes, as well as several Canadian cases against certain U.S. producers, in particular corn producers, the media has brought the public's attention to this previously obscure field. Public attention has been sustained by the claims and counter-claims of proponents and critics of the Canada-U.S. Free Trade Agreement about the effectiveness of its provisions for safeguarding Canadians from politically motivated and protectionist U.S. actions pursuant to U.S. trade contingency law. The critics of the Agreement, noting that it fails to exempt Canada from application of U.S. law, advocate that Canada should reject the Agreement with the U.S. and work instead through the General Agreement on Tariffs and Trade (GATT). These views are common in agricultural circles, but recent developments have some-what muted them: GATT panels have attacked Canada's protection of both its beer and wine industries, whereas the Americans have insisted merely that Canada dis-mantle its protection of the wine industry.

Those who suggest Canada rely upon GATT for protection against U.S., Japanese and European protectionism and scrap the Canada-U.S. Trade Agreement are unin-formed of GATT's utter weakness in enforcing the interests of a small country against those of a major trading power. Michael Hart (1988) has pointed out that the U.S. trade contingency system has become, under duress, the accepted standard in all Gatt countries. Until very recently, no other major trading country except the United States made significant use of countervail. (The 1987 Canadian corn case, analyzed later in this volume, marked the first time a U.S. product has ever been countervailed.) Because of a lack of international jurisprudence in this area, the U.S. has a virtual monopoly on defining what are and what are not countervailable subsidies.

As Chase Wilde, Klein and Richter have pointed out, GATT is not a system of enforceable and binding world trade law: "It is a contractual arrangement among member countries" (Blackhurst, 1986, cited in Chase Wilde, et al.). GATT is equally well described as an effort to codify and systematize an area of traditional diplomatic activity. Its processes are therefore not designed to protect the rights of the weak. GATT negotiations and dispute resolution mechanisms reflect a dipomatic tendency to Realpolitik, the art of the possible that recognizes the political and economic realities of those countries powerful enough to dismiss GATT rulings with impunity. Hudec (1988) stresses that in GATT the term "dispute settlement" refers to a litigation procedure:

> A process under which one government can "sue" another for the violation of its legal rights. It means a procedure in which there is a neutral tribunal of expert judges that will rule on the legal complaint, issue orders to comply if there is a violation, and sometimes, in cases of serious violation, authorize the aggrieved party to take retaliatory trade action as compensation or as a sanction. (p. 145)

Dispute settlement under GATT therefore carries the trappings of what most lay persons would identify as the rule of law. But all this is a facade for a far different reality. The expert panels that adjudicate GATT disputes merely report their findings to the GATT Council. At the Council the guilty party is able to vote against any retaliatory measures. Merely by declining to accept the panel's finding, the guilty party formally avoids GATT's remedy. Whether or not the guilty party accepts the remedy and alters its behavior depends upon the sanctions that the aggrieved nation can credibly threaten to bring to bear against it, a simple example of enforcing one's will through brute power rather than rule of law. Thus, as far as trade contingency law is concerned, GATT is an arena formalizing bilateral negotiations over trade disputes, and is not a Court adjudicating disputes with some enforcement machinery at its disposal.

Nor does anyone hold much hope that an agreement can be reached remedying the fundamental flaw in GATT. Hudec (1988) points out that current proposals "have not yet gone so far as to recommend making GATT legal rulings effective in domestic law, as are rulings of the European Court of Justice. (GATT rules are not mandatory national law enforceable by national courts.)" (p. 146). GATT may never fullfill the hope of some that nation states would subject their bi-national trade disputes to international adjudication and commit themselves to abide by the adjudicator's decisions without bringing indirect pressure to bear to alter a GATT ruling. Hudec suggests that

"The GATT cannot be a world court of trade disputes. The GATT exists at the pleasure of its signatories. When it was the predominant player in the world economy, the United States had more leverage to impose trade solutions. Today, if the GATT rules are not politically acceptable to national governments they will be ignored and ultimately the GATT as a general body of principle will be eroded." (p. 157)

GATT is clearly a useful body that helps to hold up the lofty ideal of trade liberalization as a goal before the world community, but except for negotiating tariff reductions, it is a toothless tiger. According to Hudec, to give GATT teeth is to doom it to death. Evidently, those who place all their hopes for a fairer trading world in GATT are doomed to be disappointed.

In light of the impotence of GATT, small countries are for all intents and purposes defenceless. Hart (1988) points out that few small countries have made any use of contingency trade law as a means of protection or as a means of countering a large country's subsidies, dumping or protection. There is no mystery here. A small country finds it futile to appeal to GATT if a large country has ruled against it; it is easy for the large country to delay the GATT process and in the end to disregard it, at least as long as it takes for economic conditions to change and the trade protection to become superfluous. There is little in GATT to give a small country confidence that it will be safeguarded against a large country's trade contingency law.

Why do small countries not retaliate against larger ones by deploying their own trade contingency law against them? The answer here is that small countries usually have little to gain from imposing a duty on imports from a larger trading partner since it is the small country's own consumers who suffer from the duty. In small countries domestic prices will often rise by the full amount of the duty. Therefore, any Canadian campaign to alter American behavior through increased use of national trade contingency laws against U.S. producers, whether or not the commencing of cases and the harassment of U.S. producers is justified by subsidies or dumping, imposes costs on other Canadians that generally exceed the benefits gained for the complainants (see for example Lermer, elsewhere in this volume). Klaus Stegemann (1980) has shown that in almost every conceivable case a small country can find another instrument for redistributing income to the complainant that is less costly than is a temporary duty. This fundamental asymmetry between the positions of large and small countries makes trade contingency law a weak instrument for small countries to rely upon, unless strongly bolstered by international rules and sanctions. And as noted, GATT does not provide a mechanism for such international enforcement of small countries' contingency trade law decisions.

GATT has been successful in reducing tariff barriers but, despite considerable efforts, it has made little progress in the realm of non-tariff barriers (in which category I include trade contingency law). Historically, when tariffs have been reduced there has developed an increased demand for protection through the operations of quotas and contingency trade law: as early as 1904 in Canada the government introduced anti-dumping legislation in order to diffuse political pressure for it to increase tariffs (Grey, 1973, p. 8). Today, trade contingency law has again become an active field after the member nations of GATT succeeded in negotiating reduced tariffs. The rise of recent U.S. protectionism under its trade contingency legislation dates from the 1970s, following the full implementation of the Kennedy Round of tariff reductions and the entry of the United States into a prolonged recession after the rise in Middle East oil prices. The early 1980s have witnessed an extraordinary increase in countervailing and anti-dumping cases because of U.S. trade deficits in turn related to the appreciation of the U.S. dollar.

However, one should not dismiss the role of U.S. protectionism as a bargaining tool for improving U.S. access to European and Japanese markets. The trade war in which the U.S. is engaged does not seem to be softening the Europeans, whose political intransigence remains intact on behalf of farmers especially but also automobile workers, television set producers and numerous other industries. Many believe that the Common Market's planned integration in 1992 will result in a "Fortress Europe" that will raise protectionism to a new high. In contrast, U.S. policies are having some successes in pressuring the Japanese selectively to liberalize access to their market.

Simon Reisman (1988), Canada's Chief Negotiator of the Free Trade Agreement, points out that:

> Under GATT, in the final settlement of accounts, any concessions agreed to by pairs of countries are automatically accorded to everyone else. But there is a provision in GATT that allows countries to form a free trade area or a customs union. For such groupings, the trade concessions do not have to be extended to other countries. (p.12)

Clearly, in these circumstances Canada could not hope to negotiate an exemption for itself from U.S. trade contingency law outside the scope of a comprehensive agreement that is recognized as such by GATT. For Canada to negotiate a unique exemption for itself, it would have to extend the terms it offers the U.S. to all other GATT countries and, of course, the U.S. would be bound to make the same offer.

Since the United States views its trade contingency laws as a weapon in its arsenal with which to force Europe and Japan to agree to liberalize trade, there is no prospect for Canada to be exempted from U.S. law except in the context of a comprehensive agreement. If for no other reason, Canada needs the Free Trade Agreement to avoid being sideswiped by U.S. laws and actions that are aimed at others but must under

GATT be applied evenly to all countries. Canada gets caught dangerously in this trap because of its huge two-way trade with the U.S. and because U.S. trade law is driven by the private rights of complainants who have every reason to pursue Canadian exporters in order to profit from protection, even if the U.S. government would prefer to avoid trade disputes with Canada.

In light of the continuing weakness of GATT in dealing with trade disputes concerning non-tariff barriers, the issue of international trade contingency law and the particular institutions and laws in place in Canada and the United States will likely remain a subject of interest to an audience concerned with public affairs in general and not just to an audience of public servants, consultants and lawyers for whom trade contingency law is a specialized field. The agricultural community's continued interest in trade contingency law is the rationale for all the articles appearing in this volume, but these articles and especially the case studies of anti-dumping and countervailing duty proceedings were written before anyone had a chance to analyze the full details of how the U.S.-Canada Free Trade Agreement will alter the applications of both countries' trade contingency laws to each other. Canada's agriculture and food processing sectors have more reason to be concerned about U.S. protectionism through trade contingency laws than do other segments of society. As Steger (1988) points out, "During the first half of the 1980s, 70 percent of U.S. countervailing duty cases and 60 percent of U.S. anti-dumping cases against Canada involved agricultural and food sector products" (p. 161).

A Brief History and Evaluation of Trade Contingency Law

In the United States, the Tariff Act of 1897 (the Dingley Tariff) "provided for additional duties to be levied against imports that benefited from bounties or grants(that is, subsidies)" (Lande and Van Grossler, 1986, p. 108). An anti-dumping provision entered the system in 1916, and the trade remedy system was codified in the famous Smoot-Hawley tariff legislation, known officially as the Tariff Act of 1930. That Act remains in force but has been frequently amended, "most notably by the Trade Act of 1974, the Trade Agreements Act of 1979, and the Trade and Tariff Act of 1984" (Lande and Van Grossler, p.108).

In Canada, the anti-dumping system was initiated as early as 1904, but the system of countervailing duties is comparatively modern. Rodney de C Grey is the historian of the Canadian anti-dumping system up to 1968. (A brief review of the changes after 1968 is available in Salembier, Moroz and Stone, 1986.) As reported by Grey, until 1968 the existence of dumping and injury were not subject to case by case review by a tribunal; instead, customs authorities applied general rules of law. The formal injury review system in the United States usually involved long delays at the dumping investigation stage and before the injury inquiry, often leading an exporter to settle rather than fight the case. The Canadian system was up for renegotiation during the Kennedy Round tariff negotiation together with an effort to rewrite the GATT code.

As a result, the 1968 Canadian law separated the dumping investigation (by Customs) from the injury inquiry (by the Tariff Board) from the right to appeal (to the Federal Court). Thus after 1968 Canada's trade remedy law came into conformity with GATT and the U.S. system. The 1984 revision of the law, the Special Import Measures Act (SIMA), did not fundamentally alter the system established in 1968, but it does allow Canadian authorities far more discretion in the administration of the system. A major new provision in SIMA is the voice given to consumers and others potentially affected by a special duty: after injury is found, the Canadian Import Tribunal (now incorporated into the new Canadian International Trade Tribunal) may be petitioned by users to recommend to the Minister of Finance that a lower rate of duty be imposed.

Though the Canadian subsidy law is far more recent and has been used far less frequently than the dumping law, the two laws are today administered in a virtually identical way. During the 1970s only six or seven cases of subsidy were initiated and only three reached the Tribunal for a finding of injury. (See various issues of the Annual Report of the Canadian Import Tribunal for details.) At the same time anti-dumping cases were commonplace. Both antidumping and subsidy systems conform with GATT by separating the finding of dump or subsidy from the subsequent finding of injury. Both conform also in this respect to U.S. legislation. But Canadian and American law diverge in one crucial respect: American law creates a right for a private party to commence an inquiry and press its own case for a remedy. The Canadian law gives standing to a complaining party, but the complainant has no recourse if Revenue Canada chooses not to investigate or if it declines to find that dumping or a subsidy exists. Only if Revenue Canada takes up the matter does it proceed to the Import Tribunal for a determination of injury.

Too much can be made of this difference. Certainly petitioners in the United States have been assisted by having access and by administrative changes that invited more cases. Nivola (1986) documents how the shift of responsibility for enforcing the trade remedy law from the Treasury Department to the Commerce Department has improved the odds favoring the protection seeker. Moreover, administrative changes in the U.S. legislation have reduced the costs to American petitioners by speeding up the process to the point where a final determination of the facts can be made. Indeed, Nivola notes that merely by initiating a petition U.S. producers have been able to negotiate terms directly with foreign industry, amounting to a settlement out of court without a need to bring the matter before the U.S. International Trade Tribunal. The U.S. industry merely withdraws its complaint after the foreign industry acquiesces in some form of allegedly voluntary quotas. But a Canadian government that is aware that its industry is being harassed by foreign firms using trade remedy law has no incentive to restrain officials in Revenue Canada. Given normal bureaucratic preferences for expansion, Revenue Canada can generally be expected actively to pursue the cases of all petitioners. In these circumstances, the lack of access may not be a detriment to the petitioner. The petitioner is saved the costs of following a long and complex investigation, as the Crown itself absorbs all costs.

Article XVI of the GATT defines subsidies to be "any form of income or price support which operates directly or indirectly to increase exports from, or to reduce imports of any product into, its territory." GATT distinguishes between export and domestic subsidies. Only export subsidies on industrial and manufactured goods are prohibited. Agricultural goods were expressly exempted under American duress. Services have never been included. GATT is vague about its distinction between export and domestic subsidies, but an effort to be more specific is to be found in the GATT Code on subsidies that emerged from the Tokyo Round of negotiations. The important point to keep in mind is that Article VI of the GATT restricts the use of countervailing duties. Essentially, the GATT scheme recognizes that countervailing duties can be used as a ruse for providing protection as much as an instrument for enforcing an "even playing field."

Article VI of the GATT defines dumping to be the practice "by which products of one country are introduced into the commerce of another country at less than the normal value of the products." Usually this means that dumping is said to occur when an exporter sells products at lower prices abroad than at home despite the higher costs of delivery. In Canada it is possible to find dumping even if products are sold at the same price in Canada as in the exporter's market. It need only be shown that the products are being sold in both markets at prices below cost. Evidently, dumping legislation suffers from all the weaknesses of price discrimination legislation in anti-trust law. Dumping is alleged to parallel in trade law the role of price discrimination provisions in domestic legislation. At a practical level in both cases, it is unclear how to calculate the standard cost (the normal value in the GATT definition) from which the level of price discrimination or dumping is to be measured. At a theoretical level it is difficult to find many instances in which the culprit has a motive for selling at prices which are unreasonably low. The usual refrain is that the dumper intends to injure and force his competition out of the market and then to enjoy a lengthy period during which monopolistic profits will more than repay the initial investment incurred by selling at prices below costs. However, there are few dumping cases, of which I am aware, that any opportunity exists for the defendant in the case to recover monopolistic profits. As in the case of subsidies, Article VI of GATT wisely focusses on restricting the country that is out to build protective barriers on a foundation of alleged dumping.

Rising Trend of Protectionism in the United States

The above brief review of trade contingency law in the United States and Canada is a sufficient basis for observing that trade remedy laws are usually used by private parties to seek protection and that often the government sponsor of the complainant has a parallel interest in offering that protection. Thus trade remedy law is largely a vehicle by which politicians grant protection on a selected basis to specific petitioners who will be well aware of the political benefit received. Trade remedy law is of course not just a means of providing protection. It is unthinkable that countries that agree on removing tariffs would not simultaneously seek a means of controlling subsidies and especially export subsidies. Those trade remedy laws dealing with countervail duties provide an imperfect mechanism for institutionalizing the control of subsidies that can readily be used to achieve effects similar to those banned by the agreement to remove tariffs. At the domestic level, trade remedy laws are an effective channel into which politicians hope to direct political pressure in favor of protection. If effective, small doses of temporary protection help to diffuse broader coalitions of forces that might build in favor of wider reaching protection (see Finger et al., 1982). However, the latter strategy puts the politician in considerable danger because other constituents will realize the costs, if not directly then indirectly, after other countries choose to retaliate. Better by far to have a system that offers small and temporary doses of protection in the name of fair trade.

Clearly trade remedy law is a necessary evil and is as much a tool for liberalizing trade as it is a means of erecting trade barriers. Therefore, it may not be in anyone's interest, even Canada's, for the United States to cancel its trade remedy laws or to offer Canada complete exemption from those laws. However inviting that prospect might be in the short run, it should be tempered by the realization that the trade remedy laws act as a political outlet for aggrieved parties; in the absence of the laws the aggrieved parties might be in a position occasionally to enlist political support in favor of a more damaging and long lasting bout of protectionism that cannot be avoided through a bilateral agreement.

The focus of those concerned with building a liberal trade regime should be on the degree of protectionism offered by the trade remedy laws and the arbitrariness with which the laws are applied. At what point is U.S. trade remedy law a well-managed channel for conceding limited protection and highlighting unfair subsidies, and when does it cross over the line and become the major thrust of protectionst interests? Some Canadians (see Rugman and Anderson, 1987) believe that the boundary line between a benevolent and a virulent U.S. trade remedy regime was crossed in recent years and threatens to become far worse. Certainly there is evidence (collected below by Nivola, 1986) that the protectionist sentiment continues to build in the United States:

The United States International Trade Commission(ITC) took up almost twice as many investigations of unfair trade practices (section 337 of the 1974 Trade Act) in 1984 as in 1980, over three times as many anti-dumping investigations(Section 731 of the 1930 Tariff Act), and over four times as many countervailing duty cases (section 701 of the 1930 Act)....the proportion of affirmative opinions by the Commission climbed from 56 to 66 per cent after antidumping hearings and from only 5.5 percent to 83 percent in countervailing duty cases. (p. 578)

The 1974 and 1979 laws shortened the criteria and lag times for obtaining redress in escape clause and countervailing duty cases. As a condition for passage of the 1979 bill, Carter also agreed to transfer out of the Treasury

Department the power to levy countervailing duties and to administer anti-dumping sanctions; these tasks were handed to a more zealous bureaucracy, the Department of Commerce. The result was that the number of petitions climbed and so did the probability that the ITC would find in favor of the petitioners. (p. 592)

Nivola convincingly identifies the shift in administration of the import contingency laws as a response to a broadly based protectionism that has strengthened rather than waned during the economic expansion of the 1980s.

Canadian firms canvassed by the MacDonald Royal Commission in 1985 (Hart, 1986) "indicated as their main concern increasingly protectionist attitudes and expressed their desire for 'stricter rules' on the application of anti-dumping and counter-vailing measures" (p. 286). Yet Hart points out that the actual volume of cases would not seem to warrant the concerns being expressed by Canadian businessmen. During the 1980s to mid-1987, just 67 cases were launched and only 20 of them resulted in border measures. Evidently, withdrawn cases causing harassment are not included in these numbers. U.S. firms are free to threaten action, and cases settled between the U.S. executive and the Canadian government for which no border regulations go into effect may yet disadvantage the Canadian industry. For example, in the softwood lumber case, the tax on Canadian producers imposed by the federal government has the identical impact upon the companies as does an equivalent U.S. tariff.

Destler (1986) agrees that the trade remedy laws and procedures "have been transformed politically from means of diverting protectionist pressure to handy vehicles for asserting it, particularly for large industries" (p. 165). He also foresees "a rather bleak trade future...we are likely to see, at the very least, two extensions of recent trends: a further spread of negotiated barriers to imports, or 'managed trade,'and an even more fractious trade diplomacy, as our embattled officials demand more of foreign governments—and offer them less in return" (p. 172).

If Destler is right, the usual ebb and flow of protectionist sentiment in the United States that varies with economic conditions can no longer be relied upon to bring the system back from protectionism to equilibrium. Internally, what is different about the 1980s is the massive and persistent U.S. trade deficit that is continuing despite a weak U.S. dollar. Externally, the U.S. faces a stubborn Japanese economic success story, and the Japanese are unwilling to liberalize their own marketplace. Beyond the decade the U.S. is looking forward to a seemingly far more protection-oriented European Common Market already having demonstrated a surly disposition with respect to liberalizing agricultural trade. In these circumstances it may be too much to rely upon the balance of forces within the United States to temper the strong pro-protection pressures on the U.S. Congress. It is also asking a lot of Canadians to expect them to maintain their faith in a rigid GATT structure that is unable to overcome the forces leading the world's major trading blocks into a trade war. The Canada-U.S. Free Trade

Agreement offers Canadians a haven in the event that a still more violent, widespread and bitter trade war than already is being fought should become a reality.

The Dispute Settlement Mechanism

Chase Wilde et al. briefly touch upon the dispute settlement mechanism in the FTA which, they conclude, will, "bring Canadian and U.S. trade law closer together in the future." I agree with this conclusion, but the dispute settlement mechanism in the Agreement is among its most important elements and deserves further attention. Canada settled for the weaker dispute settlement mechanism instead of a stronger exemption for Canada from all U.S. trade law. More was not attainable, and what was achieved is quite remarkable because of the unprecedented measure of sovereignty ceded by the United States to a joint panel of mixed Canadian-American membership. The future of trade contingency law as an irritant to trade and commercial relations between the two countries rests largely upon the way the dispute settlement mechanism will work in practice. Of course no one is able to predict exactly how the scheme will in fact work itself out, especially as the negotiators of the Agreement foresaw a five- to seven-year period of continuous negotiation of a more complete overhaul of the dispute settlement mechanism, possibly leading to an integration of the two countries' systems of trade contingency law.

There are two dispute resolution mechanisms in the Free Trade Agreement. One, which receives the most attention here, is under Chapter 19. It governs disputes over countervailing duties and anti-dumping. The second, under Chapter 18, concerns disputes over interpretation of the Agreement but also governs disputes arising from "escape" clause and "safeguards" measures (Robinson, 1988, p. 265) described in Chapter 11 of the Agreement. Chapter 11 has quite properly received far less attention than countervailing duties and anti-dumping. The U.S. can invoke either of the two relevant provisions when a rapid surge of imports injures U.S. producers, and Canada is rarely a source of surging imports into the U.S. market. Under Chapter 11, each country can until 1998 "suspend duty decreases or return to a given most favored nation duty rate" (Robinson, p. 267). The trigger for such an action is a sharp surge of imports from the other country that causes serious injury to the producers of the importing country. Neither dumping nor countervailable subsidization need be alleged, shown or even involved. Emergency measures can remain in effect for up to three years (Robinson, p. 267).

Furthermore, Canada and the United States "agree in Article 1102 to exempt each other from global actions under the GATT" (Robinson, p. 267). Only if the other country's exports are the cause of "serious injury" might a general emergency or safeguard action be applicable to the partner under the Agreement. Because action under the emergency and safeguards provisions is largely an American phenomenon, the Free Trade Agreement has won for Canada a likely exemption from actions that are aimed at third parties.

Shirley Coffield (1988) has described and commented on the provisions of Chapter 19. Article 1901 restricts the Agreement to goods and excludes services. Article 1902, apart from confirming the applicability of each country's trade remedy laws, stipulates that future amendments to those laws will not have application to the other party to the Agreement without prior notification and consultation, and that the changes must conform with GATT obligations and be in the spirit of the Free Trade Agreement. Article 1903 sets out the process to be followed by panels established to determine in a dispute whether statutory amendments "conform to the GATT and the object or purpose of the FTA" (p. 255). Article 1904 sets out the role for bi-national panels in anti-dumping and countervailing duties disputes. If either party to a dispute, through its government, seeks a panel resolution to a final determination by a national administrative law decision, "the final determination cannot then be subject to judicial review in either country" (p. 257).

The panels will be chosen from a roster of 50, none of whom shall be government employees, 25 being from each country. A majority of the panelists must be lawyers. Each party chooses two panelists, "normally" from the roster. A party need not select one of its own nationals. Each party has four challenges to the other side's selections. Should a party fail to make a selection within the time period, 30–45 days, the selection is to be made by lot. If the parties are unable to agree on a fifth member, the selection shall be made by lot from the roster. The Chairman of the panel, to be selected by the panelists, must be a lawyer. Decisions are due within 315 days from the date of the initial request of the panel. The conduct of the panels is to be governed by rules of procedures to be established before 1 January 1989. An Extraordinary Challenge Committee, three members to be selected from a roster of ten judges or former judges, will be convened when one party alleges "gross misconduct, bias or serious conflict of interest of the panel making the decision which has affected the integrity of the process" (Coffield, 1988, p. 261). Article 1905 allows that even those cases initiated before the coming into effect of the Agreement be handled by the bi-national panel procedure when a new final determination is made by an administrative body. Usually automatic provisions call for each country's administrative tribunal to review a finding after two years even in the absence of a petition from an interested party. Other articles are entirely technical in nature, except that the standard of review to be used by the panels is set out explicitly in Article 1911.

Coffield's analysis leads her to conclude "that the 'discipline' on the two governments will be increased" (p. 269) in two dimensions—fewer harassment cases will be taken, and "obligations undertaken in the GATT" will receive greater respect. She concludes that "the Department of Commerce will look more carefully at its earlier precedents with respect to how it treats cases involving Canada, that policy decisions which make changes similar to those made in the lumber case would be more difficult to make" (p. 268). Panels reviewing cases like the softwood lumber case would certainly have some interesting material with which to work because as D. Gale Johnson, the eminent agricultural economist from the University of Chicago, has noted, "the economic reasoning and analysis in both [the hog and the softwood lumber] cases struck me as worth no more than a D minus paper in an intermediate microeconomics course. In fact, that might be an act of generosity" (quoted in Allen, 1988, p. 191–192). Whether the panels will be free to remedy the poor and sometimes arbitrary standards of economic reasoning applied by the U.S. Trade Commission is itself in dispute. At least in the softwood lumber case there is a high probability that a panel would have reversed the decision because the first finding was not merely flawed reasoning, it was also inconsistent with U.S. precedent.

Gary Horlick and Debra Valentine maintain that Canada might have anticipated winning a reversal on the softwood lumber case had it chosen to appeal the case rather than settle the issue with the U.S. Executive. However, the lengthy delay caused by appealing a case through the U.S. system can dissuade anyone from following that route. Horlick and Valentine report that the sugar and syrup anti-dumping case spent four years and five months in the U.S. judicial review process (p. 131). In the meantime, dumping duties were being collected. The new dispute settlement mechanism established under the FTA is a significant improvement over the existing process if only because it speeds up the appeal. At present in the United States an appeal of an initial decision may easily take two to three years (p. 131) while litigants must continue to deposit duties. Not surprisingly, most parties find the cost of appeal prohibitive. Canadian appeal procedures may also extend for two to four years. These authors attribute the improvement that makes the Free Trade Agreement a model for GATT to the twinning of the binding appeal process with a tight time schedule. They also agree with Coffield that the joint administration of the Free Trade Agreement "should lead to a convergence in the application of both countries' already similar trade remedy laws" (p. 138).

On the fundamental issue, the standard of review to be adopted by the panels, Horlick and Valentine imply that Canadians have gained considerably because U.S. courts (as compared with Canadian ones) apply a far tougher standard to their reviews of decisions by administrative law bodies. They report that "under the current U.S. system, the CIT has reversed, remanded or modified final agency determinations in numerous instances" (p. 140). According to Horlick and Valentine, "In Canada, the standard for judicial review is so lenient that foreign exporters often are disinclined even to apply for judicial review" (p. 141). In this area too, commentators hope that Canadian and American practices will converge.

All informed practitioners appearing regularly before both American and Canadian trade tribunals whose writings I was able to find agree that the Free Trade Agreement marks an important improvement on current practice and on GATT procedures. The key to the improvement is the speedier resolution of appeals by a system of bi-national panels whose precise composition can never be known in advance by the protection-seeking private. Both the speed of the process and the uncertainty about the composition of the panel raise the cost to an initiating private party that is seeking advantage through harassment. If an appeal can be made quickly and inexpensively, the initiator of the case can anticipate a higher probability of facing an appeal. The price of harassment rises by the costs of defending an appeal, and the probability of successfully harassing the exporter falls because harassment depends upon dissuading the exporter from appealing even those cases that are likely to be won by the appellant. Even the adjudicators of the facts in the administrative tribunal of first instance will be conscious of the likelihood of review by a bi-national panel selected from a roster of independent experts. Decision makers cannot be sanguine about frequent and speedy reversals of their decisions; and even if their decisions are upheld, they cannot appreciate having a review panel offer derisive asides about the quality of their fact finding.

Canada clearly gains through the bi-national panel system of adjudicating disputes. Does it gain much? This is more difficult to determine. At the outset it needs to be admitted that the trade remedy laws are a puny threat against the United States when employed by Canada. So the Americans evidently have little to gain taking this issue in isolation. Canada has the most to gain on the trade remedy law dispute resolution issue and may have needed to concede some points elsewhere to get it. Canada has gained a speedier and certainly fairer appeal mechanism, but it has not gained exemption from U.S. law. The scope of the review remains the same as under present U.S. law. But the American standard of review of U.S. administrative decisions is higher than the Canadian standard. Moreover, American law is not appreciably different from Canadian trade remedy law (which is indeed patterned on the U.S. law). And U.S. trade remedy law, in so far as it is to apply to Canada, cannot under the Free Trade Agreement be changed without Canada's assent. The latter provision is an unprecedented concession by the United States. One might well argue that the Free Trade Agreement prevents the United States from further broadening the definition of a countervailable subsidy. At the moment, under GATT articles most subsidies of general application to industries and regions, especially those not geared directly to export promotion, are non-countervailable. Many Americans would like to expand the range of subsidies that are countervailable. However, in so far as U.S. trade remedy law is applicable to Canada, the U.S. is prevented from expanding the range of countervailable subsidies unless the bi-national panels themselves should repeatedly interpret the current law in a broad rather than narrrow context. This seems most unlikely.

Conclusions

In the final analysis one must admit that the Free Trade Agreement does not fundamentally alter the power relations between the United States and Canada. Canada may find it difficult to compensate for or overturn measures adopted in the U.S. in response to political pressures for protecting a domestic interest from a Canadian exporter. If the U.S. insists on imposing a duty even after a bi-national panel rules against that action, it would be clearly acting in violation of the Free Trade Agreement.

Canada would be legally entitled to raise its own duties in a strategic way to damage a particular U.S. interest, even one entirely unconnected to the original dispute. In this manner a trade and diplomatic war would emerge that might well see the Trade Agreement being scuttled.

Canada has few trade instruments to wield as a means of holding the Americans to the Agreement, but U.S.-Canada relations are not a one-way street. The United States would be unlikely to seek to tarnish its reputation in world diplomatic circles by muscling a smaller country in the face of a valid trade agreement. If anything, one can imagine few issues of such fundamental importance to the U.S. that it would choose to risk its reputational capital by violating the Free Trade Agreement in order to get its way in a dispute with Canada. But one can think of issues that a Canadian government would take to be so fundamental that it would choose to risk violating the Agreement and thus expose Canadians to the economic consequences rather than the government to the political consequences. Protection of cultural industries is one example where Canada might draw the line in the face of U.S. intransigence. However, on balance, I think the forces on both sides of the border that support the Agreement should be able to overcome any threats to its survival and pull the two sides back from the brink if the Agreement is seriously theatened.

From Canada's point of view the Free Trade Agreement is just what it was advertised as being, an insurance policy to bring us under the protective umbrella of the United States free trade zone should the present trade dispute between the U.S., Asia and Europe develop into a more extreme trade war, pitting one protectionist block against another. Informed American opinion overwhelmingly takes the position that Congress will be unable to resist selective pressures for protection. Given the Democratic Party's strength in Congress, the Executive will necessarily compromise on trade matters. Europe heading into 1992 is similarly going in a protectionist direction. Hope seems dim that the current round of trade negotiations under the auspices of GATT will see a breakthrough in favor of a more liberal trading world. The opposite outcome is the more realistic forecast, and Canada is fortunate to have negotiated a treaty with the United States that will largely deflect the effect of American protectionism away from Canada.

REFERENCES

Allen, K. and D. MacMillan (Eds.). (1988). *U.S.-Canadian Agricultural Trade Challenges: Developing Common Approaches*. Washington, D.C.: Resources for the Future.

Coffield, S. (1988, January). Dispute Settlement Provisions on Anti-dumping and Countervailing Duty Cases in the United States/Canada Free Trade Agreement. Ottawa: University of Ottawa.

Destler, I.M. (1986). *American Trade Politics: System Under Stress*. Washington, D.C.: Institute for International Economics.

Finger, J.M., K.H. Hall and D.R. Nelson. (1982). "The Political Economy of Administered Protection." *American Economic Review*, 72, 452–466.

Grey, R. de C. (1973). *The Development of the Canadian Anti-Dumping System*. Ottawa: The Canadian Economic Policy Committee and the Private Planning Association.

Hart, M. (1988, 29 January). *Trade Remedy Law and the Canada-United States Trade Negotiations*. American Bar Association National Institute on U.S./Canada Free Trade Agreement.

Horlick, G.N. and D. A. Valentine. (1988, January). *Improvements in Trade Remedy Law and Procedures Under the Canada-United States Free Trade Agreement*. Paper presented at a conference on the Canada-U.S. Free Trade Agreement: Analysis of the text. Ottawa: University of Ottawa.

Hudec, R.E. (1988). "Dispute Settlement in Agricultural Trade Matters: the Lessons of the GATT Experience." In Kristen Allen and Katie MacMillan (Eds.). *U.S.-Canadian Agricultural Trade Challenges: Developing Common Approaches*. Washington, D.C.: Resources for the Future, 145–153.

Lande, S.L. and C. Van Grasstek. The Trade and Tariff act of 1984: Trade Policy in the Reagan Administration. Lexington, MA: D.C. Health.

Nivola, P.S. (1986). "The New Protectionism: U.S. Trade Policy in Historical Perspective." *Political Science Quarterly, 101*, 577–600.

Reisman, S.S. (1988). *The Canada-U.S. Free Trade Agreement: The Canadian Perspective*. Vancouver: The Fraser Institute.

Robinson, D.R. (1988, January). *Dispute Settlement Under Chapter 18 of the United States-Canada Free Trade Agreement*. Paper presented at the American Bar Association National Institute on the United States-Canada Free Trade Agreement, Washington, D.C.

Rugman, A.M. and A.D.M. Anderson. (1987). *Administered Protection in America*. London: Croon Helm.

Salembier, G.E., A.R. Moroz and F. Stone. (1987). *The Canadian Import File: Trade, Protection and Adjustment*. Montreal: The Institute for Research on Public Policy.

Stegemann, K. (1980, November). *The Efficiency Rationale of Anti-dumping Policy and other Measures of Contingency Protection.* (Discussion Paper #387), Queen's University, Kingston, Ontario.

Steger, D.P. (1968). "Canadian-U.S. Agricultural Trade: A Proposal for Resolving Disputes." In Kristen Allen and Katie MacMillan (Eds.). *U.S.-Canadian Agricultural Trade Challenges: Developing Common Approaches.* Washington, D.C.: Resources for the Future, 161–168.

CHAPTER 4

ECONOMIC ISSUES IN THE U.S. COUNTERVAIL CASE AGAINST CANADIAN HOGS AND PORK

K. Meilke and E. van Duren

Since the United States imposed a countervailing duty on Canadian hog exports in 1985, the gross revenues of Canadian hog producers have declined by approximately 70 million dollars per year (Meilke and Scally, 1987). The decision to impose a countervailing duty on Canadian hog, but not pork, exports has been the subject of continuous debate and many appeals. The breadth of the issues debated and the varied subjects of the appeals suggest there are aspects of U.S. countervailing duty law which are unclear and in need of change if such contentious decisions are to be avoided in the future.

The development of proper economic procedures and rules of evidence for countervailing duty cases becomes even more important given the recently negotiated Canada-U.S. Free Trade Agreement (FTA) and the Multilateral Trade Negotiations (MTNs) being conducted under the auspices of the General Agreement on Tariffs and Trade (GATT). If there is to be progress towards liberalizing international agricultural trade, the negotiators must agree not only on what measures constitute trade-distorting and potentially countervailable subsidies, but also on new procedures and rules of evidence for settling trade disputes.

Our objective in reviewing the countervailing duty case involving hogs and pork from Canada is to aid in the development of a more appropriate economic framework for analyzing the issues involved in trade disputes. Before proceeding to discussion of the specific issues involved in the hogs and pork case, we review selected portions of U.S. countervailing duty law and discuss the insights economic theory provides with regard to the process of settling trade disputes. (A Case History of the hogs and pork countervail case appears in Appendix One.)

Countervailing Duty Law

According to the GATT Subsidies Code of 1979 a country may impose a countervailing duty if government assistance available to foreign producers or exporters of a product materially injures the domestic producers of that product. The GATT Subsidies Code implies that this test can be implemented properly for cases involving domestic production subsidies by making the following three decisions:

(1) Standing: Are the complainants representative of the domestic industry that produces the subject product?

(2) Subsidy/Causality: Are there government programs that provide a subsidy to the domestic industry, and if so, to what degree do they cause a shift in, and/or movement up, the supply curve?

(3) Injury/Causality: Is the complainants' industry materially injured or threatened with material injury as a result of the subsidized imports and, more importantly, not other factors which could be harming the industry?

In the U.S. the International Trade Administration (USITA) makes the preliminary standing and subsidy determination and the International Trade Commission (USITC) makes the preliminary injury determination. The USITA then makes the final subsidy determination and the USITC the final standing and injury determinations. USITA and USITC decisions are made independently of each other, under strict time constraints and according to the U.S. interpretation of the GATT Subsidies Code. The decisions made under American countervailing duty law may not be entirely consistent with the GATT Subsidies Code (van Duren and Martin, 1987). In addition, given the complexity of U.S. countervailing duty law, decisions are not always consistent with those made in previous cases.

Furthermore, the majority of countervailing duty (as well as anti-dumping) case law applies to manufactured products, which economists characterize as "fix-price" markets, rather than to primary and semi-processed products such as hogs and pork, for which prices are determined in "flex-price" markets. Thus, economic evidence that may be quite useful in evaluating a countervailing duty case for a product priced in a "fix-price" market (such as price undercutting) may be irrelevant or misleading in a case involving a "flex-price" market.

A Theoretical Analysis Of A Countervailing Duty Case

Economic theory provides considerable insight into the three-part test for counter-vailing duties required by the GATT Subsidies Code. In most cases the largest subsidies provided to agricultural producers are fairly easy to identify, and it is widely accepted that not all subsidies are equally trade distorting. The problem of classifying subsidies according to their trade distorting effects is the most important issue in the MTNs, and is one which we do not attempt to resolve. However, we will address the other issues involved in a countervailing duty case.

The Subsidy Determination

Economic theory and the GATT Subsidies Code recognize two types of subsidies: export and domestic production subsidies. The following discussion concentrates on domestic production subsidies, since they are relevant to the hogs and pork case.

The effect of a domestic production subsidy is illustrated by the impact of a government program on the domestic supply curve in the subsidizing country (Country 1 in Figure 1). A domestic production subsidy exists if the program causes an outward shift (from S1 to S1') and/or a movement up the domestic supply curve (from P1 to P1'). The former is an input or "upstream" subsidy and the latter an output subsidy. Either type of subsidy alters the subsidizing country's excess supply curve. Production and exports from the subsidizing country increase, and the world price falls. The amount of trade distortion induced by the subsidy is the increase in exports, from OT to OT', for both the output and input subsidies, as depicted in Figure 1.

FIGURE 1
THE ECONOMICS OF A DOMESTIC PRODUCTION SUBSIDY

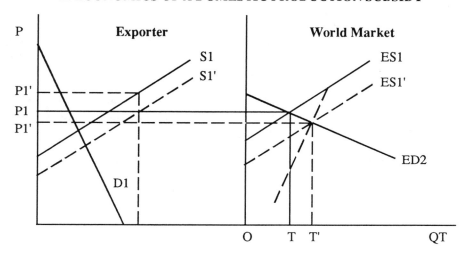

The Injury and Causality Determination

According to the GATT Subsidies Code, domestic producers in the complaining country must be materially injured by the subsidy available to foreign producers and/or exporters before a countervailing duty can be imposed. Figure 2 explains the economic concept of injury, in the case of an input subsidy.

FIGURE 2
THE ECONOMICS OF INJURY AND CAUSALITY

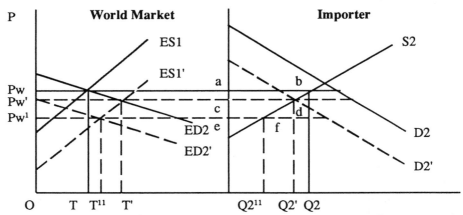

Recall from Figure 1 that an input subsidy in Country 1 induces a shift in both the domestic supply curve (from S1 to S1') and the excess supply curve (from ES1 to ES1'). Figure 2 depicts the shift in the excess supply curve. The existence and degree of injury experienced by producers in Country 2 are a function of the slope of Country 2's excess demand curve and the shift in Country 1's excess supply curve. A shift in the excess supply curve and a negatively sloping excess demand curve are necessary for injury, but the degree of injury depends on the extent of the shift in the excess supply curve and the slope of the excess demand curve. In the case shown the world price declines from Pw to Pw', trade increases from OT to OT', and producers' surplus in Country 2 declines by the area "abcd." Generally, the smaller the subsidizing country's exports are in relation to the importer's production and consumption, the less chance there is of finding material injury.

A proper determination of economic injury requires separating the impact of the subsidized imports on the domestic industry from other factors which may be harming the industry. According to the GATT Subsidies Code, "The injuries caused by other factors must not be attributed to the subsidized imports." This injury and causality test is simple at a theoretical level. Assume that an input subsidy produces the effects described above (Figure 2). Simultaneously there is a decline in consumer income in

Country 2, which causes the demand curve in Country 2 to shift from D2 to D2'. The joint effect of the subsidy and the decline in demand produces a decrease in the world price from Pw to Pw", an increase in trade from OT to OT", and a decrease in producers' surplus in Country 2 equal to the area "abef." Both factors, the subsidized exports and the decline in income, contribute to the injury. If both factors are required to produce a material effect on prices (0.5 %), then the subsidy *alone* does not cause material injury and a countervailing duty may not be appropriate.

Standing

The standing determination requires deciding whether the complaining producers have the legal right to bring a countervailing duty case. If they produce a product "like" the one subsidized by the foreign government then they can be considered the "domestic industry," and the case can proceed. A standing determination involves two issues. First, do the domestic producers produce a good that is sufficiently similar to the one being subsidized by the foreign government? This requires determining how readily or easily substitutable the domestic and foreign products are in final consumption and/or further production. The elasticity of substitution (which is either infinite for homogeneous goods, between infinity and zero for differentiated products, and zero for goods used in fixed proportions) can be used to classify products. However, the theory provides no guidance as to how large the elasticity of substitution must be before goods can be considered "similar," and the distinction between identical and similar products, while simple in a theoretical sense, is difficult to apply in the real world. Nonetheless, the decision as to whether products are similar or identical is crucial to the choice of the appropriate economic model to use in measuring the injury suffered by domestic producers. In Figures 1 and 2 the foreign and domestic products are assumed to be identical. However, if they are similar but not identical, a completely different type of analysis would have to be undertaken.

In our view, the decision whether the domestic industry produces a product sufficiently similar to the allegedly subsidized product to warrant a formal countervailing duty action should be based primarily on common sense and a detailed understanding of the markets, and secondarily on economic theory. In most cases there will be an incentive for the complainant to argue that the imported and domestic products are identical, while the defendant will argue that they are differentiated products. However, if no economic injury is found using the homogeneous product assumption it is highly unlikely the injury determination would be reversed under the differentiated product assumption.

The second issue in the standing determination is deciding whether the case involves one or more than one product (industry). The definition of the domestic industry is important in determining whether the foreign subsidies materially injure the domestic producers. This is the case because there is an economic incentive for the complainant to attempt to reduce the size of the industry to be used in the analysis.

Use of a smaller domestic industry would result in relatively larger price, revenue and income impacts. Conversely, the defendant has an economic incentive to attempt to expand the scope of the domestic industry, so the price, revenue and income impacts of the imports would be relatively smaller.

If there is more than one product involved in the case there may be an incentive to define the industries so that there is a greater likelihood of finding injury in one of them. One factor involved in an injury determination is the level of imports, or the ratio of imports to domestic production or consumption. The import ratios may differ among the products involved in the case, thereby providing an incentive for the complainant to separate the products into two or more industries if some products show higher import penetration ratios.

For products traded in more than one form, and at multiple levels of the market, incentives still exist to redefine the market, but the argument is slightly different. Since the processed product is derived from the raw product, the size of the domestic industry is largely determined by the amount of raw product produced, whether production is measured at the raw or processed level of the domestic market. Therefore, adding imports of the raw and processed product and dividing by some definition of domestic production results in a higher import penetration ratio than separating the raw and processed product industries. However, imports of one of the products, say the raw product, may be increasing at a faster rate than those of the other, and therefore of the combined raw and processed product. Since the rate of growth in import penetration is a factor that may be considered in a material injury determination, there may be an incentive for the complainant to argue for separate raw and processed product industries.

With respect to the standing decision, economic theory suggests a three-part test for determining the appropriate definition of the domestic industry when the product trades in both the raw and processed form. Throughout the subsequent discussion we assume that the product is traded at each market level and that all markets are efficient, i.e. that all arbitrage opportunities are exhausted. The first step is to document the government programs that provide subsidies, and to determine to which market level they most logically apply. The second step is to analyze the potential for the subsidies to injure the domestic industry at both market levels. A few examples will illustrate why this step is necessary.

Suppose a price support scheme for raw product producers in Country 1 results in increased production of the raw product in that country, and a lower market price for the raw product in both countries. In this case subsidies in Country 1 injure the raw product producers in Country 2, but the existence of the raw product subsidy does not injure the processing sector in Country 2. The processing sectors in both countries gain access to a lower priced input, and both sell their output for the same price.

Therefore, the processing sectors in both countries benefit, while raw product producers in Country 2 are injured and raw product producers in Country 1 benefit.

Now suppose that Country 1 provides a subsidy on the cost of fuel to its processors. Lower fuel costs allow processors in Country 1 to bid up the price of the other inputs, including the raw product. This causes injury to Country 2's processing sector and benefits raw product producers in both countries. Finally, suppose Country 1 offers a subsidy on every unit of raw product purchased from domestic sources. In the long run such a scheme increases the supply of the raw product in Country 1 and the raw product price in both countries declines. Therefore, raw product producers and processors in Country 2 would be injured.

The variety of possible scenarios suggests it is crucial to evaluate the potential effects of the existing subsidies on the various market participants before defining the domestic industry.

The final step in properly defining the domestic industry is a consideration of what effect a countervailing duty applied at one level of the market will have on trade flows and prices at other market levels. A countervailing duty applied on the raw product by Country 2 has the short-run effect (prior to any production response) of raising raw product prices in Country 2, reducing them in Country 1, and leaving processed product prices unchanged. Consequently, if Country 2 places a countervailing duty only on the raw product, it puts its processing industry at a competitive disadvantage. If the country imposing the duty on the raw product is relatively large it may be willing to ignore this effect, but in many cases a lack of response would be counterproductive.

The Case: Hogs and Pork from Canada

In this section we apply the general economic arguments presented above to the case of hogs and pork from Canada. Table 1 summarizes the arguments and evidence considered by the USITC in its decision that U.S. hog producers were materially injured, but that U.S. pork producers were not materially injured or threatened with material injury as a result of subsidized hog and pork imports from Canada.

The GATT Subsidies Code states that a country may impose a countervailing duty if the domestic producers of that product are materially injured as a result of government assistance provided to foreign producers or exporters of that product. We contend that this test was not applied properly in the case of hogs and pork from Canada. To develop this argument we assess on theoretical grounds the economic content of the standing, subsidy, and injury and causality determinations made by the USITC. We then present alternatives and, we believe, more correct estimates of the injury experienced by U.S. hog and pork producers as a result of Canadian subsidies for hog production.

TABLE 1
EVIDENCE USED BY THE USITC IN ITS FINAL INJURY AND CASUALTY DETERMINATION FOR HOGS AND PORK FROM CANADA

Decision Change: Level:	1981 to 1982 $1982	1982 to 1983 $1983	1983 to 1984 $1984	1984(I) to 1985(I) $1985(I)
I HOGS - INJURY				
1. U.S. Production	9% decrease	9% increase	7% decrease	slight increase
2. U.S. Domestic Shipments (sold for slaughter)	10% decrease	6% increase	4% decrease	6% decrease
3. Financial Experience				
- average profit margin farrow to finish/per hog	$24.09 increase	$2.62 decrease	$4.45 decrease	
- net profit margin of U.S. feeders/per cwt	$2.24 increase	$5.52 decrease	$4.44 decrease	
II PORK - INJURY				
1. U.S. Production		12% increase	2% increase	5% increase
2. U.S. Production Capacity		33% increase	constant	constant
Capacity Utilization		16% increase	2% increase	4% increase
2. U.S. Domestic Shipments	10% increase	7% increase	2% decrease	4% decrease
3. Total Exports (lbs.)	117,102	124,846	93,140	32% decrease
4. Numbers of Production Workers	12,783	13,216,	11,667	4% increase
Hours Worked (000's)	25,810	25,632	24,147	8% increase
Total Compensation ($000's)	319,774	307,950	239,599	8% increase
Labor Productivity (lbs./hour)	234	265	287	3% decrease
Unit Labor Cost (cents/lb.)	5.3	4.5	3.5	3% increase
5. Financial Experience of Selected Firm: Operating Income (mil.$)	21.4	-11.4	-14.7	85% decrease
- as per cent of sales	0.4	-0.2	-0.2	N/A

TABLE 1 (Continued)
EVIDENCE USED BY THE USITC IN ITS FINAL INJURY AND CASUALTY DETERMINATION FOR HOGS AND PORK FROM CANADA

Decision Change: Level:	1981 - 1982 $1982	1982 - 1983 $1983	1983 - 1984 $1984	1984(I) - 1985(I) $1985(I)
III HOGS - CASUALTY				
1. Imports from Canada	102% increase	52% increase	196% increase	97% increase
2. Import Penetration (% of apparent U.S. consumption)	0.4%	0.5%	1.6%	2.6%
3. Published U.S. Prices for Barrows and Gilts, $/cwt	$55.00	$48.00	$49.00	$48.00
Impact on prices ($/cwt)		$.19-.38 increase	$.64-1.27 decrease	$.18-.36 decrease
4. Impact on Gross Revenue (mil. $)		36-73 $ increase	118-234 $ decrease	32-64 $ decrease
IV PORK - CASUALTY				
1. Imports (mil./lbs)	269	266	345	
2. Import Penetration (% of apparent U.S. consumption)	40% increase	1% decrease	30% increase	32% increase
	1.9	1.7	2.2	2.8
3. Impact on Prices	- found no discernible trends			
	- price of pork in the U.S. increased at the same time that pork imports were increasing			

V PORK - THREAT OF INJURY

1. Production in Canada	- levels reached in early 1985 approximately equivalent to 1980 levels
2. Canadian Pork Consumption	- declined only slightly from 1980 to 1984
3. Canadian Pork Exports	- did not show consistent increase
4. Import Penetration	- Canada's share of the U.S. pork market remained low
5. Inventories	- U.S. holds virtually no inventories of Canadian pork
6. Canadian Hog Slaughter Capacity	- is adequate for slaughtering the hogs produced in Canada
7. Canadian Production Potential	- there has been a decline in breeding potential in the Canadian hog sector; this will reduce export ability
8. Product Shifting	- only conjecture that imposing a countervailing duty on hogs will lead to increase in pork exports from Canada

Standing

The USITA's preliminary standing decision on hogs and pork from Canada was that hog and pork producers were members of the same industry. It made this preliminary assessment on the basis of information obtained from experts in the industry, and it was consistent with the USITC's preliminary assessment of injury. The USITA's preliminary ruling relied primarily on four arguments. First, the packing stage of the production process contributes only a minor amount (10 per cent) to the "value added" of the product. Second, the demand for hogs is almost entirely dependent on the demand for pork, and thus hogs enter a "single continuous line" of production resulting in one end product, pork. Third, there is a commonality of economic interest between hog and pork producers, evidenced by the fact that several pork producers supported the hog producers' petition. Fourth, Canadian hog producers would be able to circumvent a countervailing duty placed only on hogs by exporting pork instead.

The USITC overturned this preliminary decision, ruling that the U.S. hog and pork industries were separate industries. In reaching this decision the USITC relied on the following arguments. First, hogs and pork have different end uses and are produced in different facilities. Second, the USITC, unlike the USITA, found that substantial value is added to hogs at the packing stage. Third, there is little interlocking ownership between the hog and pork industries, and the prices of hogs are not linked by contract to the price of pork. Oddly, the USITC did agree that the hog and pork production processes met the "single continuous line" of production criterion, but the Commission rejected the argument that economic integration could be established solely by the high correlation between hog and pork prices.

Some members of the USITC raised the question whether a countervailing duty placed only on hogs would result in increased imports of pork from Canada. Although some Commissioners agreed it was possible, in the majority decision the probability of product shifting was viewed as conjectural. Therefore the hog and pork industries were treated as separate industries, and only the U.S. hog industry was deemed to be injured.

The USITC decision to treat hog and pork producers as members of separate industries at the beginning of the formal hearings resulted in several problems. The expert witnesses based their analyses on the USITA's preliminary decision that hog and pork producers were members of one industry. Thus, much of the evidence used to make the injury and causality determinations for hogs and pork was flawed, and this eventually resulted in the U.S. Court of International Trade remanding the decision for reconsideration of the price elasticities of demand used in the injury determination for hogs.

The Subsidy Determination

The USITA applies its "specificity test" to determine which programs available to foreign producers of the subject good are countervailable. Under U.S. law, if a program is available to a "specific enterprise or industry or group of industries or enterprises" then it provides a countervailable subsidy.

In calculating the level of the subsidy, per unit of production, payments made to foreign producers or government expenditures for each program are divided by the level of production in the relevant political jurisdiction. Limitations on producer participation and program benefits are not considered, and the potential production response to a program is not a factor in the calculation. There are a number of features of this method of calculating subsidies that could be challenged. But it is important to note that the USITA's method of calculating the amount of the foreign subsidy is equivalent to the procedure that the U.S. and several other countries are advocating for calculating subsidy levels (producer subsidy equivalents, PSEs) in the current round of GATT negotiations. In fact, the PSE normally incorporates all government programs, even those that are generally available. Therefore, any criticism of the procedure that the USITA uses to calculate subsidies is equally applicable to the PSE.

Table 2 lists the federal and provincial programs available to Canadian hog producers that were considered to be countervailable by the USITA. The subsidies provided by each program are listed on both a live and dressed weight basis. Output subsidies, provided through federal and provincial stabilization payments to hog producers, account for 90 per cent of the estimated total subsidy of $4.39 cwt/live. Several smaller provincial programs which provide a variety of input and output subsidies account for the remainder of the estimated total.

The Final Injury and Causality Determination for Hogs

The USITC's final decision that U.S. hog producers were materially injured as a result of Canadian subsidies was based on the evidence summarized in Table 1. First, the import penetration ratio of Canadian hogs and pork in the U.S. market was increasing, and there was some evidence of a negative correlation between this increase in imports and the erratic decline in U.S. market hog prices from 1982 to the first quarter of 1985 (Figure 3). Using quarterly data from the first quarter of 1982 to the second quarter of 1985, the simple correlation coefficients between U.S. hog prices and Canadian hog exports, pork exports and hogs plus pork exports, are -0.4, -0.3 and -0.4, respectively, while the correlations with U.S. pork prices are slightly higher.

The degree of correlation between Canadian exports and U.S. hog prices is low, and very sensitive to the time period selected for analysis. This point is also illustrated in Table 3. When the correlation coefficients are calculated using four additional quarters of data (for 1981), three of the six correlation coefficients switch signs—from

TABLE 2
FEDERAL AND PROVINCIAL PROGRAMS AVAILABLE TO CANADIAN HOG PRODUCERS DEEMED TO CONFER COUNTERVAILABLE SUBSIDIES, AND CALCULATION OF SUBSIDY LEVEL

	Live Weight[a]	Dressed Weight[a]
Countervailable Government Programs		
Federal Programs		
Agricultural Stabilization Act	1.7890	2.2510
Joint Federal-Provincial Programs		
Record of Performance	0.1140	0.1440
Provincial Programs		
B.C. Swine Producers Farm Income Plan	0.0480	0.0600
Manitoba Hog Income Stabilization Plan	0.1040	0.1310
New Brunswick Hog Price Stabilization Plan	0.0540	0.0680
Newfoundland Hog Price Support Program	0.0130	0.0170
Nova Scotia Pork Price Stabilization Program	0.0680	0.0860
P.E.I. Stabilization Program	0.0450	0.0570
Quebec Farm Income Stabilization Insurance Program	1.6960	2.1330
Saskatchewan Hog Assured Returns Program	0.1220	0.1530
Total Provincial Stabilization Programs	**2.1500**	**2.7050**
	Live Weight[a]	Dressed Weight[a]
Countervailable Government Programs		
New Brunswick Swine Assistance Program	0.0004	0.0006
New Brunswick Loan Guarantees and Grants Under the Livestock Incentives Program	0.0030	0.0040
New Brunswick Hog Marketing Program	0.0060	0.0080
Nova Scotia Swine Herd Health Policy	0.0010	0.0010
Nova Scotia Transportation Assistance	0.0050	0.0060
Ontario Farm Tax Reduction Program	0.2700	0.3390

TABLE 2 (Continued)
FEDERAL AND PROVINCIAL PROGRAMS AVAILABLE TO CANADIAN HOG PRODUCERS DEEMED TO CONFER COUNTERVAILABLE SUBSIDIES, AND CALCULATION OF SUBSIDY LEVEL

Countervailable Government Programs	Live Weight[a]	Dressed Weight[a]
Ontario (Northern) Livestock Programs	0.0000	0.0000
P.E.I. Hog Marketing and Transportation Subsidies	0.0060	0.0070
P.E.I. Swine Development Program	0.0020	0.0020
P.E.I. Interest Payments on Assembly Yard Loan	0.0000	0.0000
Quebec Meat Sector Rationalization Program	0.0040	0.0050
Quebec Special Credits for Hog Producers	0.0040	0.0050
Saskatchewan Financial Assistance for Livestock and Irrigation	0.0360	0.0450
Total Other Provincial Programs	**0.3375**	**0.4227**
Total Provincial Programs	**2.4875**	**3.1277**
Total Countervailable Programs	**4.3905**	**5.5227**

[a]Canadian cents/lb.

Source: U.S. Federal Register, Vol. 50, No. 116, Monday, June 17, 1985.

Notes: The subsidies per program on a live weight and dressed weight basis were reported by the USITA in its final determination.

negative to positive. More importantly, these simple correlation coefficients do not provide evidence that changes in Canadian hog and pork exports result from production subsidies available to Canadian hog producers, or that these subsidies cause lower prices.

FIGURE 3
IMPORTS OF CANADIAN HOGS AND PORK AND U.S. HOG AND PORK PRICES

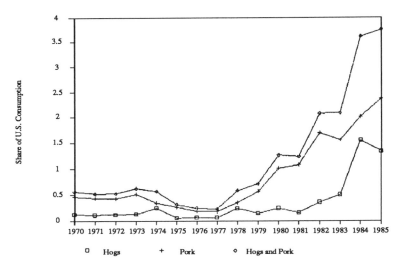

The second piece of evidence the USITC used to support its affirmative injury determination was the economic analysis conducted by Commission staff economists. This intriguing analysis was partially based on evidence provided by the expert witnesses at the formal hearing. These witnesses provided a range of estimates of the price flexibility of demand—the percentage change in price given a one per cent change in the quantity supplied-for pork in the United States. The flexibilities ranged from the low of -2.0 provided by the complainant's witness to the high of -1.0 provided by the defendant's witness. These price flexibilities could have been used in conjunction with the increase in Canada's share of U.S. pork consumption to estimate, albeit incorrectly, the impact of Canadian imports on U.S. hog prices and U.S. hog producers' revenues. For example, Canada's import penetration ratio for hogs increased from 0.4 per cent in 1982 to 0.5 per cent in 1983. If the USITC had assumed that the entire increase in import penetration was due to Canadian subsidies, then U.S. prices would have declined by 0.1 to 0.2 per cent, allegedly as a result of Canadian subsidies. Figure 4 shows hog and pork imports as a percentage of U.S. consumption.

TABLE 3
SIMPLE CORRELATION COEFFICIENTS OF CANADIAN HOG,
PORK AND HOG PLUS PORK EXPORTS
WITH U.S. HOG AND PORK PRICES

Variables	Hog Price		Pork Price	
	1981–85	**1982–85**	**1981–85**	**1982–85**
Hog Exports	-0.10	-0.41	-0.12	-0.56
Pork Exports	+0.15	-0.29	+0.03	-0.47
Hog plus Pork Exports	+0.01	-0.41	-0.05	-0.54

FIGURE 4
CANADIAN IMPORT PENETRATION RATIOS FOR HOGS
AND PORK IN THE U.S.

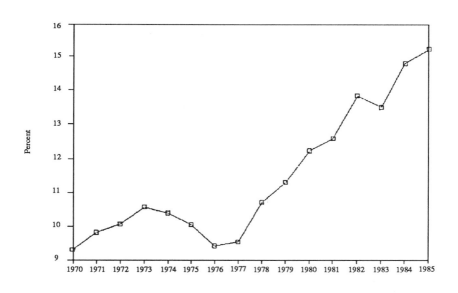

FIGURE 5
CANADA'S SHARE OF NORTH AMERICAN HOG MARKETINGS, 1970 TO 1987

U.S. Hog and Pork Prices

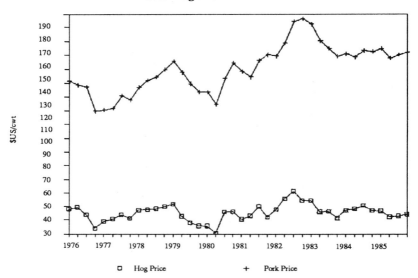

Canadian Hog and Pork Exports

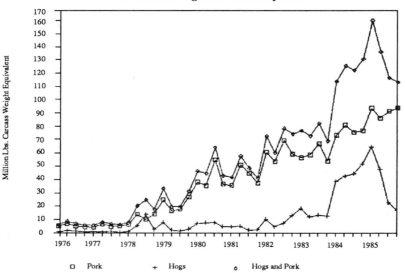

However, the USITC did not do this. The USITC staff economist argued that the North American pork market should be treated as an "integrated" or single market. This approach is reasonable and one with which we largely agree. However, it assumes implicitly that the North American pork and hog markets arbitrage perfectly and that the cost of transferring hogs and pork between the two markets is either zero or a constant percentage markup on the price. The USITC estimated injury to hog producers by:

(1) Calculating the ratio of Canadian hog marketings to North American hog marketings.

(2) Determining the change in this ratio from year to year.

(3) Using the change in this ratio as the change in quantity in the price flexibility expression to determine the impact of Canadian production subsidies on U.S. hog prices.

As shown in Figure 5, Canada's share of the North American hog market has been increasing by about 0.6 percentage points per year, almost without exception since 1976. Nonetheless, the USITC assumed that any increase in Canada's share of North American hog marketings was due to subsidies on Canadian hogs. Consequently, the Commission argued that the decline of 0.4 percentage points in Canada's share of the North American market in 1983 increased U.S. hog prices by 0.4 to 0.8 per cent over the prices that would have prevailed without Canadian hog subsidies. They did not take into account the fact that Canadian production had increased by 2.8 per cent between 1982 and 1983. When Canada's share of the North American market increased by 1.3 per cent in 1984 and 0.4 per cent in 1985, the increase was assumed to be entirely the result of Canadian hog subsidies, and the estimated decline in U.S. hog prices was 1.3 to 2.6 per cent in 1984, and 0.4 to 0.8 per cent in 1985.

The analytical approach used by the USITC to quantify injury to the U.S. hog industry can only be justified by assuming that the American and Canadian hog sectors are identical. Specifically, one must assume that in the absence of Canadian government programs hog producers in both countries would change production levels identically (in percentage terms) for a given price change, which implies that the price elasticity of supply in both countries is identical. However, there is nothing in economic theory, or the history of the North American hog market, to support this assumption. Even if the USITC's assumption was correct, the procedure still fails to relate declines in U.S. hog prices to increases in hog imports from Canada. This must be done under U.S. countervailing duty law. The USITC's analysis also ignores the possibility of increased Canadian production being consumed in Canada or in third country markets.

In summary, the USITC's economic analysis of the hog sector did not relate changes in Canada's exports to the U.S. to price changes in that market and did not, as required by law (Bryan, 1980), attempt to separate the impact of imports from Canada from other factors which could have depressed U.S. hog prices.

The final piece of evidence used by the USITC in its affirmative injury determination was the observation by one of the Commissioners that when Canada exported hogs, hog prices in Ontario were below hog prices in the U.S. and this price spread tended to increase as Canadian exports increased. This was interpreted as strong evidence of price undercutting by Canada. While this interpretation may be valid for a "fix-price" market, it is incorrect when applied to a "flex-price" market such as the North American hog market. But the fact that the practice of price undercutting is completely inconsistent with the assumptions underlying the economic analysis conducted by the USITC economists went unnoticed.

The Final Injury and Causality Determination for Pork

The USITC's final decision that U.S. pork producers were not injured or threatened with material injury as a result of imports of pork from Canada was based on the following arguments.

The U.S. pork industry was experiencing material injury, but not as the result of pork imports. The finding of material injury was supported by several facts. First, the industry's financial situation had deteriorated from 1982 to 1985, even though productivity was increasing and wage rates were declining. Second, the number of workers employed declined irregularly from 1982 to 1984. Third, an increase in production levels and production capacity resulted in a decrease in the capacity utilization rate. However, the fact that packers' operating income as share of their net sales was 0.4 per cent in 1982, and then declined to a negative margin of 0.2 per cent in 1983 and 1984, appears to be the key piece of evidence that the USITC used in its decision.

The Commission then had to determine whether imports of pork, but not hogs, from Canada caused the material injury being suffered by the U.S. pork industry. They determined that pork imports from Canada were not the cause of the material injury. The argument was as follows. First, the level of pork imports increased, from 192 million pounds in 1982 to 345 million pounds in 1984, but Canada's share of U.S. consumption remained low, at 2.8 per cent by the first quarter of 1985. Second, the USITC could find only one instance in which a U.S. processor lost a sale to a Canadian pork processor. Third, the USITC could not find any discernible relationship between Canadian pork imports and U.S. pork prices, and they noted that U.S. pork prices generally rose during the time that imports from Canada were increasing.

The USITC's economic analysis for the injury and causality determination for pork was deficient in several ways. First, there is no theoretical or legal reason and there is nothing in the history of the North American hog market to suggest that a Canadian share of 2.8 per cent of U.S. consumption is "low." This is a matter of judgment, and the numbers could be used to support either the argument that it is "high" or that it is "low" (see Table 1). Second, the statement that there was only one instance of a confirmed lost sale to a Canadian processor implies that USITC is using logic that applies to "fix-price" markets rather than to "flex-price" ones. Third, the apparent lack of a relationship between U.S. pork prices and imports from Canada was derived from casual observation of the trends in U.S. pork prices and Canadian imports, as shown in Figure 3. Although the USITC is not required to explain how it "reviewed the pricing data" with respect to the effect of imports of Canadian pork, the fact that they did explain the procedure used for hogs, and refer only to tables containing price and import data for pork, suggests that the Commission did not conduct an econometric analysis of this issue.

Since the USITC determined that U.S. pork producers were not materially injured as a result of pork imports from Canada, it was required to determine whether U.S. pork producers were *threatened* with material injury by Canadian pork exports. The countervailing duty placed on hog imports from Canada made this question an especially interesting one.

Section 612 of the U.S. Trade and Tariff Act directs the USITC to consider several factors in determining if there is a threat of material injury. (These factors are listed in Table 1.) The USITC decided that the following facts indicated there was no threat of injury to the U.S. pork industry. First, although Canadian pork production increased during the period of investigation, it had only reached the 1980 level by the first quarter in 1985. Second, Canada's share of U.S. pork consumption remained "low," only reaching 2.8 per cent by the first quarter of 1985. Third, there were virtually no U.S. inventories of Canadian pork. Fourth, the Canadian processing industry had adequate capacity to slaughter Canadian hogs. Fifth, the breeding potential of the Canadian hog industry had declined, which indicated that Canadian pork exports would likely decrease. Last, the possibility that Canadian exporters would switch from hog to pork exports in response to a countervailing duty on hogs was viewed as speculation only, and therefore not permissible as evidence of a threat of material injury under U.S. law.

Again, several aspects of the USITC's decision were deficient in economic reasoning. The potential for product shifting in Canada, from hog to pork exports, in response to U.S. countervailing duties on hogs, was argued incorrectly. A duty on hog exports reduces hog prices in Canada, raises them in the U.S., and provides a competitive advantage to the Canadian packing industry since North American pork prices remain unchanged in the short run. The existence of adequate slaughter capacity in Canada only makes it easier for Canada to increase its pork exports to the United States. If the Canadian industry had inadequate hog slaughter capacity the potential for product shifting would be less, but this is contrary to the argument presented by the USITC.

Although the majority USITC opinion found that the potential for product shifting, from hog to pork exports, was too speculative an area, one Commissioner disagreed quite strongly with the majority reasoning and we believe correctly so. Commissioner Eckes stated that in the absence of a countervailing duty on pork it was extremely likely that Canadian exporters would increase pork shipments in order to circumvent countervailing duties on hogs.[1]

The Remand

In August, 1987 the U.S. Court of International Trade (USCIT) remanded the final determination on hogs and pork from Canada for reevaluation of evidence concerning the price flexibilities/elasticities relied on by the USITC. The price flexibilities estimated by the expert witnesses were based on a quantity variable defined as pork disappearance, which was consistent with the USITA's preliminary determination that hog and pork producers were members of the same industry. However, when the USITC determined that hogs and pork were separate industries, these flexibilities were no longer appropriate for evaluating the impact of hog and pork imports from Canada on U.S. hog and pork prices, respectively. Nevertheless, the USITC did use them in its final determination.

Therefore, the USCIT directed the Commission either to obtain new data for its price flexibility estimates *or* to identify and explain what data in the existing record supported the redetermination. The USITC staff economist erroneously advised the Commissioners that the former option was not possible since the data were not readily available. He suggested that the latter option be pursued, and specifically that any bias in the price elasticities that resulted from aggregating U.S. hog slaughter and U.S. net imports of pork (instead of treating hogs and pork separately) was quite small. Consequently, he "adjusted" the price flexibilities provided by the expert witnesses to arrive at new estimates of hog price flexibilities ranging from -0.97 to -1.98 rather than -1.0 to -2.0. A complete discussion of this issue is contained in Meilke (1987), but it is obvious that the staff economist failed to come to grips with the issue of how to measure injury in an open trading environment involving both a raw and a processed product.

In its redetermination the USITC could only consider the effect of the revised elasticity estimates on the outcome of the case. However, two of the four Commissioners considered other evidence, and one dismissed the relevance of "elasticity analysis." A tied vote resulted from the remand, and the countervailing duty of $4.39 cwt was maintained on imports of Canadian hogs.

Alternative Estimates of Injury

Having criticized the methods used by the USITC to calculate injury, we feel compelled to provide a more satisfactory alternative. To accomplish this we use a quarterly econometric model of the North American hog and pork sector developed by Meilke and Scally (1987). This model explains pork consumption and inventories, hog slaughter, hog production and prices and trade for both hogs and pork in the U.S. and Canada.

To allow comparison with the method used by the Commission to estimate injury, we approximated the USITC's procedure by simulating the model. The results for hog prices were consistent with those obtained by the USITC for 1983 and 1984, but we estimated considerably larger declines in hog prices for 1985. This was likely caused by the fact that the USITC considered only the first quarter of 1985, while our simulation used a full year's data and also allowed for feedback effects not considered by the Commission.

The USITC's definition of injury implies that a finding of injury to U.S. producers would only have been avoided if Canada had maintained its share of North American hog production at the 1982 level. Our estimates of the effects of holding Canada's share at 13.9 per cent (the average value in 1982) for 1983 through 1985 are shown in Table 4. Canadian hog production would have been reduced by an average of 5.2 per cent and prices in Western Canada would have increased by 3.8 per cent. Gross revenues from hog production in Canada would have decreased by 2.7 per cent. Hog processors would also have experienced losses in economic welfare ranging from 4.0 per cent in Canada to 0.3 per cent in the United States.

Since we have argued that the USITC's method of determining injury is incorrect, what is the correct method? The correct process is illustrated in Figures 1 and 2. These figures show that an output subsidy pivots the subsidizing country's excess supply curve to the right at the domestic support price. To simulate this effect we subtracted the USITA's estimate of the subsidy ($4.39 cwt/live) from the market price for hogs used in the model's Canadian hog supply equations. This approach assumes that producers perceive a decline in subsidies identically to a decline in hog prices when they make their supply decisions. Analyses by Martin and Goddard (1987) and Gilmour and Cluff (1987) have suggested that this approach overstates the impact of the subsidy on production, and the extent of the overestimate is a salient issue in the controversy over the causality test. The results of our analysis to determine injury are presented in Table 4.

Reducing the supply price of hogs by the USITA's estimate of the subsidy lowers Canadian hog production by an average of 1.3 per cent between 1983 and 1985. Canadian hog exports decline by 8.7 per cent and net pork exports fall by 3.2 per cent. U.S. hog prices increase by 0.3 per cent and pork prices rise by 0.2 per cent. Gross revenues of U.S. hog producers also increase by 0.3 per cent. Consequently, all the price and revenue variables in the U.S. sector increase by less than the threshold (*de minimis*) level of 0.5 per cent. This suggests that the USITC should have found there was no injury to U.S. hog or pork producers. Of course this finding would be predicated upon the USITC conducting a proper economic analysis.

TABLE 4
ALTERNATIVE METHODS OF DETERMINING INJURY, AVERAGE
PERCENTAGE CHANGE, 1983 TO 1985

Variable			Method
1	2	3	
Canada:			
Hog Production	-5.2		-1.3
Hog Slaughter	-2.0		-0.5
Hog Exports	-34.9	-76.7	-8.6
Gross Revenues (Hog Producers)	-2.7		-0.6
Hog Price (East)	+3.1		+0.6
Hog Price (West)	+3.8		+0.8
Packers' Welfare	-4.0	-31.5	-1.0
Pork, Net Exports	-12.6		-3.2
Pork Price	+0.8		+0.2
United States:			
Hog Production	+0.0	+0.3	+0.04
Hog Slaughter	-0.6	-0.6	-0.1
Gross Revenues (Hog Producers)	+1.6	+2.7	+0.3
Hog Price	+1.6	+2.4	+0.3
Packers' Welfare	-0.3	+0.3	-0.02
Pork Price	+1.0	+1.8	+0.2

Method 1: Fix Canadian share of total North American hog production at its 1982 level of 13.87 per cent.
Method 2: Fix Canada's exports of hogs and pork to their average values for the period 1980 (1) to 1982 (4).
Method 3: Subtract Canada's alleged subsidy on hog production of $4.39 cwt/live from the actual market prices incorporated in the Canadian hog supply functions.

Source: Meilke and Scally

In devising new rules for settling trade disputes there will always be a temptation to institute simple, but incorrect, procedures, rather than requiring the use of more complex, but proper, economic analysis. One simple, but incorrect, procedure is to measure injury by determining the price effects of restricting exports to the level of some base period. To illustrate the danger involved in this approach we have simulated the impacts of restricting Canada's hog and pork exports to their average values over the three years prior to 1983 (57,530 head of hogs and 49.5 million pounds of pork). As presented in Table 4 the price impacts estimated using this method are even larger than those obtained by the USITC's method, which fixed Canada's share of the North

American production. The estimated impact on U.S. hog prices is eight times larger than the price effect estimated using the correct method described earlier.

Conclusion and Implications of the Canada-U.S. Free Trade Agreement

It is our conclusion that the economic analysis relied on by the USITC in its determination that U.S. hog producers were materially injured as a result of the subsidies available to Canadian hog producers was fundamentally flawed. Based on our review of the hogs and pork case we conclude that the process for settling countervailing duty cases could be improved by recognizing the following:

First, different procedures will be required for cases involving "flex-price" markets than for cases involving "fix-price" markets.

Second, there is a desperate need to incorporate more economic logic in the methods used to measure injury. In particular, the market level at which the subsidies apply must be identified carefully, and the potential impact of the subsidy must be separated from the effects of other factors which may be having a negative influence on the industry.

Third, the standing decision, with regard to whether producers of raw and processed products are members of the same industry, should rely on criteria such as those developed earlier in this chapter rather than on current procedures.

Fourth, the question of what is a trade distorting subsidy will have to await the outcome of the current round of MTNs. However, if a proper procedure for analyzing material injury is used, the definition of a countervailable subsidy becomes far less important.

Two questions certain to be raised by the above analysis are: (1) what impact will the FTA have on the countervailing duty placed on Canadian hog exports if it is ratified; and (2) what impact would FTA have had on the countervail decision if had it been in effect at the time the case was heard?

The first question is the easiest to answer because the FTA contains no special provisions for the hogs and pork case. Therefore, the current duty of $4.39/cwt live will remain in place until the USITA conducts a review of the case. Normally, a review of the case can be conducted if the "circumstances" involved in the case have changed and there is a good reason for conducting a review. A change in circumstances may include a change in the level of the estimated subsidy, and therefore the estimated countervailing duty. Normally, a review is not conducted within two years of the final determination, and any application for revocation of the final countervailing duty order will not be considered until no imports of the subject good have occurred for a two-year period (Bryan, 1980).

Whether the FTA would have influenced the decision on hogs and pork from Canada, had it been in effect, is more difficult to answer. All provisions for settling disputes over subsidies and dumping will apply to agricultural trade. However, the provision of FTA most likely to have affected the hogs and pork case is the replacement of judicial review by domestic courts of countervailing and anti-dumping orders by a bilateral panel, whose findings will be binding on both countries. This five-member bilateral panel, composed of at least two mutually agreed upon members from each country, will have the power to determine whether a case has been conducted in a manner consistent with the relevant national law. Had this panel existed when Canada appealed the final decision in hogs and pork it would have been responsible for determining whether the economic evidence used in the final affirmative determination was correct under U.S. countervailing duty law. We hope that the panel would have:

(1) found that the economic analysis used by the USITC did not separate the potential injury caused by Canada's hog subsidies from other sources of injury.

(2) decided that the USITC's finding that the hogs and pork were separate industries required new economic evidence.

There are other provisions of the FTA that could have influenced the hogs and pork case, but none as fundamentally as the bilateral panel mentioned above. The FTA's dispute settlement provisions for subsidies imply that much work remains to be done in order to arrive at mutually acceptable rules and procedures for settling these disputes. We hope that the lessons of the hogs and pork case will prove to be valuable in avoiding past errors.

NOTES

1. Evidence to support this argument included information obtained by the USITC which indicated that Canada has increased both its ability and need to boost pork exports to the U.S. Canada already has adequate slaughter capacity, and capacity could be increased without substantial investment or reorganization, since most slaughter houses in Canada operate only one shift. Canadian per capita consumption has also been decreasing, as in the U.S. during this period. Last, Canada has become increasingly reliant on the U.S. market to absorb its surplus production; in 1981 the U.S. absorbed 61.4 per cent of Canadian pork exports, and by 1984 this share had increased to 75 per cent.

REFERENCES

Bryan, G. (1980). *Taxing Unfair International Trade Practices: A Study of U.S. Antidumping and Countervailing Duty Laws.* Lexington, D.C.: Heath and Company.

Canada. (1987). *The Canada-U.S. Free Trade Agreement.* (Copy 10–12–87). Ottawa: External Affairs.

Gilmour, B and M. Cluff. (1986). "Canadian Stabilization Initiatives and Their Effects on the Welfare of American Pork Producers." *Canadian Farm Economics, 20,* 9–18.

Martin, L.J., and E.W. Goddard. (1987, October). *The Economics of Canadian Hog Stabilization Programs and U.S. Countervailing Import Duties.* Guelph, Ontario: University of Guelph, Department of Agricultural Economics and Business.

Meilke, K. (1987, October). *Measuring the Impact of Canadian Swine Exports on U.S. Swine Prices.* Unpublished manuscript prepared for the Canadian Pork Council.

Meilke, K. and M. Scally. (1987, February). *Trade in Vertically Related Markets: The Case of Hogs and Pork.* Unpublished Manuscript, University of Guelph, Department of Agricultural Economics and Business.

Moschini, G. and K. Meilke. (1987, May). *An Analysis of Spatial Price Differences in the North American Livestock Sector.* (Working Paper 7/87). Ottawa: Agriculture Canada.

Steger, D. (Ed.). (1988, February). *A Guide to the Canada-U.S. Free Trade Agreement.* Toronto: Fraser and Beatty Barristers and Solicitors.

Subsidies and Countervailing Duties Agreement of Interpretation and Application of Articles VI, XVI and XXIII of the General Agreement on Tariffs and Trade. April 5, 1979.

U.S. International Trade Commission. (1985, July). *Live Swine and Pork from Canada, Determination of the Commission in Investigation No. 701–TA–224 (Final) Under the Tariff Act of 1930.* (Publication 1733).

van Duren, E. and L. Martin. (1987, October). "The Role of Economic Analysis in Trade Law and Trade Disputes." *Canada-U.S. Trade in Agriculture: Managing the Disputes.* University of Guelph and Ontario Ministry of Agriculture and Food, Department of Agricultural Economics and Business.

APPENDIX 1
Case History of Hogs and Pork from Canada

May 21, 1984   Senator Robert J. Dole, Chairman of the U.S. Senate Finance Committee, requests that the U.S. International Trade Commission (USITC) investigate the competitive and economic factors affecting the U.S. and Canadian hog and pork industries in U.S. markets under Section 332(g) of the U.S. Tariff Act of 1930. The investigation is initiated on June 25, 1984.

Nov. 2, 1984   A petition for imposition of countervailing duties on hogs and pork imported from Canada is filed with the U.S. Department of Commerce (USDOC), and supported by a number of U.S. packers.

Nov. 9, 1984   The USITC commences a preliminary investigation of injury under Section 703(a) of the Tariff Act of 1930.

Nov. 21, 1984   The USITC's findings in the Section 332(g) investigation are delivered to the U.S. Senate Finance Committee. The major conclusion of the report is that Canadian hogs and pork are being unfairly traded in the U.S. market.

Nov. 23, 1984   The U.S. International Trade Administration (USITA) commences a preliminary investigation of subsidization under Section 701 of the Tariff Act of 1930.

Nov. 26, 1984   Hearings for the preliminary investigation by the USITC are held.

Dec. 17, 1984   The USITC makes an affirmative preliminary determination. It states that "There is a reasonable indication that an industry in the United States is materially injured by reason of imports from Canada of live swine and fresh, chilled, or frozen (except meat offal) of swine." The hog and pork industries are considered to be one domestic industry.

Jan. 4, 1985   The USITA decides that the subsidy investigation is "extraordinarily complicated" and gains 65 additional days for making its preliminary subsidy determination.

Apr. 3, 1985   The USITA makes a preliminary affirmative subsidy determination. The USDOC instructs U.S. Customs Service to suspend liquidations of all entries of hogs and pork products from Canada. A bond of C$0.04390/lb. live weight is required. On this date the final subsidy and injury investigations are formally initiated. (The preliminary duty is 5.3 cents/lb. on pork and 3.8 cents/lb. on hogs.)

May 9, 1985   The USITA conducts hearings to determine the existence and level of subsidy. The defendants argue that the upstream provision of Section 613 of the Trade and Tariff Act of 1984 should be applied, in order to measure the amount of any benefit received by hog growers which is passed through to pork packers.

June 17, 1985   The USITA makes an affirmative final subsidy determination. Several federal and provincial programs available to Canadian hog producers are deemed to be countervailable. The net subsidy is estimated to be C$0.04390/lb. live weight.

June 25, 1985   The USITC conducts hearings to determine whether the U.S. hog and pork industry is materially injured as a result of imports of hogs and pork from Canada.

July, 1985   The USITC determines that the U.S. hog industry is materially injured by reason of hog imports from Canada. It determines that the U.S. pork industry is not materially injured or threatened with material injury, and that the establishment of an industry in the U.S. is not materially retarded by reason of pork imports from Canada.

Vice Chairman Liebeler dissents. She doubts the USITC's determination that the hog and pork industries are separate industries. She determines that the U.S. hog industry is not materially injured as a result of hog imports from Canada.

Commissioner Eckes dissents. He determines that both the U.S. hog and pork industries are materially injured by reason of hog and pork imports from Canada.

May 15, 1987   The U.S. Court of International Trade (USCIT) remands the USITA subsidy determination. It decides that the USDOC should have conducted an upstream subsidy investigation with respect to the pork industry. The successful appeal was made by the Canadian Meat Council.

May 28, 1987   The USCIT upholds the USITC's final determination that the hog and pork industries are separate industries and that the pork industry was not materially injured or threatened with material injury as a result of pork imports. The unsuccessful appeal was made by The National Pork Producers' Council and Wilson Foods Corporation.

June 1, 1987   U.S. Senate Amendment 326 to the Omnibus Trade Bill is proposed. It states that "In the case of an agricultural product processed from a raw agricultural product in which (1) the demand for the prior stage product is substantially dependent on the demand for the latter stage product, and (2) the processing operation adds only limited value to the raw commodity, subsidies found to be provided to either producers or processors of the product shall be deemed to be provided with respect to the manufacture, production, or exportation of the processed product."

Aug. 7, 1987   The USCIT remands the USITC's affirmative injury determination for reevaluation of evidence concerning price elasticities relied on by the USITC in making its decision. The successful appeal was made by the Alberta Pork Producers' Marketing Board. The USITA's decision that the Ontario Farm Tax Reduction program is a countervailable subsidy holds, but the method for calculating the benefit is remanded.

Sept.16, 1987   The USITC decision in the Remand Determination is that the U.S. hog industry "is materially injured by reason of imports of live swine which are subsidized by the Government of Canada." The decision is based upon adjusted econometric estimates of hog price flexibilities. The vote is evenly divided.

Oct. 6, 1987   The Alberta Pork Producers' Marketing Board and the Canadian Meat Council appeal the USITC decision in the Remand Determination of Sept. 16, 1987 to the USCIT. They state that the USITC exceeded the scope of the USCIT's remand because two Commissioners voting in the affirmative did not rely solely on the revised price elasticities analysis.

Mar. 22, 1987   The USCIT does not re-open the case with respect to the elasticities analysis used in the injury and causality determination.

CHAPTER 5

STABILIZATION PROGRAMS AND COUNTERVAILING DUTIES: CANADIAN HOG EXPORTS TO THE UNITED STATES

A. Schmitz and D. Sigurdson

Recently there have been a number of cases investigated by the United States Department of Commerce (DOC) and the International Trade Commission (ITC) involving the exportation of agricultural and forest products to the United States either under production subsidization schemes by competitors or via unfair trade practices which fall under the general classification of dumping (Schmitz, Firch and Hillman, 1981). Most attention has been on products exported under production price stabilization programs, which are common in many countries including Canada.

These authors argue that current United States trade law results in countervail duties which are not justified according to an econometric evaluation. We examine the case of the 1984-85 investigation by the DOC and the ITC into alleged export subsidization of Canadian hogs and pork products shipped into the U.S. market, in which the source of subsidization was deemed to be various pork production stabilization schemes in Canada. The DOC found that subsidies did exist and the ITC found injury to United States hog producers; the Commission supported a countervailing duty on live hogs although not on pork products.

On 2 November 1984, the U.S. National Pork Producers Council (NPPC) launched a formal complaint to the ITC against the imports of live hogs, pork and processed pork products from Canada. The NPC argued that Canadian hog production subsidies were causing injury to the industry due both to the expanded market share of Canadian imports and to reduced prices.

The U.S. complaint arose from the increasing amounts of Canadian live hogs and pork products that were being imported into the United States. Canada's market share in the U.S. had been increasing while the American share of the Canadian market had been decreasing. From 1974 to 1984, Canada's pork exports to the United States had increased from 85,850 thousand pounds to 573,630 thousand pounds; during that period, Canada had switched back and forth from being a net importer to being a net exporter. More recently Canada had been increasing its exports, and the NPPC argued that Canada would have a permanent position as a net exporter to the United States.

The NPPC claimed that Canadian pork producers had increased production and exports to the United States because of the substantial subsidies through stabilization programs for Canadian producers. Their formal complaint to the ITC was referred to the DOC, which ruled that hog exports to the U.S. were being subsidized through production subsidies. In December 1984, the ITC reviewed these findings and in a preliminary determination ruled that U.S. producers and processors were being injured as a result of the subsidies. The NPPC attended the hearing on behalf of American pork producers, and the Canadian Pork Council represented Canadian pork packers. As the NPPC had also alleged that pork products were being subsidized, the Canadian Meat Council represented the interests of Canadian packers. In June 1985 the ITC gave its final ruling that only Canadian live hog exports were subsidized and that it was this subsidy which resulted in injury to U.S. producers. Exports of pork and pork products, while also found to be subsidized, were not ruled to have resulted in injury.

In the first section of the paper we establish the economic principles that should be used in a countervail duty case. Next, we examine both the General Agreement on Tarrifs and Trade (GATT) and United States trade laws as they apply to a countervail duty case. We then review the U.S. countervail imposed on Canadian hogs in light of an appropriate economic analysis. Finally, we consider the effect that the bilateral free trade agreement will have on such countervail duty cases.

Theoretical Economic Framework

In an analysis of government programs for agriculture, we focus on two main issues: supply response and subsidy effect. Does the program cause increased production and does that increased production result in a significant price decline? Also, if a subsidy does result in a significant decrease in price, what should the countervail duty be and should it also be applied to processed products? Finally, if the program provides a subsidy on production, does the benefit pass through to processors in that country? What generally needs to be established is whether a government payment is a subsidy or is simply a transfer. It has been recognized in the recent trade negotiations, both bilateral and multilateral, that the programs differ in their effect on production and trade.

Supply Response and Injury as Result of a Subsidy

The first issue to be addressed is whether a government program provides a subsidy which encourages production sufficiently that the exports cause significant damage to the importing country.

A government program should be viewed as an unfair trade practice if the program is subsidized by government. But in consideration of the magnitude of the subsidy, only the government portion should be included; if the producers also make a contribution into the program, their payments should be netted out of the subsidy calculation.

The question is whether these government contributions do cause significant harm to the importing nation, and if so, what size of duty is required to restore prices. What needs to be considered is the elasticity of the supply and demand curves and the nature of the subsidy, and whether it causes a shift, a movement, or no change to the supply curve.

Supply Shift

In Figure 1 the supply curve for the exporter is S_f and the domestic demand schedule is D_f; S_d is the supply curve in the importing nation and D_d is the corresponding demand curve. With free trade the price is P_f and imports are Q (determined by the intersection of the excess demand curve ED and the excess supply curve ES assuming no transportation costs).

FIGURE 1
SHIFT IN SUPPLY CURVE

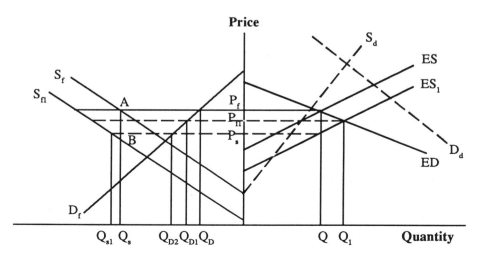

Suppose a per unit input subsidy is put into place resulting in the exporting supply curve shifting to S_{f1}. Output increases and exports increase from Q to Q_1. Accordingly, the increased production in the exporting country because of the subsidy causes the equilibrium price to decline from P_f to P_{f1}. Clearly a program which shifts the exporter's supply curve results in a decline in the price to producers in the importing country.

However, whether exports should be countervailable depends on the extent to which the increased production causes a significant price decline. The extent to which the price drops for producers in the importing country will depend on the price elasticity of demand D_d and on the price elasticity of ED. Note that with the price drop from P_f to P_{f1} as a result of the subsidy, domestic consumption increases from Q_D to Q_{D1}; hence not all of the increase in output due to the subsidy goes to the importer. The more price elastic D_d, the smaller is the price drop resulting from a subsidy. Also, note that the price elasticity of ED for a given price is greater than the elasticity corresponding to D_f. Thus, a large increase in exports due to a subsidy may result in only a small drop in world prices.

To restore prices back to P_f to producers in the importing country, exports need to be reduced to Q from Q_1. The countervailing duty needed to accomplish this would be $P_f P_s$; prices in the exporting country would be lowered to P_s. It should be noted that prices to the exporting country are lowered for both producers and consumers. Production in the exporting country is still higher than it would be without the subsidy by $Q_{s1}-Q_s$, but this is offset by higher consumption $Q_{D2}-Q_D$. The net result is that Q is exported and prices return to P_f in the importing country.

The countervailing duty which would be needed to offset the subsidy program is less than the actual subsidy. In Figure 1 a subsidy of AB results in supply shifting from S_f to S_{f1}. The duty required to restore prices is $P_f P_s$, which is less than the subsidy of AB.

Supply Movement

Suppose now that a guaranteed price of P_s is given to producers in the export country, which results in a movement along the original supply curve S_f (Figure 2). A guaranteed price of P_s would result in a new equilibrium price of P_{f1} to producers in the importing country. In the exporting country producers would increase P_{f1} along with a subsidy of P_s-P_{f1}. The new quantity produced would be Q_{s1} and the exports would increase from Q to Q_1. Hence a subsidy which results in a movement along a supply curve leads to a price decline in the importing country and should be considered for countervailing action. Whether or not a countervailing duty should be placed would again depend on whether the price decline was significant.

FIGURE 2
MOVEMENT ALONG A SUPPLY CURVE

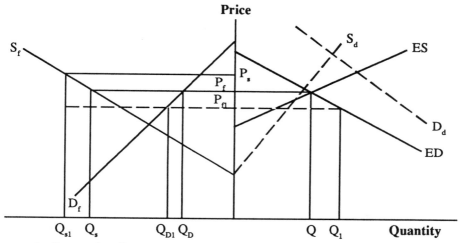

As discussed earlier, the more price elastic D_d and ED the smaller is the price drop as a result of increased exports. Also, the more price inelastic S_f the smaller is the expansion of exports and hence the damage from the producer export subsidy to importing country producers. In addition, the percentage increase in producer price in the exporting country resulting from a production subsidy can be much higher than the accompanying percentage producer price drop in the importing nation.

The reason for considering whether a subsidy resulted in a shift of or movement along the supply curve is not necessarily to examine injury, as it is the same in either case. However, the duty necessary to restore prices is different depending on whether exports increased because of a shift of or movement along the supply curve. In the exporting country producers would receive P_{fl}. In the case of a movement along a supply curve, producers in the exporting country receive a subsidy of P_s-P_{fl} and production increases from Qs to Qsl. To restore prices in the importing country back to P_f, exports should be reduced to Q. A duty of P_s-P_f would be necessary to increase price from P_{fl} back to P_f. With a duty of P_s-P_f, price in the exporting country net of the duty would be P_f. The duty needed to restore prices to P_f is again less than the value of the subsidy.

No Supply Response

If a government were to provide a subsidy of P_sP_f after the production period to producers in the exporting country, no change in production would occur (see Figure 3). Such a program would not be countervailable as it would not lower prices in the importing country.

FIGURE 3
NO PRODUCTION RESPONSE DUE TO A SUBSIDY PROGRAM

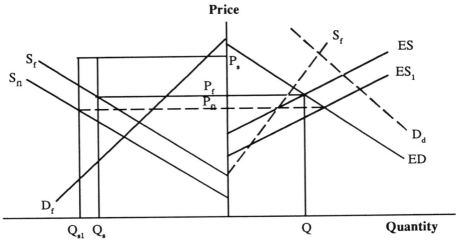

If such a program were in place over time, a shift in the supply curve might occur as a result either of new technology or of reduced risk because of the subsidy. If this were the case and supply shifted to S_{fl}, the price in the importing country would decline to P_{fl}. Therefore, if the government program resulted in a supply shift which led to a significant price decline, then the program should be countervailable.

It has been shown that the extent to which a government program results in an increase in production depends on whether a shift, a movement, or no response of the supply curve occurs in the exporting country. In a case for a countervailing duty, simply establishing that a subsidy exists is not sufficient reason for imposing a duty. It must be shown that the program bestowing the subsidy is the type which results in either a shift or movement of the supply curve. Once having established that a shift or movement has occurred, it needs to be determined that the increased production results in a significant price decline in the importing country. In determining whether a significant decline has occurred, the price elasticity of the importing demand curve and the exporting supply curve must be considered. The more price elastic the importers' demand curve or the more inelastic the exporters' supply curve, the smaller will be the price decline as a result of the subsidy.

Subsidy Effect on Processors

The second issue to be examined is whether a production subsidy of the primary product is passed through to processors in the exporting country.

In Figure 4, the effect of a subsidy on the primary product is shown. Prior to the subsidy the equilibrium primary price is P_F and the equilibrium processed price is P_r. The amount Q is exported as raw product and the amount Q_R is exported as processed product. Consider now a subsidy which shifts the supply curve in the exporting country from S_f to S_{fl}. As a result, production increases and the new equlibrium price is P_{fl}. Processors received a margin of P_RP_f prior to the subsidy and now receive an equivalent margin of $P_{R1}P_{fl}$.

FIGURE 4
EFFECT OF A PRIMARY PRODUCT SUBSIDY ON THE
PROCESSING SECTOR

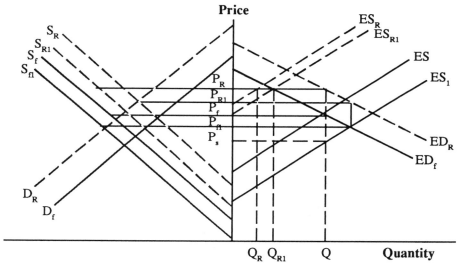

The processor in the exporting country receives no pass through benefit from the production subsidy since the margin remains unchanged. The processor would receive a benefit only if a condition of the subsidy were that the product be processed domestically. Since there is no subsidy passed through to the processor in the exporting country, no countervailing duty should be applied. A duty of P_fP_s should be applied only on exports of the raw product; such a duty would restore prices to the original level of P_f.

An interesting situation develops when the duty is placed on the raw product. With the duty, the price of the raw product is P_s in the exporting country and P_f in the importing country. With a lower input price in the exporting country, the processed supply curve shifts from S_r to S_{rl}. With the shift in the supply curve exports of the processed product increase from Q_R to Q_{Rl}. The processed price, however, remains the same at P_r, so any loss to processors in the importing country would be lost volume, which would be the case if the bulk of trade were in the primary product.

Having examined the theoretical economic framework for imposing countervailing duties, we now turn to the laws which govern them.

International and United States Trade Law on Countervailing Duties

The General Agreement on Tariffs and Trade is an international agreement which provides the guidelines member countries must follow in their own respective trade laws. The primary objective of the GATT in the area of countervail law was to provide a mechanism through which members could establish a duty to offset the impact of imports which were the result of subsidies. The intention of GATT was not to dictate to member countries how they could internally transfer funds between sectors, but rather to ensure that these transfers did not injure individuals in other countries (Gray, 1980). Article VI of the General Agreement deals with countervailing duties; of particular interest to this study are those parts which define injury and size of countervail duty. In determining injury the agreement states that:

A determination of injury ... shall involve an objective examination of both ... the volume of subsidized imports and their effect on prices in the domestic market for like products ... (GATT, 1979, p. 14)[1]

There are two key principles being addressed here. The first is that in determining injury a country shall concern itself only with subsidized imports. Article VI does not directly state that in determining injury a country should address only the incremental increase of imports which is the result of the subsidy (and not the total level of imports). It is inferred, however, that this is what is meant, as "subsidized imports" are referred to throughout the text of the Agreement.

The second principle is that in determining injury a country can only consider the effect the subsidized imports have on like products. The definition of "like products" is taken to mean "identical." Therefore, a subsidy on an input or raw product cannot be taken into account in determining the damage from the finished products. In determining injury from imports the Agreement also states in Article VI.4 that injury must be the result of subsidized imports and not the result of other factors that at the same time are causing injury to an industry.

A further point of interest to this case study is the size of duty to be applied once a countervail has been deemed justified. The General Agreement gives the authority to set the duty to the importing country. The Agreement only mandates that the duty not be more than the amount of the subsidy, although it does suggest that it would be desirable if the duty were less, and equal to the amount required to nullify injury.

As a signatory to the GATT, the United States must set its trade laws concerning countervailing duties in accordance with the Agreement. There are important differences, however, between U.S. definitions, both written and in practise, and those laid out in Article VI (Gray, 1980; Langford, 1985; Rugman, 1986). The most important difference is the linkage which is made between subsidized imports and injury. In determining injury, U.S. trade law requires that the volume of imports be evaluated in determining the effect on price (Stowell, 1986). In contrast with Article VI of the GATT, there is no mention of *subsidized* imports. The United States requires only that there be evidence of a subsidy; the necessity to establish a linkage between the subsidy and the increased imports is not clearly stated or practiced (Gray, 1980; Langord, 1983; Rugman, 1986).

Furthermore, U.S. trade law is not explicit in stating that the injury to the industry must be the result of the imports and not of other factors. The law directs the ITC to examine the impact imports have had on the affected industry by observing industry indices such as output, sales, market shares, profits and other related indicators. The law does not direct the ITC to ensure that they separate the injuries and consider only injury resulting from the subsidized imports. In Canadian trade law, in contrast, causality on the linkage between the subsidized imports and injury must be clearly established.

The United States does allow for input or upstream subsidies to be considered in an investigation. It must be proven that the subsidy of an input which is used in the manufacture or production of a good provides a competitive benefit, the benefit occurring because the purchase price of the input to the manufacturer is lower than what it would be if there were no subsidy on the input.

Results of United States Trade Law

International Trade Commission's Ruling

In the case of the countervail suit against Canadian hogs and pork, in their final subsidy determination the DOC ruled that certain benefits which constituted subsidies were being provided to Canadian producers and exporters of live swine and fresh, chilled and frozen pork products. The net subsidy and thus the countervailing duty rate was determined to be Can $0.05523/lb. dressed weight (Can $0.4390/lb. live-weight). The ruling was submitted to the ITC, which in turn held hearings as to whether or not the Canadian subsidies materially injured U.S. pork producers and by how much. Because of conflict of interest, only three Commissioners from the ITC heard the case.[2] The Commissioners ruled that live hogs were countervailable but pork and pork products were not. On an individual basis, however, one of the Commissioners voted that neither was countervailable because the impact of increased imports due to Canadian subsidies was insignificant. Of the other two Commissioners, one voted that live hogs were countervailable but pork products and unprocessed pork were not, while the other voted that both live hogs and all the products derived from them were countervailable.

The Department of Commerce has defined live swine and fresh, chilled, or frozen pork as being "like products." The ITC Commissioners, however, ruled that they were "two like products" (i.e., live swine (1) and fresh, chilled or frozen pork (2)).[3] The ITC ruling brought about an interesting situation: since the DOC had ruled the two were like products, according to U.S. trade law the complainants only had to show that a subsidy occurred on one product. An upstream issue investigation was not required.[4] Therefore, when a subsidy on live swine was demonstrated, it was interpreted that by default there was a subsidy on fresh, chilled or frozen pork products. In light of this ruling, the request for exclusion by the packers of unprocessed pork was not considered. In essence, the DOC had ruled that live hogs, processed pork, etc., are all the same product and hence if a subsidy exists to producers, part of it is passed through to packers. Therefore, countervailing duties could be placed on live hogs as well as on unprocessed pork and pork products.

The DOC argument that live hogs, processed pork, etc. are all the same product, competing for or fulfilling the same end demand, is the correct one. This is illustrated in Figure 4 where the supply and demand curves S_f, D_f are for hogs and the supply and demand curves S_r, D_r for processed pork are derived from the live hog supply and demand curves.

According to U.S. law if two products are ruled to be like products, it is not necessary to prove that a subsidy on one product is passed through to the next. It is simply assumed to be the case since they are like products. But in view of the previous theoretical discussion, it is clear that the raw product subsidy in the exporting country did not result in a benefit to the processors in the exporting country. Since processors in the exporting country were facing the same price as processors in the importing country, any benefit which occurred because of the subsidy was shared equally. It is further apparent from the theoretical analysis that a duty is only needed on the raw product to restore prices back to their original level. With this duty, producers in the importing country are no longer injured, but processors may be injured as they lose market share to the exporting processors.

The ITC Commissioners, according to procedures set down in U.S. trade law, could not rule on the subsidy issue; hence, they had to take the Department of Commerce subsidy ruling as given. The task of the ITC Commissioners was to determine if the subsidies resulted in injury to the U.S. industry, and the Commission found subsidies on live swine had caused injury while the subsidy on processed pork had not.

The ruling that the Canadian stabilization programs conferred a subsidy on producers was consistent with economic analysis. The ITC ruling that these subsidies also injured the U.S. industry, however, was not consistent with economic arguments. The ruling noted that the U.S. hog industry was experiencing difficult times, as evidenced by a decline in hog production and low to negative profits at the farm level.

Second, the Commission concluded that there is a relationship between American and Canadian prices (i.e., prices move together) and prices are related to pork production. Third, they found that Canadian exports to the United States and their share of the market had been increasing for the period examined (1981 to 1984). These factors together with the fact that Canadian producers were being subsidized led the ITC to conclude that Canadian exports of hogs were the cause of the decrease in hog production and profits in the United States hog industry.

The case under investigation poses a conflict between law and economics; the ITC, while correct according to U.S. trade law, would have reached a different conclusion based upon a proper economic evaluation. The legal definition of a product allowed the DOC to consider live hogs and product as one good and therefore it only had to show a subsidy existed, which then by definition applied to both live hogs and products. The ITC, which considered them as separate products, had to accept the DOC ruling that a subsidy existed on live hogs as well as processed pork and pork products, even though no investigation was undertaken to see if this was true. Based on an economic evaluation rather than U.S. trade law, the conclusion would have been that there was no subsidy on processed pork. The ITC, by default, ruled correctly because it felt that processed pork exports did not cause injury to American producers. However, in their decision to impose duties on live hog imports, the ITC did not examine the effect the stabilization subsidy payment had on Canadian production and hence the actual effect on Canadian exports to the U.S. market.

Economic Results

In Appendix A a model is developed which demonstrates that the effect of a price subsidy in one country is diluted by the market share of the other country. The price of a product which is traded is determined by the total demand and supply in the two countries; any change in supply/demand which occurs in one country impacts on the total supply/demand, and the equilibrium price adjusts accordingly. The country which represents a proportionally larger share of the market will influence price more by a shift in its supply/demand than will a shift in the supply/demand of the smaller country. In essence, the model shows that the Canadian government subsidies, passed through producers by hog stabilization programs, are diluted by the American share of the market.

Table 1 provides an example of the various price effects on the United States if an 8 per cent subsidy on price exists in Canada. As our theoretical model suggests, when elasticities in two countries are equivalent the effect of a subsidy on the importing country is dependent on the relative size of the markets and not on the supply elasticity (Regier, 1978). The price effect on the importing country is simply the change in producers' price in the exporting country because of the subsidy, divided by the relative size of the two countries. The example shows that the larger the size of the importing country, the smaller the effect of an exporters' subsidy. From 1980 to 1984, American hog production was 8.7 to 7.6 times Canadian production. With the subsidy of $5.52/cwt representing approximately an 8 per cent increase in the Canadian price, the price decline in the United States market is between 1.14 and 0.8 per cent.

TABLE 1
PERCENT DECLINE IN UNITED STATES PRICES:
8% SUBSIDY IN CANADA

Market Size: United States/Canada	0	2	5	7	10	20	30
Supply Elasticity							
0.5	0	4.0	1.6	1.14	0.8	0.4	0.27
1.0	0	4.0	1.6	1.14	0.8	0.4	0.27
1.5	0	4.0	1.6	1.14	0.8	0.4	0.27
2.0	0	4.0	1.6	1.14	0.8	0.4	0.27

This example assumes that a subsidy has the same effect on production as does a change in price. However, it has been argued by Martin and Goddard (1985) and Agriculture Canada (1985) that this is probably not true, since the subsidy payment does not occur in the production period and also is not known in advance. Therefore, the 1.14 to 0.8 per cent price effect represents an upper bound.

The commodity price stabilization programs for hogs differ among provinces, but essentially they require producers who join a program to pay a levy on each hog sold. In return, producers receive a payout from the stabilization fund when the market price falls below the support level (cost of production formula). The levy paid by a producer is matched by the government of the province in which they live. The federal stabilization program is the Agricultural Stabilization Act (ASA) fund, which works somewhat differently than the provincial programs. The ASA fund is based on federal contributions, and pays producers when the market price is below 90 per cent of the 5 year average price adjusted by the change in cash costs. The level of support, while usually established by an economic evaluation, can also be influenced by political decisions. The government has the authority to set the level of support above 90 per cent if it believes that more support is required.

A strong argument can be made that the size of a subsidy measured *ex post* may be overstated. Producers do not know for certain, at the time they join a program, whether or not they will receive a subsidy. Stabilization schemes are viewed by producers as income insurance schemes just as is, for example, crop insurance. Risk-taking firms generally do not belong to stabilization schemes, nor do they take out crop insurance. In view of this, the actual amount of an *ex post* subsidy should be discounted heavily in order to determine the true *ex ante* subsidy (Just, Jueth and Schmitz, 1982).

Work done by Martin and Goddard has found that in all areas of Canada, excepting Manitoba and the Atlantic provinces, provincial stabilization payments were not significant variables in determining the supply of hogs. They concluded that federal and provincial programs do nothing towards reducing risk, since the support levels are based on occurrences in the production period. The hog sector studies done by Martin and Goddard (1985), Gilson and St. Louis (1986), Martin and Meilke (1986), and Charelebois and Cluff (1986) concluded that the production response to the various stabilization programs have ranged from one to 3.4 per cent. These empirical studies support our suggestion—that in modeling the effects of stabilization programs subsidies should be diluted to account for the nature of the programs.

In Table 2 the effect of both market size and dilution on prices are shown over a range of prices and market shares. Table 2 shows that if a subsidy through a stabilization program has half the effect of an 8 per cent market price increase, prices in the United States would be reduced by between 0.57 per cent and 0.4 per cent.

These economic results suggest that Canadian production and exports of hogs due to subsidies had not caused injury to the U.S. industry, and the results support the hypothesis that producers do not respond in the same way to a subsidy through a stabilization program as they do to an increase in price.

TABLE 2
PRICE DECLINE IN UNITED STATES PRICES: AN 8 PER CENT
SUBSIDY IN CANADA UNDER VARIOUS DILUTION SCENARIOS

Market Size: United States/Canada	0	2	5	7	10	20	30
Dilution Effect							
0.25	0	1	0.4	0.29	0.2	0.1	0.07
0.50	0	2.0	0.8	0.57	0.4	0.2	0.14
0.75	0	3.0	1.2	0.55	0.6	0.3	0.20
1.00	0	4.0	1.6	1.14	0.8	0.4	0.20

Upon determining that Canadian hog programs provided a subsidy to Canada for producers and resulted in injury to the U.S. industry, the ITC set the duty at the level of the Canadian subsidy. This ruling, while consistent with U.S. trade law, is not supported by an economic evaluation. The models developed here demonstrate that, depending on the type of the subsidy, the duty necessary to restore prices is less than the actual subsidy. In the case of a subsidy given after the production period, as in the Canadian programs, no duty is required as the subsidy does not result in a production response.

Impact of Canada-U.S. Free Trade Agreement on the Hog
Countervailing Duty Case

On 2 January 1988, the leaders of the government of Canada and the government of the United States signed a bilateral free trade agreement which establishes new trading rules between the two countries. The agreement had been initiated and negotiated because of increasing trade disputes between the two countries, and its objective is to facilitate trade by creating a fair and secure trade environment.

If the Free Trade Agreement had been in place during the United States' countervailing duty suit against Canadian hogs, it is questionable whether the outcome would have been any different. The agreement, in Article 1902, gives each country the right to apply its own countervailing duty law as it has in the past. This means that the United States could apply its definition of injury as set out by law and past cases. As a result, the ruling in this case would have been the same even with a free trade agreement.

If the Free Trade Agreement were to have had an influence on the ruling, it would have been of Article 1904, which allows appeal of a final countervail determination to a bi-national panel review rather than to a domestic judicial review. The bi-national panel would consist of two members from each country, plus an equally acceptable fifth member. The panel was proposed because of complaints that countervailing and anti-dumping cases were being influenced by political pressures. The purpose of the review panel is to provide an impartial review of a final determination, and to ensure that the laws of the importing country are interpreted fairly.

In the Canadian hog countervailing duty case a bi-national review panel might have ruled differently on whether Canadian hog exports were causing injury to the U.S. industry. Even given the vague U.S. trade law definition of injury, an impartial panel might have found that the relative size of the two countries are such that Canada's exports have no significant influence on the U.S. industry. It should be noted at this point, however, that the exact powers this panel would have are not yet clear.

There is hope that through the Free Trade Agreement countervailing duty laws in both the U.S. and Canada can incorporate some basic economic principles, and a seven-year time framework has been set up for this development. The Agreement allows for the framing of mutually acceptable rules governing subsidies and private anti-competitive pricing practices, such as dumping; these would then replace current countervailing and anti-dumping rules in the respective countries.

Conclusions

In the decision about hog exports to the United States market, the inconsistent voting of the ITC Commissioners is noteworthy. Of the three, one voted that countervailing duties should not be placed on either live hogs or their products, one argued that both were countervailable, and the remaining Commissioner contended that only live hog exports were countervailable. This outcome is not consistent with the economic theory and empirical results presented in this case study.

A strong case has been made as to why live hogs and their products should enter the United States from Canada duty free. First, it is questionable whether commodity stabilization schemes such as in the Canadian case provide producer subsidies which do lead to increased production and exports. Second, while one can argue that live hogs and their products are "like products," it is difficult to show that subsidies are passed through to the processors. Third, even if subsidies exist, it is difficult to argue that the impact on the U.S. market is significant, largely because of the extremely small market share Canadian pork has in the U.S. market. Furthermore, U.S. excess demand for Canadian pork is highly price elastic while the Canadian supply response is highly price inelastic—diminishing further the real price effect of the subsidies.

The U.S. ruling on Canadian hog stabilization programs was consistent with U.S. trade law, but it certainly was not consistent with a proper economic evaluation. U.S. trade law does not stipulate that in a countervail suit it must be proven that a subsidy results in increased production and therefore increased exports. Yet if economic principles were used this would be the first condition that would need to be met. Here the GATT rules appear to be better than U.S. law, in that they recognize it is the subsidized exports that need to be considered in a countervail case.

If economic principles were the basis for countervail decisions, the second condition that would have to be met in a countervailing duty case would be showing that the increased exports have directly resulted in injury to the importing country's industry. Current U.S. trade law only requires that it be shown that the industry has been experiencing injury; this injury does not have to be linked with the subsidized exports. In contrast, the GATT rules themselves are quite clear in stipulating that subsidized exports and injury do need to be linked.

Finally, the trade laws of both GATT and United States allow a countervailing duty to be set at the level of the relevant subsidy. If the purpose of the duty is to restore price, economic analysis suggests that the duty should be less than the subsidy, depending on the nature of the subsidy and the market. Certainly, all countries should be able to retain the right to transfer funds within their own boundaries, but a countervailing duty should only be imposed when that transfer injures parties in an importing country. The purpose of a countervailing duty is to restore prices in the importing country; but the over- or misapplication of countervailing duties can itself be an unfair trade practice.

NOTES

1. Agreement on Interpretation and Application of Articles VI, XVI and XXIII of the General Agreement on Tariffs and Trades, GATT, 1979, p. 14.

2. Our assessment is that the two Commissioners did not participate because one was a major hog producer and the other represents the major hog producing areas.

3. One has to interpret this to mean that the two products are not like products.

4. An upstream issue investigation is done to determine if a subsidy on inputs results in a subsidy to the processed product.

REFERENCES

Charlesbois, P. and M. Cluff. (1986). "Benefits of Stabilization Programs and Their Incidence: The Canadian Livestock Sector." In M. Cluff & H.B. Huff (Eds.). *Modelling Livestock Stabilization*. Ottawa: Agriculture Canada, 55–105.

GATT. (1979). *Agreement on Implementation of Article VI of the General Agreement on Tariffs and Trade*. Geneva: GATT.

GATT. (1979). *Agreement on Interpretation and Application of Articles VI, XVI and XXIII of the General Agreement on Tariffs and Trade*. Geneva: GATT.

Gilmour, B. and M. Cluff. (1985, February). "Canadian Stabilization Initiatives and Their Effects on the Welfare of American Pork Producers." Ottawa: Agriculture Canada.

Gilson, J.C. and R. Saint-Louis. (1986). *Policy Issues and Alternatives Facing the Canadian Hog Industry*. Ottawa: Agriculture Canada and Canadian Pork Council.

Grey, R. de C. (1982). *United States Trade Policy Legislation: A Canadian View*. Montreal: The Institute for Research on Public Policy.

Just, R., D. Hueth, and A. Schmitz. (1982). *Applied Welfare Economies and Public Policy*. Scarborough, Ontario: Prentice Hall.

Langford, Jock R. (1985). "American Investigations Involving Temporal, Perishable Agricultural Commodities." Winnipeg. Unpublished manuscript.

Martin, L. and K. Meilke. (1986). "Trade Implications of Canadian Stabilization Programs: Reality and Perception." In M. Cluff and H.B. Huff (Eds.). *Modeling Livestock Stabilization*. Ottawa: Agriculture Canada, 121–152.

Martin, L. (1985). Testimony Before The United States International Trade Commission on Hog Countervail. Washington, D.C.

Martin, L.J. and E.W. Goddard. (1985, February). The Effects of Government Payments to Hog Growers of the Canadian Pork Packing Industry. Guelph, Ontario: University of Guelph.

Regier, D.W. (1978, September). *Livestock and Derived Feed Demand in the World GOR Model*. (Statistics, and Cooperative Service Foreign Agriculture Report No. 152) Washington, D.C.: United States Department of Agriculture Economics.

Rugman, Alan M. (1986, July/August). "United States Protectionism and Canadian Trade Policy." *Journal of World Trade Law*, *20*, 363–380.

Schmitz, A. (1984). *Commodity Price Stabilization: The Theory and Its Application*. (World Bank Staff Working Paper 668.) Washington, D.C.

Schmitz, A. and C. Carter. (1986, April). "Sectoral Issues in a United States-Canadian Trade Agreement: Agriculture." *United States-Canadian Relations*. Workshop conducted at the University of Western Ontario, London, Ontario.

Schmitz, A., R.S. Firch, and J.S. Hillman. (1981). "Agricultural Export Dumping: The Case of Mexican Winter Vegetables in the United States Market." *American Journal of Agriculture Economics*, *63*, 645–654.

Stowell, Alan M. (1987). *United States International Trade Laws*, Washington, D.C.: The Bureau of National Affairs.

United States International Trade Commission. (1985, July). *Live Swine and Pork from Canada*. (USITC Publication 1933).

APPENDIX A

Theoretical Market Share

When trade occurs between two countries, the price for a good is determined by the total demand and supply in those countries. The total demand and supply curves are derived simply by adding each country's demands and supplies together. Any supply/demand shift that occurs in one country impacts on the total supply or demand curve and the equilibrium price is adjusted accordingly. The country which represents a proportionally larger share of the market will influence price more by a shift in its supply/demand curve than will a shift in the supply/demand curve of the smaller country.

The model can be stated mathematically. The demand and supply curves for the importing country are:

$$D_I = A_1 - B_1P_t \qquad (1)$$
$$S_I = A_2 + B_2P_t \qquad (2)$$

The demand and supply curves for the exporting country are:

$$D_E = A_3 - B_3P_t \qquad (3)$$
$$S_E = A_4 + B_4P_T \qquad (4)$$

The equilibrium price is determined by equating the excess demand and supply curves:

$$ED(P_t) = (D_I - S_I) \qquad 0 \qquad (5)$$
$$ES(P_t) = (S_E - D_E) \qquad 0 \qquad (6)$$

Equating equations 5 and 6 the equilibrium price is determined by:

$$P_t = \frac{A_1 - A_2 + A_3 - A_4}{EB_i} \qquad (7)$$

In countries which use the same technology and face the same prices, the price elasticities of supply are the same.

For the supply functions in equation 2 the price elasticity can be represented by:

$$E_{SI} = B_2 Q_1 \frac{P_t}{} \qquad (8)$$

and for equation 4 by:

$$E_{SE} = B_4 \frac{P_t}{Q_E} \qquad (9)$$

Equating these 2 equations obtains:

$$E_{SI} = E_{SE} = B_2 \frac{P_t}{Q_E} = B_4 \frac{P_t}{Q_I} \qquad (10)$$

With identical prices, the quantity in one country can be represented as some factor R of the other. The factor R represents the market share of the United States relative to that of Canada ($R \times Q_E = Q_I$). Thus:

$$\frac{B_2}{R} = B_4 \tag{11}$$

The effect of a supply shift that occurs in Canada because of a subsidy can now be shown by rewriting equation 4 to reflect the subsidy:

$$S_E = A_4 + B_4 P_t \ (1 + K) \tag{4a}$$

Where K is the amount of the subsidy, substituting 11 into 4a and then rewriting equation 7 obtains:

$$P_t = \frac{A_1 - A_2 + A_3 - A_4}{B_1 + B_2 + B_3 = B_2 = \frac{KB_2}{R} \quad R} \tag{7a}$$

The effect on the price subsidy which causes output to increase in Country 1 is diluted by the market share of Country 2. When that market share is large, like that of the United States in the pork industry, the effect on price from a supply shift in Canada can be quite small. The price effect on the importing country of a subsidy in the exporting country is equivalent to the percent change in price in the exporting country because of the subsidy, divided by the market share of the importing country. This holds true regardless of the supply elasticities involved as long as they are equivalent.

The above model assumes that government contributions to a stabilization program affect a producers' production the same way as a price increase or decrease in the marketplace does. This may not be true, since a payment from a stabilization program is often calculated from a complicated formula. These payments seldom if ever are payed out in the period during which the production occurs. For this reason the effect on production may be less than if a comparable increase came from the market price.

Equation 4 is redefined to account for the government contributions:

$$S_E = A_4 + B_4 P_t \ (1 + dk) \tag{4b}$$

where d is a discount factor on the subsidy. Substituting equation 4b into equation 7 and 7a leaves us with an equilibrium price of:

$$P = \frac{A_1 - A_2 + A_3 - A_4}{B_1 + B_2 + B_3 = B_2 + \frac{dKB_2}{R} \quad R} \tag{7b}$$

Thus, whether or not prices decline in the importing country because of stabilization programs in the exporting country depends both on market share and on the supply effect of stabilization programs.

CHAPTER 6

THE DISPUTE CONCERNING CANADIAN IMPORTS OF IRISH BEEF: A PROBLEM OF MULTILATERAL PRODUCT SUBSTITUTION

W.A. Kerr and D.B. McGivern

On 25 July 1986 the Canadian Import Tribunal issued the *Finding* for its investigation of imports of beef from Ireland and Denmark.[1] The Tribunal found that subsidized Irish beef exported to Canada:

> has not caused, is not causing, but is *likely to cause* material injury to the production of like goods (emphasis added).

This carefully worded statement provided the legal justification for countervailing duties to be imposed on any beef produced in Ireland which received subsidies under the Common Agricultural Policy (CAP) export refund system—European Community (EC) Regulation No. 885/68. Although the imposition of countervailing duties is allowed under the rules of the General Agreement on Tariffs and Trade (GATT) when it can be shown that a subsidy is threatening to cause material injury to an established domestic industry (King, 1979), such a justification must clearly require conjecture on the part of the importer. In the event of an appeal to the GATT, such conjectural arguments are likely to be strongly contested and closely scrutinized.

Imports of European beef have never exceeded 15 per cent of the Canadian market, while total annual imports of like product have generally been in excess of 20 per cent of total consumption. To understand why the Tribunal was sufficiently concerned about the Irish imports to support imposition of countervailing duties based on such a criterion, and why the Canadian government would risk a further deterioration in its trade relations with the EC when the direct threat did not appear substantial, it is necessary to examine the multinational complexities of international trade in beef.

93

Although Ireland and Denmark are the only countries of the EC able to export beef to Canada, the trade dispute directly involves the U.S., Australia, New Zealand, and the other members of the EC. The dispute encompasses many of the major problems facing the international trading system for agricultural commodities, including export subsidies, defence of market shares, predatory pricing, product displacement, voluntary export restrictions; and non-tariff barriers such as quantitative restrictions and health regulations. The case illustrates the weakness of the GATT system in terms of its ability to deal with agricultural disputes and underlines the need for major reforms at the Uruguay Round of negotiations, which is expected to run from 1986 to 1990.

Theoretical Models

International trade in beef is extremely complex. It is conducted over a large range of commodities, from live cattle to various qualities of fresh beef to chilled and frozen beef and, of course, canned product. Although these products can be perceived as separate commodities it must always be remembered that they are close substitutes, so that changing markets or administrative distortions manifest for one commodity will affect the markets for other beef products. The dispute between Canada and Ireland involves only the standardized internationally traded frozen commodity known as "eighty-five per cent chemical lean boneless beef" or "low quality beef" (hereafter "manufacturing quality"). This product is produced by Canada and Ireland as well as by Australia, New Zealand, other members of the EC and the U.S. In North America, its major uses are as ground beef and as product for the fast-food sector of the restaurant trade. It is considered a low quality product and, hence, not suitable for unprocessed consumption in the home. The in-home-consumption beef market is supplied by the "high quality" specialized grain-fed beef sector.

Manufacturing quality beef comes from three major sources in Canada. The first source is cows culled from dairy herds at the end of their useful milking lives. The second source is cull cows from the breeding herds in the grain-fed beef sector. The final source is less preferred cuts and trim from grain-fed beef carcasses. Hence, all of the sources of manufacturing quality beef in Canada are the result of residual production. This is important because it implies that, since no one produces manufacturing quality beef as a primary output, the domestic supply is price inelastic. This characteristic has led to the development, in North America, of a unique international trading system for manufacturing quality beef.

This can be explained through the use of Figure 1, which illustrates the Canadian market in the absence of trade with Ireland. Domestic demand in Canada is illustrated by the curve D_C and domestically produced supply by S_C. In the absence of trade the price in Canada would be determined at the level where S_C equals D_C in Figure 1(a). Given the price instability associated with products with inelastic supplies, there has traditionally been an open market in manufacturing quality beef between the U.S. and Canada. As the Canadian market is approximately one tenth the size of the U.S. market, it is possible to use the usual small-country-price-taker model to illustrate the Canadian market. Canadian prices are constrained by a price band defined by the U.S. price plus or minus transportation.

FIGURE 1
CANADIAN BEEF MARKET—NO TRADE WITH IRELAND

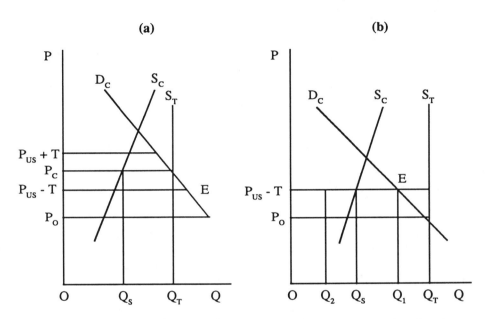

To illustrate, suppose that the domestic demand and supply situation is as illustrated in Figure 1(a). At any Canadian price above the U.S. domestic price plus transportation costs between the U.S. and Canada, it will pay U.S. producers to export to Canada. Hence, the effective maximum price in Canada becomes $P_{US} + T$. On the other hand, if domestic supply and demand were such that the U.S. price minus transportation (e.g. the Canadian price plus the cost of transportation to the U.S.) was above the Canadian price, it would be profitable for Canadian producers to export to the U.S. This would be the case if S_C intersected the demand curve to the right of point E. Therefore, in the absence of other suppliers, the Canadian price would be free to fluctuate between $P_{US} + T$ and $P_{US} - T$.

The market is further complicated, however, by imports from offshore. Tradition-ally, Australia and New Zealand have been the major sources of manufacturing quality beef in Canada. Oceanic manufacturing quality beef has been used in both the U.S. and Canada to moderate the price of domestic manufacturing quality beef; hence, the U.S. price of manufacturing quality beef is in part determined by such supplies. Again, in the U.S. there is a realization that domestic production of manufacturing beef is inelastic and that, with inexpensive sources of supply available offshore, a closed market would be to the detriment of consumers. Consumer interests, however, are balanced against those of producers, and access to the U.S. market is controlled. Although the U.S. has the power to impose import quotas, imports from Oceania are restricted by agreement and are, in effect, "voluntary export restrictions" with guarantees of historic levels of access.

In the absence of imports from Oceania, Canadian prices would likely remain at the import ceiling price of $P_{US} + T$. This would have two effects. First, Canadian consumers would pay a consistently high price. Second, Canadian users of manufacturing beef would be forced to purchase imports from the U.S. at $P_{US} + T$ when they are available at the lower Oceanic supply price, P_O. Of course, the desire of importers to obtain beef at import price P_O has to be balanced against the interests of domestic suppliers. To this end, Canada has also negotiated a "voluntary export restriction" agreement with Oceanic suppliers. Under this scenario the total supply in Canada is equal to S_T, and the Canadian market clearing price is P_C. The total supply is composed of quantity Q_S (the domestic supply at P_C) and Q_T minus Q_S, the negotiated quantity of imports from Oceania. The latter quantity can be assumed to be fixed although it may not always be filled.

When total Canadian supply S_T exceeds domestic demand at $P_{US} - T$ as in Figure 1 (b), then P_C equals $P_{US} - T$ and Canada exports to the U.S. a quantity equal to Q_T minus Q_1. However, to prevent circumvention of the U.S. agreements regarding imports of Oceanic beef, such product must be produced in Canada. Hence, quantity Q_S minus Q_2 (= Q_T minus Q_1) of Canadian product is shipped to the U.S. and Q_T minus Q_1 displaces that product in Canadian consumption. Such displacement is allowed by the U.S., as similar displacements take place in the U.S. market when the relative prices lead to U.S. product moving into Canada.

Hence, the North American beef market has evolved through political compromise into a system whose market characteristics satisfy most participants even if they are not the most desired characteristics from the point of view of each individual participant. Market price fluctuations are somewhat reduced for both consumers and producers in each country through cross-border movements. Processors are allowed access to some low priced imports from Oceania, while domestic producers receive a price higher than would be the case if they were forced to compete freely with Oceanic product. Oceanic suppliers receive virtually guaranteed access at the specified levels which, while they may not be optimal, are at least secure. This facilitates planning and is increasingly important in a world which is becoming more protectionist.

It is important for the subsequent discussion to realize that the conditions whereby P_C converges to the price floor at $P_{US} - T$ can arise for a number of reasons. Given that Q_T minus Q_S is unchanging, a rightward shift in S_C or a leftward shift in D_C could move the Canadian market from a position such as that in Figure 1(a) to that in 1(b). An increase in the U.S. domestic price would produce a similar result.

The only two nations in the EC which are considered by Canadian veterinary officials to be free of hoof-and-mouth disease are Ireland and Denmark, and therefore only they are allowed to export to Canada. The market for beef in Ireland can be illustrated by Figure 2. As Ireland is a member of the EC, if the equilibrium market price falls below that acceptable under Common Agricultural Policy agreements, there will be a policy intervention to support the price at an agreed level. There are two major CAP policies available, the "Intervention System" (EC Regulation 1302/73) and the "Export Refund System" (EC Regulation 885/68). The Intervention System is basically an offer-to-purchase policy by which, when market forces indicate that prices will fall a set amount below an annual "guide" price established by CAP Management Committee for beef and veal, the intervention agencies will purchase beef offered to them for sale at the buy-in or intervention price. This becomes the effective price in the Community and is denoted P_E in Figure 2. Such stocks are retained in storage until prices increase above the "guide" price, at which time they are returned to the market. In the period before Canada imposed countervailing duties, however, the intervention price had been set at a level which was in excess of that where zero annual net carryover stocks could be achieved. The Community's stocks increased from 207,000 to 770,000 tonnes between 1981 and 1984 (Irish Livestock and Meat Board, 1985).

FIGURE 2
IRELAND - CANADA TRADE IN BEEF

CANADA   IRELAND

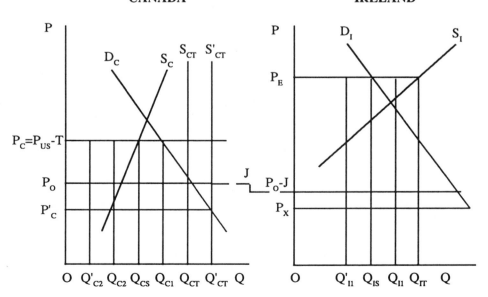

The Export Refund System allows a processor to apply directly for reimbursement for the difference between the domestic price within the EEC and the price received for extra-Community sales. Administratively, the amounts of export refunds are established on a periodic basis by the Management Committee for Beef and Veal. The size of the subsidy varies with the foreign market to which the beef is to be exported. If the export price, in the absence of trade with Canada, is P_X in Figure 2, then the exporter will receive P_E minus P_X for each unit exported. If Q_{IT} minus Q_{I1} is that proportion of the Irish surplus exported outside the Community, the budgetary cost to the CAP is area (P_E minus P_X) x (Q_{IT} minus Q_{I1}).

As P_E becomes the effective price in the EC[2], it also becomes the price at which intra-EC trade is conducted. Hence, there are three destinations for total Irish surplus production Q_{IT} minus Q_{IS}: (1) export to other members of the EC, (2) storage under the intervention system, and (3) export to countries outside the EC under the Export Refund System. Since, under the principles established in the Treaty of Rome, direct controls on the movement of commodities are not allowed (Blumental, 1984), the means by which to apportion beef among the three destinations are the letting of storage contracts and the establishment of the level of export subsidization, both by administrative fiat. Whether beef moves into storage or is exported to other EC members is not material to our argument, so such quantities will be combined in the remaining analysis.[3]

Now assume that trade with Canada can take place. The domestic price at which Irish beef can compete in Canada is the landed price of Oceanic beef in Canada minus the cost of transportation to Canada, denoted J, in other words, P_O - J. Exports to Canada will take place when P_O - J is greater than P_X. If it is assumed that export refunds are granted for quantity Q_{IT} minus Q_{I1}, the budgetary saving for the CAP equals area (P_O - J minus P_X) x (Q_{IT} minus Q_{I1}).

Irish product enters the Canadian market at P_O or possibly at a slight discount. There are two possible outcomes. Either Irish product replaces Oceanic product in the Canadian market, or it becomes a net addition to Canadian supplies. The success of an attempt to acquire market share from Oceania will depend upon the reaction of the Oceanic suppliers. If they attempt to defend their market share by undercutting the price, then it will pay the CAP to continue undercutting the Oceanic price until P_O - J declines to P_X. However, such price wars are to the detriment of both parties and, hence, are not likely to arise. This is because additions to Canadian supplies can simply displace further Canadian product in the Canadian domestic market through increased exports of Canadian product to the U.S. In other words, if quantity Q_{IT} minus Q_{I1} enters the Canadian market, then it represents a shift in the total supply available in Canada from S_{CT} to S'_{CT} (Q_{IT} minus Q_{I1} = Q'_{CT} minus Q_{CT}). As the Irish product cannot be re-exported to the U.S. without directly contravening the U.S. quota on imports of subsidized EC beef, additional quantities of Canadian produced beef will be exported. This shifts Q_{C2} leftward to Q'_{C2}, equal to amount Q_{IT} minus Q_{I1}. Neither Ireland nor Oceanic suppliers need suffer any decrease in price.[4]

Since any additional quantities of beef exported to Canada reduce the budgetary cost of CAP programs, there is an incentive for the CAP authorities to increase the amount of·Irish beef moving to Canada through the granting of additional export refunds. Initially these exports to Canada could come from quantities normally moving into storage or could be diverted from other extra-EC exports. Further, in the short run, product would be available from Irish product held in storage. In the longer term it would reduce CAP budgetary expenditures to divert all surplus Irish product into the Canadian market rather than to have it move to the rest of the EC with its chronic beef surplus (e.g. moving Q_{I1} leftward to coincide with Q_{IS}). In fact, in the absence of any Canadian action to restrict imports it would further reduce CAP budgetary expenditures to divert beef normally produced and consumed in Ireland to the Canadian market (moving Q_{I1} further leftward to, say, Q'_{I1}) and allow that displacement to be filled from imports from the remainder of the EC. Hence, the effective maximum for Irish exports to Canada appeared to Canadian officials to be the quantity represented by O - Q_{IT}.[5] Of course, health regulations prevent any re-export of beef from other areas of the EC to Canada. From the point of view of U.S. officials, the effective upper bound on EC displacement of Canadian product was either the same quantity of Irish beef plus a similarly determined Danish quantity or O - Q_{CS}, the maximum displaceable Canadian product, whichever was less. Naturally, the growth in exports either to Canada and the U.S. would depend, in the short run, on the time it takes to develop market channels. Certainly officials in Canada or the U.S. did not expect to have to deal with such quantities as their respective global meat import quotas could have triggered. Basically, North American cattlemen and officials perceived that there was no soon-to-be-reached threshold which would be likely to limit Irish exports to Canada.

Empirical Evidence

Total Irish beef exports ranged between 217,253 and 350,000 metric tonnes between 1979 and 1984. As Table 1 shows, the great majority of Irish exports go to other EC members, with the U.K. and France receiving the largest quantities. In addition, 46,300 metric tonnes of Irish beef were added to EC stocks in 1984 and total Irish stocks at the end of November stood at 87,828 metric tonnes (Irish Livestock and Meat Board, 1985). Total EC stocks stood at approximately 770,000 metric tonnes by the end of 1984 and the Community as a whole was in a position of 112 per cent self-sufficiency. Total EC exports had grown by 19 per cent between 1981 and 1984 and stocks of beef by 221 per cent. Clearly, from the Canadian and U.S. perspective, there appeared to be no likelihood that the EC beef regime would be able to correct its over-production in the short run, and the motivation for increased Irish exports to Canada was likely to remain. This is supported by the data on export receipts as is the model developed in Figure 2. Clearly the unit value received for Irish product within

TABLE 1
IRISH BEEF EXPORTS

Destination	1980 Quantity (metric tons)	1980 Value ('000 US$)	1980 Unit Value (US$/metric ton)	1981 Quantity (metric tons)	1981 Value ('000 US$)	1981 Unit Value (US$/metric ton)	1982 Quantity (metric tons)	1982 Value ('000 US$)	1982 Unit Value (US$/metric ton)
EC	248,719	834,487	3,355	163,369	460,794	2,821	152,860	423,329	2,769
Bene-Lux	13,297	43,934	3,304	3,723	12,099	3,249	2,708	8,247	3,249
France	57,339	187,972	3,278	35,111	114,258	3,254	31,979	100,553	3,144
W. Ger.	15,288	57,844	3,784	10,057	39,509	3,929	9,480	29,157	3,076
Neth.	32,691	98,004	2,998	9,431	27,133	2,877	7,308	19,807	2,710
U.K.	162,189	428,734	2,643	100,938	251,208	2,489	97,612	238,775	2,446
USSR	17,373	29,714	1,710	9,839	17,852	1,814	5,287	8,561	1,619
Lybia	0	0	-	0	0	-	4,639	6,630	1,429
Egypt	7,487	17,182	2,295	0	0	-	104	133	1,279
Algeria	2,667	5,968	2,238	0	0	-	10,215	16,320	1,598
U.S.	9,616	21,845	2,272	3,808	6,765	1,777	3,642	7,585	2,083
Canada	0	0	-	829	1,822	2,198	1,925	3,964	2,059

Destination	1983 Quantity (metric tons)	1983 Value ('000 US$)	1983 Unit Value (US$/metric ton)	1984 Quantity (metric tons)	1984 Value ('000 US$)	1984 Unit Value (US$/metric ton)
EC	142,219	335,811	2,361	124,678	279,826	2,244
Bene-Lux	1,651	4,385	1,715	5,372	14,243	2,651
France	31,883	89,475	1,690	23,201	56,814	2,449
W. Ger.	6,085	18,855	3,099	7,923	22,606	2,853
Neth.	2,661	6,026	2,265	2,489	6,824	2,742
U.K.	95,715	198,953	2,079	83,259	162,270	1,949
USSR	23,840	33,687	1,413	391	538	1,376
Lybia	6,616	7,133	1,078	1,989	2,296	1,154
Egypt	9,694	13,450	1,387	17,661	23,545	1,333
Algeria	16,120	26,471	1,642	10,436	13,962	1,338
U.S.	5,070	11,380	2,245	1,944	3,823	1,967
Canada	7,470	17,409	2,331	17,544	33,843	1,929

Source: U.N. Commodity Trade Statistics

the EC was considerably higher than that received for exports outside, giving an indication of the degree of export subsidization.

There were no Irish exports to Canada before 1981. At that time Ireland was concentrating its export efforts on the lucrative Middle Eastern market, which was expanding as a result of growing oil revenues. The small quantities shipped to the U.S. market in those years and the unit value received suggests that North America would have been a less preferred market for Irish product. However, prices in North America and the Middle East were converging. By 1981 North American prices were, on average, above those received for Irish product in the Middle East, and exports to Canada commenced while those to the U.S. decreased considerably. This represented a budget saving to the CAP, since P_O - J was now above P_X. This trend continued, and exports to Canada expanded rapidly from 829 tonnes in 1981 to 1,925 tonnes in 1982. This more than tripled in 1983 to 7,470 tonnes and in 1984 increased again by almost two and a half times to 17,544 tonnes. As the relative unit values suggest, the budgetary benefits to the CAP of sales to Canada relative to the Middle East or the USSR were clearly evident by 1984.[6] Initially, the attractiveness of the Canadian market was, in part, the result of supply conditions in Oceania which had driven P_O up, and Irish product was, in part, simply replacing Oceanic product as the price of EC imports remained below those of Australia (Pugh and Kemp, 1986). However, when supply conditions eased in Australia, Australian beef producers served notice that they were going to move to recapture their market share.

The Countervail Suit

It is not surprising that the Canadian Cattlemen's Association reacted with alarm to the rapid increases in imports of subsidized Irish beef, first pressuring the Canadian government to invoke the quota provisions of the Meat Import Act as an interim measure in 1985 and then initiating a countervail suit in October of that year under the Special Import Measures Act. The case was referred to the Canadian Import Tribunal, and the arguments were heard in late 1985 and early 1986. The claim of the Canadian Cattlemen's Association was contested by the Commission of the European Communities, the Irish Livestock and Meat Board, and one Canadian importer.

Although the defense was also fought on a number of legal points, the major economic argument was that material injury had not been sustained by Canadian producers as a result of Irish and Danish imports. In the final analysis the Canadian Import Tribunal concurred with this view. Their conclusion is easy to understand in the context of the model developed above. For the Canadian producers of manufacturing quality beef to have suffered material injury, the imports from Ireland would have had to cause a decline in the Canadian domestic price, P_C. This could only happen if, in the absence of Irish and Danish imports, the Canadian market could be represented as in Figure 1(a) with P_C above P_{US} - T. Then an increase in subsidized imports would shift S_T to the right, driving P_C down. If, however, the situation was as in Figure

1(b), then the Canadian market price would already be at the export floor price, $P_C =$ P_{US} - T, and a shifting of S_T to the right as a result of increased Irish imports would have no effect on the revenues of Canadian beef producers. Of course, there would have been increased displacement of Canadian manufacturing quality beef and, hence, increased exports to the U.S.

At the same time as Irish imports were increasing, demand for manufacturing quality beef was declining in Canada (a leftward shift in D_C), and supplies of cull cows had increased (a rightward shift in S_C) as a result of a rationalization of the national grain-fed beef cattle herd in response to the declining demand for high quality beef. Further, over the period there had been an appreciation of the U.S. dollar against the Canadian dollar, leading to a relative increase in the price of U.S. manufacturing quality beef. All of these events could move the Canadian market into a position such as depicted in Figure 1(b) rather than 1(a) and, therefore, the Canadian Import Tribunal could not confirm the Canadian Cattlemen's Association's claim of material injury.

The rapid increase in Irish and Danish beef imports into Canada did not, however, go unnoticed in the U.S. The displacement of Canadian beef and the subsequent increase in movements to the U.S. was perceived as a circumvention of the 5,000 metric tonne U.S. quota on imports of subsidized EC beef. This concern was expressed by the National Cattlemen's Association (NCA) of the United States in a letter to the Canadian Cattlemen's Association on 17 July 1985. The letter expressed the sentiment that:

...Canada's importing of large amounts of E.E.C. beef has us very concerned. With relatively unrestricted trade between the U.S. and Canada there is evidence of Canadian beef being displaced into our market at levels above what can be considered normal.

This distortion in trade creates several problems for us. For example, our cow prices, particularly on a regional basis, are affected by the greatly increased number of Canadian cows competing for our slaughtering and processing facilities and for our manufacturing beef markets....

For these reasons, I want to let you know that if you are not successful in your efforts in obtaining countervailing action against the E.E.C., and beef continues to be imported into Canada, the NCA has an obligation to pursue action by our government to address the displaced beef imports from Canada into the U.S. (Canadian Import Tribunal, p. 20)

More disturbing was the direct introduction in the U.S. Congress of a number of Bills to restrict imports of Canadian beef. For example, Representative Ron Marlenee of Montana introduced "A Bill Relating to the Importation of Certain Beef Products" into the U.S. House of Representatives on 15 April 1986. This legislation proposed an import moratorium such that:

> Canadian beef products may not be entered, or withdrawn from warehouse for consumption, in the customs territory of the United States... (Marlenee).

Canadian beef products were broadly defined to include both "live cattle" and "fresh, chilled or frozen beef." Hence, if enacted, the Bill would have meant a total ban on Canadian cattle and beef exports to the U.S. The rationale presented to support the introduction of the Bill was that:

> ...exports from the European Community to Canada may be displacing the Canadian market to such an extent that Canadian beef articles have been, and are being, imported into the United States in increased quantities (Marlenee).

Given the interdependent nature of the North American cattle market, it would not be sufficient for the U.S. to impose restrictions solely upon manufacturing quality beef imports. As can be seen from the model, prohibiting the export of Canadian manufacturing beef would cause a fall in the price of that product in Canada.[7] Given that manufacturing and high quality beef both have high positive cross-price elasticities, such a fall in the price of manufacturing beef would lead to a decline in the price of high quality beef. As the Canadian price of high quality beef declined in relation to the U.S. price, exports of that product would increase and the circumvention of U.S. restrictions would continue. In a similar fashion the fall in the price of manufacturing quality beef would be reflected in the price of Canadian live cattle and one would expect increased exports of cattle to the U.S. Consequently, the U.S. had no reasonable option but to limit the import of all beef and live cattle. Of course, restrictions on the export of cattle and beef to the U.S. would clearly lead to material injury for Canadian beef cattle producers.

Hence, the Canadian Import Tribunal was forced to base its judgement on speculations relating to the Canada-U.S. trading environment. Clearly protectionism was on the rise in the U.S., with Canadian hogs recently subject to U.S. countervail actions and with over 100 protectionist Bills introduced into Congress over the previous twelve months. The Tribunal felt that U.S. action to limit Canadian exports was a real possibility. In the summation to its *Statement of Reasons* the Tribunal stated:

> ...given the deep discontent of the United States with the Common Agricultural Policy of the EEC (a matter of public knowledge); given the fact that EEC exports to the United States of subsidized meat products are limited to 5,000 metric tonnes annually; given the fact that the level of EEC subsidized exports into Canada in 1984 alone was almost five times that amount; given the Canadian export imperative; given the conviction of the Tribunal that in the absence of an injury finding EEC exports of subsidized boneless

manufacturing beef will resume in significant volume; and noting the vulnerable state of the Canadian beef industry, the Tribunal concludes that the subsidizing of EEC subject goods entering Canada is likely to cause material injury to the production in Canada of like goods. (Canadian Import Tribunal, p. 21)

As Table 2 illustrates, the imposition of countervailing duties on EC beef effectively eliminated Irish exports to Canada, and the ruling of the Canadian Import Tribunal was subsequently appealed to the GATT. On 29 October 1986 a GATT panel was established to hear the appeal, which centred around legal rather than economic issues pertaining to the case.[8] In essence, the appeal was based on whether the complainant, the Canadian Cattlemen's Association, had "standing" to bring suit before the Canadian Import Tribunal. Only those who are considered producers of "like" product are considered to have "standing." The Panel ruled that as cattle producers produce live cattle rather than beef, a processed product, they did not produce "like" product. Acceptance of the Panel decision by the GATT Committee on Subsidies and Countervailing Measures requires consensus. The U.S., Australia and New Zealand have not yet accepted the Panel's report (this is probably not surprising given their vested interest in a continuing Canadian countervail), and the countervailing measures remain in force at the time of writing.

TABLE 2
CANADIAN BEEF IMPORTS
(FRESH, FROZEN, BONELESS)
(METRIC TONNES)

	1981	1982	1983	1984	1985	1986	1987
Ireland	584	1,938	6,593	17,438	8,610	1,007	0**
Denmark	625	1,581	0*	5,190	2,380	124	0**

* Imports from Denmark curtailed due to outbreak of hoof and mouth.
** January to September only.
Source: Statistics Canada: 65–203 and 65–007.

Conclusion

International trade in agricultural commodities can be extremely complex both because of the high degree of substitutability between products and because of the multiplicative effects of government policies. Although the GATT rules allow countervailing duties on the basis of conjectured damages, the rules are primarily established for cases of two-country confrontations where the injury can be directly attributed to subsidized exports. As is illustrated by the dispute between Ireland and Canada, considerable conjecture is involved when the actions of third parties are the potential cause of the material injury. Further, the material injury caused by a third party may be significantly more substantial than that attributable to subsidy itself. It would seem that direct action at the Uruguay Round of GATT negotiations to address the question of export subsidies will be required if the GATT system is to continue to have any merit for agricultural products. Although this is not a new conclusion, the complexity of the dispute between Ireland and Canada illustrates the difficulties which will continue to arise if recourse to the currently established rules of international trade is relied upon as the sole method of resolving disputes.

NOTES

1. Much of what follows could also apply to Denmark but only Ireland is considered for institutional brevity.

2. Of course this is somewhat of a simplification, as it abstracts from the daily volatility of beef markets and differences in quality and preferences as well as the interaction of these factors. This simplification, however, does not alter the general conclusions of the argument.

3. In the case of chronic annual additions to storage as is currently exhibited in the EC, it is assumed that, net of stock rotation, all removals from storage would have to be eventually disposed of in the export market. This situation is less preferred, as the products cost the CAP not only the amount of the export subsidy but also storage costs. Of course storage decisions will, in part, depend on the availability of capacity and seasonal marketing variations.

4. Of course, if the quantities become sufficiently large, this would begin to have a depressing effect on the entire U.S. market and, hence, Canadian producers and importers would suffer from the decline in P_{US} - T. Quantities had not reached a sufficient level to create a clearly identifiable effect on the large U.S. market prior to the Canadian action to limit Irish imports.

5. Realistically this would be moderated by the preferences of Irish consumers for beef produced in their own country relative to beef produced elsewhere in the EC.

6. Such comparisons must only be approximations due to possible quality differences in the product.

7. In the very short run, to P'_C in Figure 2 and subsequently to P_O.

8. For a complete discussion of the legal aspects of the Canadian Import Tribunal's ruling see Kerr (1987).

REFERENCES

Blumental, M. (1984). "Implementing the Common Agricultural Policy." *Northern Ireland Legal Quarterly, 35*, 28–51.

Canadian Import Tribunal. (1986, 25 July). *Finding of the Inquiry Under Section 42 of the Special Import Measures Act Respecting: Boneless Manufacturing Beef Originating in or Exported from the European Economic Community.* Ottawa.

Irish Livestock and Meat Board (CFB). (1985). *Annual Review 1985, Livestock and Meat Industry.* Dublin: Irish Livestock and Meat Board.

Kerr, W.A. (1987). "The Recent Findings of the Canadian Import Tribunal Regarding Beef Originating in the European Economic Community." *Journal of World Trade Law, 21*, 55–65.

King, D. (1979). "Results of the Tokyo Round of GATT Multilateral Trade Negotiations with Special Reference to Developing Countries." *World Agriculture, 21*, 15–26.

Marlenee, R. (1986, 11 April). *A Bill Relating to the Importation of Certain Beef Products.* (H.R. 4591, in the House of Representatives, 99th Congress, 2nd Session). (Discussion Draft #2).

Pugh, G. and D. Kemp. (1986, 21 May). *Boneless Manufacturing Beef Originating in or Exported from the European Economic Community* (Public Pre-Hearing Staff Report, Inquiry No. CIT–2–86). Ottawa: Canadian Import Tribunal.

CHAPTER 7

THE IMPACT OF SUBSIDIZED IMPORTS OF LOW QUALITY BEEF FROM THE EC ON THE CANADIAN CATTLE INDUSTRY

E. van Duren and L. Martin

International trade disputes have become a frequent occurrence in recent years. Although the majority of these disputes have been anti-dumping, escape clause and countervailing duty disputes conducted under U.S. trade laws, Canadian producers have become more active in seeking relief from unfair import competition since Canada implemented its rights and obligations under the GATT Subsidies Code in the Special Import Measures Act (SIMA) of 1984. The first major countervailing duty case heard under the SIMA dealt with the impact of subsidized imports of boneless manufacturing (low quality) beef from the European Community (EC) on the Canadian cattle industry. Canadian and American cattle producers welcomed Canada's decision to impose a countervailing import duty but the decision was criticized by European exporters, who subsequently appealed it to the GATT. The GATT panel of experts disagreed with the Canadian decision, but neither the EC nor Canada has taken further action.

According to the GATT Subsidies Code and Canada's SIMA, a countervailing duty may be imposed if government assistance programs available to foreign producers and/or exporters of the subject product cause material injury to domestic producers of the product. Revenue Canada and the Canadian Import Tribunal (CIT) are jointly responsible for administering the test for the imposition of countervailing duties. The test requires making the following four related decisions:

First, do the complainants have *standing* to bring the case? Do they produce the subject product and represent the domestic industry? Second, does the foreign government provide a *subsidy*, and in what amount? Third, are domestic producers of the subject product experiencing *material injury* or threatened with material injury? Fourth, is there a *causal link* between the foreign subsidy, imports of the product and the injury to domestic producers?

Revenue Canada makes the preliminary determination on standing and subsidy and the Canadian Import Tribunal (CIT) makes the preliminary injury and causality determination. Revenue Canada makes the final subsidy determination, and the CIT makes the final standing, injury and causality determination. This delineation of responsibilities parallels U.S. countervailing duty law.

In low quality beef from the EC, Revenue Canada and the CIT determined that the conditions required to impose a countervailing duty were satisfied, although not without debate. The purposes of this paper are to analyze how Revenue Canada and the CIT applied the test for countervailing duties on low quality beef from the EC and to discuss whether or not the decisions were economically sensible. To do this we provide a brief review of Canada's countervailing duty law and the final standing and subsidy determinations. The remaining sections discuss the economic issues involved in determining injury and causality, the research approach used to estimate the actual and potential future impacts of subsidized beef imports from the EC on the Canadian cattle industry, and selected results of this analysis. A previous study of the relationship between imported beef from the EC and prices of beef and cattle in Canada (Martin and van Duren, 1986), commissioned by the CIT, was part of the evidence used in its final decision. Therefore, we conclude with a discussion of the factors that the CIT considered in its determination that subsidized imports of low quality beef from the EC did pose a threat of material injury to the Canadian cattle industry.

Canada's Countervailing Duty Law

Canada's countervailing duty law (SIMA) guides Revenue Canada and the CIT in their conduct of countervailing duty investigations. The SIMA implements Canada's rights and obligations under the GATT Subsidies Code of 1979—the agreement reached on subsidies and the use of countervailing duties in the Tokyo Round of the GATT. The GATT Subsidies Code provides some guidance on the four components of the test for imposing countervailing duties.

First, for the standing determination it states that the complainants must produce a product like, or sufficiently similar to, the one being investigated. Second, for the subsidy determination the existence and the amount of the domestic production and/or export subsidy must be established.

Third, material injury, threat of material injury, or the threat of material retardation of the establishment of a domestic industry must be shown. This requires examining prices, import levels, and revenues and incomes in the industry, as well as any other relevant factors.

Fourth, a causal link between the subsidy and the material injury to domestic producers must be established. The GATT Subsidies Code suggests that a proper causality test consists of two parts. First, the impact of the alleged subsidy on production and/or exports of that product in the foreign country must be demonstrated. Second, it must be shown that the subsidized imports, and not "other factors" that could be injuring the domestic industry, are causing the material injury.

The Standing Determination: Do "Canadian Cattlemen" Produce Low Quality Beef?

The Canadian Cattlemen's Association (CCA), asserting that its members represent the majority of Canada's low quality beef industry, petitioned Revenue Canada for a formal countervailing duty investigation on 18 October 1985. The Association argued that low quality beef from the EC could only enter Canada with export subsidies, and that the resulting increase in beef supplies in Canada caused a decline in Canadian beef and cull cow prices, since excess supplies of beef and cattle produced in Canada had to be exported to the United States. In addition, U.S. producers perceived these exports as a contravention of the EC quota in the U.S. market (5000 tonnes annually). This in turn could lead to U.S. retaliation against Canadian cattle producers in the form of tariffs or quotas on cattle and/or beef imports.

On 28 October 1985 Revenue Canada began a formal investigation, thus accepting that cattle producers had standing to bring a case against beef exported from the European Community. In support of this decision Revenue Canada stated that the production process for low quality beef consisted of a "single continuous line" starting with the raw material (the cull cow) which yielded only one commercially significant end product—low quality beef. (The decision to treat beef and cattle production as one industry contrasted with the decision made in the 1985 U.S. case against Canadian hogs and pork, in which the production of the raw and processed products was deemed to occur in two separate industries.) Furthermore, although cow-calf producers, as represented by the CCA, were not exclusively representative of the industry, Revenue Canada determined that they constituted a major portion of the industry (44 per cent) and thus had standing to bring the case.

Demonstrating that cattle producers were not representative of the low quality beef industry would have been the most convenient way of defeating the CCA's attempt at obtaining countervailing duty protection. Thus, the issue of standing remained important to the defendants. At the formal hearings, held in June of 1986, counsel for the EC and Canadian importers contended that the CCA had no right to bring a case because "it was not representative of the industry concerned," which should be limited to the low quality beef industry. He argued that cull cows were not low quality beef and there was no evidence put forward that the CCA represented the Canadian beef industry.

The CIT ruled in favor of the CCA, finding that the CCA's position was more in accord with the purposes of the SIMA than the narrow interpretation urged by the defendants. The CIT provided the following reasons. First, low quality beef is an intermediate agricultural product destined for processing into something else, and without the contribution of cattle producers there could be no low quality beef. And second, the cattle producer has no control over cow prices and for him the value of a cow is its value as low quality beef. In its decision the CIT examined the economic relationships among various participants in the Canadian beef industry, thereby improving on U.S. precedents, which until now have placed undue emphasis on the legal relationships among industry participants.

The Subsidy Determination

Revenue Canada determined that several assistance measures available to beef exporters and cattle producers in the EC were countervailable subsidies. The Export Refund, originally intended to compensate exporters in the EC for the difference between internal and world prices, was the major countervailable subsidy. Programs such as the Export Refund, which provide export subsidies, cause a shift in the exporting country's excess supply function. Therefore they confer a countervailable subsidy, by definition.

For domestic production subsidies the issue of whether or not a program confers a countervailable subsidy is not as straightforward. Canada's SIMA does not require the use of a strictly legal test, like the specificity test used in the United States. Thus, the criterion of whether a program is available to a specific industry or group of industries is only one factor in the subsidy determination. In this case Revenue Canada determined that several domestic programs were countervailable.[1]

The amount of the export subsidy was calculated by dividing the financial benefits made available to beef exporters by the tonnes of beef exported. For domestic production subsidies the financial benefits made available to cattle producers were divided by the tonnes of beef produced. These subsidies were calculated for each program in European Currency Units per tonne of beef produced or exported. These per unit subsidies were summed and converted to Canadian dollars. Irish subsidies were estimated at $0.81/pound and the Danish subsidies at $0.74/pound. Under Canadian law a countervailing duty equal to the estimated value of the subsidy could be imposed, but the countervail is not mandatory if it is not in the public interest.

Determining Injury and Causality: The Economic Issues

Before 1982 Canada did not import low quality beef from the EC, although it did import from Oceania and the United States. By 1984, annual imports from the EC had reached 22,400 metric tonnes, accounting for about 15 per cent of Canadian production. Figure 1 depicts the composition and level of Canada's imports of low quality beef from 1977 to 1985. Since low quality beef is a homogeneous product, subsidized beef from the EC competes directly with domestic beef and beef imported from Oceania and the United States.

FIGURE 1
CANADIAN IMPORTS OF LOW QUALITY BEEF FROM 1977 TO 1985

Economic Relationships in the Beef Industry

The CCA felt that the EC's export subsidies enabled its exporters to undercut domestic and other exporters' prices, thereby depressing low quality beef prices in Canada. Decreased low quality beef prices were alleged to cause Canadian cow, fed cattle and feeder cattle prices to fall. Consequently, profits in the cow-calf and feedlot sectors of the industry were alleged to decline. In addition, cattle producers in the U.S. north-west perceived that subsidized beef from the EC was being transhipped to the U.S. in the form of increased cow exports from western Canada. Consequently, they threatened to take action against Canadian imports of cattle. In the next section we explain why the chain of events alleged by the CCA was possible. This involves a discussion of the complex biological and economic relationships in the beef industry.

Approximately 55 to 60 per cent of low quality beef is derived from the slaughter of beef and dairy cows, and the remainder is a by-product from the slaughter of fed cattle. If low quality beef prices decline, then packers bid down the price of cows because their derived demand for low quality beef has declined. Decreased low quality beef prices could also have a negative impact on fed cattle prices. First, decreased low quality prices could reduce fed cattle prices because part of the value of fed cattle is derived from the value of the low quality beef in their carcasses. Second, decreased low quality prices could induce consumers to purchase low quality beef instead of high quality beef. This would result in downward pressure on high quality beef prices at the retail level. Then, since high quality beef is predominantly derived from fed cattle carcasses, fed cattle prices would also decline. Last, lower fed cattle prices would induce feedlot operators to bid down the price of feeder cattle (Martin and Haack, 1977).

Sales of feeder cattle account for about 80 per cent of the cow-calf sector's revenue and sales of cows for the remainder (CCA, 1986). The feedlot sector sells fed cattle and purchases feeder calves, feed and other inputs, but feeder calves account for about two-thirds of production costs (CCA). Therefore, in this chain of events, income earned by both the feedlot and cow-calf sectors of the cattle industry could also decline due to subsidized imports of low quality EC beef.

Complicating Factors: The Cattle Cycle and Canada-United States Trade in Beef and Cattle

The impact that subsidized beef from the EC could have on Canadian cattle prices and cow-calf and feedlot sector income in Canada is complicated by two additional factors: the nature of production relationships in the cattle industry, and the domination of Canadian cattle and beef markets by the larger U.S. beef and cattle markets.

The Cattle Cycle

The biological lag between the decision to expand production and its realization, and the economic risk that cattle and feed prices will change during this time, are the most important influences on the numbers of cows and fed cattle marketed. Since portions of both cow and fed cattle carcasses are used to produce low quality beef, the following production relationships are important to this case.

The slaughter of beef cows is predominantly a function of the expected price of feeder cattle (Martin and Haack, 1977). An expected increase in the level of calf prices leads to a decline in the number of cows and calves marketed in the short run. Producers retain more female calves for breeding, and then lower calf supplies reinforce expectations of higher calf prices. As calf prices remain high, cattle producers' expected discounted present value of future calf production also remains high. Thus, the value of a breeding cow remains high and fewer cows are marketed. During the expansionary phase of a cattle cycle, cow marketings decrease (Jarvis, 1974; Gracey, undated).

However, in the long run the number of calves marketed increases and calf prices begin to decline. Then producers' expected discounted present value of future calf production begins to decline. They retain fewer calves for breeding and the least productive cows are culled. During the contractionary phase of a cattle cycle cow marketings increase.

Producers' expectations of fed cattle prices are an important influence on the number of fed cattle marketed at a given time. Expectations of lower fed cattle prices induce feedlot operators to increase marketings of steers and heifers in the short run, and usually at lower weights. This reinforces the price decrease and producers' expectations of lower fed cattle prices. During a contractionary phase of the cattle cycle, cattle feeders also try to reduce costs by bidding down the price of calves.

Therefore, subsidized beef from the EC could have both direct and indirect effects on Canadian cattle prices. The direct effect would be the short-run impact that beef from the EC has as a substitute source of supply, as has already been discussed. The indirect effect would follow from the existence of the cattle cycle. If Canadian cattle producers expect imports from the EC to reduce Canadian cattle prices, they would reduce the size of their breeding herds and marketings of fed cattle, cows, and feeder cattle would increase. Larger supplies of cattle would exert further downward pressure on Canadian cattle prices.

Whether this indirect impact on prices would be the result of imports from the EC or "other factors," as referred to in the GATT Subsidies Code, is debatable. One could argue that the response was induced by imports of beef from the EC and, therefore, that the injury should be attributed to the subsidized imports. However, one could also argue that the additional or indirect price response was the result of producers' erroneous interpretation of the situation, and that the injury should not be attributed to the subsidized imports. In our analysis for the CIT, we estimated both the direct and indirect impact of beef imports from the EC on cow prices from 1983 to 1985 in order to provide information for either interpretation.

Canada-United States Trade in Beef and Cattle

Canada's beef and cattle markets are dominated by the much larger U.S. beef and cattle markets. There are few impediments to trade and thus Canadian cattle and beef are priced in relation to American cattle and beef. This relationship between Canadian and American cattle prices is central to the CCA's contention that Canadian prices were being depressed by imports from the EC, and its claim that U.S. cattle producers could have retaliated against Canada. Figure 2 contains a simplified depiction of this pricing relationship for the low quality beef market. We use it to explain the arguments of the cattle producers and the EC about material injury and threat of material injury in this case. Throughout this discussion a reference to low quality beef refers to both cows and low quality beef; they are assumed to be the same product.

Supply and demand for low quality beef in the U.S. interact to produce an equilibrium price (Pus) in the United States. If Canada's internal supply and demand

FIGURE 2
PRICING RELATIONSHIP FOR THE LOW QUALITY BEEF MARKET

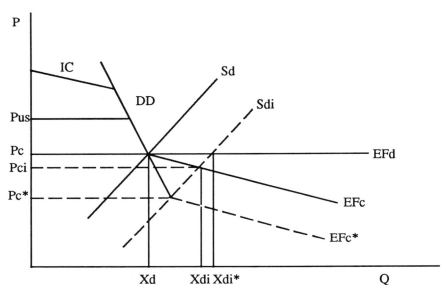

balance leads to a Canadian price which is below the U.S. price by more than the cost of transfer (transportation, shrink, death loss, tariffs, etc.), it becomes profitable for Canadian sellers to sell more in the U.S. market and less in the Canadian market. As the Canadian price decreases, it becomes profitable for Canadian sellers to compete with American sellers in increasingly distant U.S. markets, while absorbing the cost of transferring the product. The volume of Canada's exports and the difference between Canadian and American prices would therefore be negatively, but not necessarily linearly, related. Transfer costs would be expected to be an increasing function of export volumes, and therefore the "export floor" would be downward sloping.

Canada's demand for beef imports, or the "import ceiling" (IC), is downward sloping for similar reasons. The domestic demand curve (DD) is as usual downward sloping, but is always less elastic than the export floor or import ceiling. Since Canada has been a consistent net exporter of low quality beef and cows to the U.S. in the last 10 years, the "export floor" is relevant to the investigation of the impact of beef imports from the EC on Canadian cattle prices.

In this case, the determination of material injury, the complainant argued that imports of subsidized beef from the EC caused the supply of low quality beef in the Canadian market to increase. This is depicted by a rightward shift of the supply curve from Sd to Sdi along the sloping export floor (EFc) and results in increased exports of low quality beef and/or cows to the American market and lower Canadian prices relative to the American prices. The increase in exports is given by the difference between Xd and Xdi and the decrease in Canadian prices by the difference between Pc and Pci.

Counsel for the defendants argued differently. He asserted that beef prices in Canada were almost exclusively determined by U.S. prices, and did not move in relation to EC imports. In terms of Figure 2, he implied that the export floor was flat (EFd). If this was the case, an increase in supply in the Canadian market from Sd to Sdi would produce a larger increase in exports (Xd to Xdi') but no effect on Canadian prices.

For the threat of material injury determination the complainant argued that the possibility of U.S. action against Canadian cattle exports constituted a threat to the Canadian cattle industry. In terms of Figure 2, U.S. retaliation, either in the form of a countervailing duty or an import quota, can be depicted by a fall in the export floor, to EFc* for example. Both types of retaliation are an extra transfer cost to Canadian producers when they are in an export position. Thus, the Canadian price would decline further relative to the American price (to Pci*), as would incomes in the Canadian cattle industry. Counsel for the defendants argued that the possibility of U.S. retaliation against Canadian cattle exporters was conjectural and thus did not present an argument that could be depicted in terms of Figure 2.

In the next section we discuss how we developed quantitative estimates that the CIT could use to determine whether the argument of the complainant or the defendant was correct.

Method for Estimating Injury

To estimate the impact of subsidized beef imports from the EC on Canadian cattle prices and cow-calf and feedlot sector income in Canada we used econometric estimates of key economic relationships in the North American beef industry. Figure 3 depicts the conceptual model used to measure the impact of beef imports from the EC on Canadian cattle prices and incomes in the cow-calf and feedlot sectors of the Canadian cattle industry.

This conceptual model was quantified using a variety of methods. Wherever possible we used the equations estimated for Agriculture Canada's Food and Agriculture Regional Model (FARM). We estimated some of these equations over an extended time period to test for stability of the parameters, and some equations were re-estimated using specifications more appropriate to this study. The economic relationships most important to determining the impact of subsidized imports on Canadian cattle prices were estimated with Ordinary Least Squares using monthly data for the years 1980 to 1985.

FIGURE 3
**IMPACT OF IMPORTS FROM THE EC ON THE CANADIAN
CATTLE INDUSTRY**

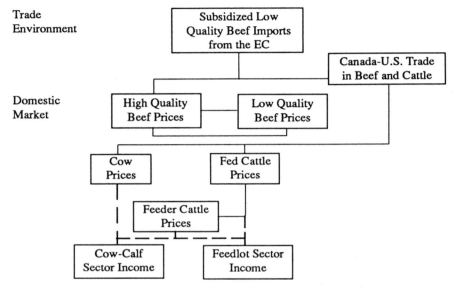

First, we estimated an equation for the "export floor" in the cow and low quality beef market. The difference between Canadian and American cow prices would be expected to be a positive, but not necessarily a linear function of exports, a positive function of transportation costs, and would be expected to display some seasonal variation. Seasonal variation in the price differential would be expected since Canada's exports increase in the fall. Canadian cow slaughter rises relative to American slaughter during this period as a result of climatic differences.

Several specifications of an equation for the export floor were estimated. The best results were obtained in the following specification where the explanatory variables are exports of cows, exports of cows (squared), private transportation cost component of the Canadian consumer price index, and quarterly dummy variables.

This specification implies a quadratic export floor; therefore, only the decreasing portion of the estimated relationship is relevant. The majority of the historical data lies along this portion of the estimated export floor, and the estimated turning point of the equation (1,500 metric tonnes) is above the average level of monthly exports (900 metric tonnes) but well below the maximum (2,700 million metric tonnes). Therefore, it cannot be used to evaluate the impact of cow exports above 1,500 metric tonnes. The relevant portion of the estimated export floor and the econometric results are provided in Figure 4.

FIGURE 4
CANADA'S ESTIMATED EXPORT FLOOR FOR COWS
AND LOW QUALITY BEEF

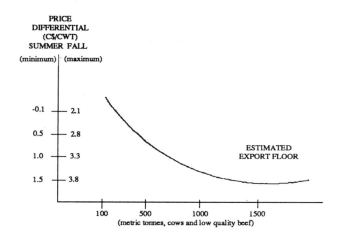

Pus-Pc = - 4.01 Winter + 2.67 Exports - 0.9 Exports^2 + .0485
Transport Index.   (2.1)   (-1.8)   (1.4)

 - 4.76 Spring

 - 5.73 Summer

 - 3.45 Fall

R^2 = .48   F-statistic = 10.1   Durbin-Watson = 1.99   N = 71

Where:

Pus-Pc is price of commercial cows in Omaha minus the price of D1/D2 cows in Saskatoon in Canadian dollars;

Exports and exports squared refer to Canadian cows exported to the U.S.;

Transport Index refers to the private transportation component of the Canadian Consumer Price Index.

Statistical tests of significance appear in brackets. A joint F-test was used to determine if the quarterly dummy variables were statistically significant and t-statistics were used for the other variables.

Second, we estimated the relationship between beef imports from the EC and Canada's exports of low quality beef and cows to the United States. To estimate the impact of subsidized imports of beef from the EC and Canadian cow prices we substituted the estimated relationship between beef imports from the EC and Canadian exports to the U.S. into the regression for the export floor. Because of data and time constraints, the relationship between beef imports from the EC and Canadian exports to the U.S. was estimated using an ad hoc approach. Canada's exports of low quality beef and cows to the U.S. were estimated as a function of Canadian imports of low quality beef from the EC and Oceania, production of low quality beef in the U.S. and Canada, per capita income in the U.S. and Canada, and a set of quarterly dummy variables. Although the econometric results were not completely satisfactory, they indicate that at the margin about 22 per cent of the beef imported from the EC was transhipped to the U.S. market, either in the form of low quality beef or cows.

Evidence of Actual Injury: Did Imports from the EC Injure the Canadian Cattle Industry from 1983 to 1985?

Subsidized imports from the EC had the potential to injure Canadian cattle producers directly through lower cattle prices, and perhaps indirectly by inducing higher cow slaughter rates, resulting from expectations of lower profits. The impact of the imports on cattle prices and incomes of the cow-calf and feedlot sectors was calculated using the econometric results discussed above. Tables 1 and 2 present these results for 1983 to 1985. The estimates for 1984 show the maximum injury experienced by cattle producers due to past imports of subsidized beef from the EC, since imports from that region peaked in 1984. In 1984 cow prices fell by 5.3 per cent due to imports of subsidized low quality beef from the European Community. A very small portion of this decline was due to the indirect effect explained earlier. Fed cattle prices declined by about 0.7 per cent and feeder cattle prices declined by about 0.9 per cent. Total cattle industry income declined by about 43 million dollars in 1984 as a result of the subsidized imports.

Evidence of Threat of Injury: Could Imports from the EC Injure the Canadian Cattle Industry in 1987 and 1988?

If the Canadian Import Tribunal does not find evidence of material injury in the past or present it must determine whether there is a "threat of material injury." This may involve determining whether material injury would have occurred in the past if action to stop the imports had not been taken, whether imports occurring in the past or present could produce injury in the future, or whether injury could occur in the future if the imports were allowed to continue either at their present or at increased levels.

In this case, the CIT had to consider whether Canadian cattle producers risked loss of access to the U.S. cattle and beef markets as a result of the subsidized beef imports from the European Community. In order to accommodate this task we developed

TABLE 1
ESTIMATED IMPACT OF SUBSIDIZED BEEF IMPORTS FROM THE EC
ON CANADIAN CATTLE PRICES, 1983 TO 1985

Cattle Prices	Actual Price ($/cwt)	Total Price ($/cwt)	Percent Effect	Indirect Effect ($/cwt)
Cows:				
1983	46.85	-0.68	-1.45	-0.07
1984	48.21	-2.56	-5.30	-0.11
1985	48.52	-1.34	-2.76	-0.33
Fed Cattle:				
1983	78.98	-0.17	-0.21	
1984	85.30	-0.60	-0.71	
1985	81.63	-0.31	-0.38	
Feeder Cattle:				
1983	86.31	-0.24	-0.27	
1984	87.12	-0.80	-0.92	
1985	88.50	-0.44	-0.50	

TABLE 2
ESTIMATED IMPACT OF SUBSIDIZED BEEF IMPORTS FROM THE EC
ON CANADIAN CATTLE INDUSTRY INCOMES, 1983 TO 1985

Decline in Industry Incomes (Mil. $)	Cow-Calf Sector Cull Cow Sales	Calf Sales	Feedlot Sector	Industry Total
1983	6.2	3.3	2.3	11.8
1984	24.1	10.6	8.6	43.3
1985	13.0	5.8	4.2	23.0

Cow Prices refer to D1/D2 cow prices in Saskatoon, fed cattle prices refer to A1/A2 steer prices in Toronto, and feeder cattle prices to 500–600 feeder cattle prices in Toronto.

several "trade scenarios." First, we considered a continuation of the current situation of relatively free trade. This represented the most optimistic situation that Canadian cattle producers could expect. Second, we considered a situation in which Canada could no longer export cows to the U.S.; this scenario was relevant because cattle producers in the U.S. northwest had complained that subsidized beef imports from the EC were being displaced into U.S. markets in the form of Canadian cow and low quality beef exports. Third, we considered a situation in which the U.S. imposed a countervailing duty on Canadian cattle imports. If the United States were to proceed with a countervailing duty action against the Canadian cattle industry, Canada could face a duty of $5.70 per cwt.

Where appropriate, we considered two levels of imports from the EC for each of these three scenarios. The two levels were a low level of imports of 10,820 metric tonnes (the average level of imports from 1982 to 1984) and a high level of imports of 45,000 metric tonnes (doubling of the previous highest level of imports). Tables 3 and 4 contain the results of these analyses of the "threat of injury."

Retaliation by the U.S. in either the form of a zero import quota for cows or a countervailing import duty on Canadian cow and low quality beef exports could have a substantial effect even if imports from the EC were restricted to the level they offered in March 1986, the low level of imports. Cow prices could decline from about 14 to 37 per cent, fed cattle prices from about 2 to 5 per cent, and feeder cattle prices from about 1.5 to 3.7 per cent. Incomes in the Canadian cattle industry could fall from 123 to 306 million dollars. If imports from the EC were to increase, as they could in the absence of a countervailing import duty, cattle prices and the incomes of producers would decline further.

The Canadian Import Tribunal's Final Decision

On 25 July 1986 the Canadian Import Tribunal determined that subsidized beef imports from the EC had not caused and were not causing material injury to the Canadian cattle industry, but were likely to cause material injury to Canadian cattle producers in the future.

In the CIT's statement of its considerations of material injury it recognized that the North American cattle market is a continental one in which the supplies and demands of many sellers and buyers interact to produce cattle prices that are differentiated by location and grade. The Tribunal found that cattle prices in Canada and the U.S. were depressed for a variety of reasons, such as declining per capita consumption of beef in both countries, the current stage in the cattle cycle, the impact of government programs in the U.S. directed to reducing the size of the dairy herd, weather conditions, and other factors. Then the CIT stated that it had to consider causality—whether there was additional price suppression in Canada due to the subsidized imports of low quality beef from the European Community.

TABLE 3
FORECAST IMPACT OF SUBSIDIZED BEEF IMPORTS FROM THE EC
ON CANADIAN PRICES FOR SELECTED TRADE SCENARIOS,
AVERAGE OF 1987 AND 1988

Cattle Prices by Trade Scenarios	Base Price ($/cwt)	Total Price ($/cwt)	Per Cent Effect
Cows:			
Unrestricted Trade			
Low Imports	48.00	- 1.25	- 2.6
High Imports	48.00	- 4.99	-10.4
Zero Cow Exports			
Low Imports	48.00	-17.80	-37.1
Countervailing Duty			
Zero Imports	48.00	- 5.70	-11.8
Low Imports	48.00	- 6.95	-14.5
High Imports	48.00	-10.69	-22.3
Fed Cattle:			
Unrestricted Trade			
Low Imports	80.00	- 0.30	- 0.4
High Imports	80.00	- 1.18	- 1.5
Zero Cow Exports			
Low Imports	80.00	- 4.23	- 5.3
Countervailing Duty			
Zero Imports	80.00	- 1.35	- 1.7
Low Imports	80.00	- 1.65	- 2.1
High Imports	80.00	- 2.53	- 3.2
Feeder Cattle:			
Unrestricted Trade			
Low Imports	85.00	- 0.22	- 0.3
High Imports	85.00	- 0.88	- 1.0
Zero Cow Exports			
Low Imports	85.00	- 3.14	- 3.7
Countervailing Duty			
Zero Imports	85.00	- 1.00	- 1.2
Low Imports	85.00	- 1.22	- 1.4
High Imports	85.00	- 1.88	- 2.2

TABLE 4
FORECAST IMPACT OF SUBSIDIZED BEEF IMPORTS FROM THE EC ON CANADIAN CATTLE INDUSTRY INCOMES FOR SELECTED TRADE SCENARIOS, AVERAGE OF 1987 AND 1988

Decline in Industry Incomes (Mil. $)	Cow-Calf Sector		Feedlot Sector	Industry Total
	Cull Cow Sales	Calf Sales		
Unrestricted Trade				
Low Imports	12.5	2.9	6.7	22.1
High Imports	49.9	11.7	26.5	88.1
Zero Cow Exports				
Low Imports	167.0	43.6	95.8	306.4
Countervailing Duty				
Zero Imports	57.6	13.4	30.2	101.2
Low Imports	70.3	16.4	36.7	123.4
High Imports	108.6	25.1	56.6	146.6

On the basis of econometric estimates and expert testimony that supported the existence of a downward sloping export floor for Canadian cows and low quality beef, the CIT determined that Canadian cattle prices had declined as a result of subsidized beef imports from the European Community. However, the CIT found that the actual losses, in terms of lower prices, were not large enough to warrant a finding of material injury. It also accepted that Canada's exports of cull cows to the U.S. increased as a result of subsidized beef imports from the EC. The Tribunal considered that this was significant because it linked lower cattle prices in Canada to the imports of subsidized low quality beef.

Having determined that there had been no material injury from 1983 to 1985, the CID then had to consider the threat of material injury. In its reasons the CIT stated that it had little doubt that, without a countervailing duty, exports of low quality beef from the EC would resume in substantial volume, and that these exports could not enter Canada without the benefit of massive subsidies. It cited as evidence the virtual disappearance of imports of low quality beef from the EC since the imposition of provisional countervailing duties.

The CIT then noted that in the past the Canadian cattle industry had been insulated from the adverse effects of imports of subsidized beef by its free access to the U.S. cattle market. However, if the U.S. retaliated against Canadian cattle and beef exports, this protection would be threatened. In the CIT's opinion the threat was real—given two American initiatives in this retaliatory direction. Therefore, it ruled that the threat of U.S. retaliation against Canadian beef and cattle exports due to Canada's imports of subsidized low quality beef from the EC was sufficient to warrant an affirmative threat of injury determination.

Conclusions

The CIT's decision was subsequently criticized on several grounds. First, its determination that cattle producers produce low quality beef was rejected by a GATT panel of experts. In September, 1987, this panel ruled that Canadian cattle producers had not had standing to bring a countervailing duty action against EC beef exporters. The GATT decision was unfortunate in that it highlighted the inability of current GATT rules and procedures to deal with subsidy disputes in agriculture, and increases the frustration of agricultural producers and governments in dealing with unfair trade practices.

Second, the CIT's decision on the threat of material injury was criticized as being "too conjectural" by some international trade lawyers (Steger, 1987). Presumably, this criticism is based on the fact that the threat of retaliation would require political action either by the U.S. government or by U.S. cattle producers. Perhaps the possibility of collusion between Canadian and American cattle producers against beef exporters and cattle producers in the EC is also an element in this criticism of the decision.

Finally, the CIT's decision highlights several elements that are important to the settling of international subsidy disputes. First, national countervailing duty laws have been designed to deal with these disputes in a bilateral fashion, when frequently a problem has been caused by and is affecting several countries. The complex economic and political relationships among governments and cattle producers in the U.S., the EC, and Canada, for example, suggest that unilateral application of countervailing duties is a solution subject to abuse and problems and that a multilateral approach to such disputes is preferable. And second, given the complexity of subsidy disputes, economic logic, quantitative evidence, and expert testimony on the operation of the market in which the subject product is priced are all required to establish the information base needed to make a proper decision regarding the imposition of countervailing duties.

NOTES

1.   Domestic programs deemed to be countervailable were the Intervention System for Beef and Veal, Calf Birth and Suckler Cow Premium and Grants for the Development of Beef Cattle Production in Ireland and Northern Ireland.

2. The general form of the equation we estimated was: Canada-U.S. Dow Price Differential = some function (exports, transportation cost index, seasonal dummy variables).

REFERENCES

Canadian Cattlemen's Association. (CCA). (1986, October). Subsidization Complaint in Respect of Boneless Manufacturing Beef Originating in or Exported from the European Communities. (Two Volumes). Calgary, Alberta.

Canadian Import Tribunal. (1986, 25 July). *Final Determination in Boneless Manufacturing Beef Originating in or Exported from the European Economic Community.*

Gracey, C. (Undated). *The Cattle Cycle.* Calgary, Alberta: The Canadian Cattlemen's Association.

Jarvis, L.S. (1974, May/June). "Cattle as Capital Goods and Ranchers as Portfolio Managers: An Application to the Argentine Cattle Sector." *Journal of Political Economy, 82* (3), 489–519.

Livestock Market Review. (1980–86). Marketing and Economics Branch.

Martin, L. and E. van Duren. (1986, June). *The Relationship Between Imported Beef from the EC and Prices for Beef and Cattle in Canada.* (Report Prepared for the Canadian Import Tribunal).

Martin, L.J., and R. Haack. (1977, November). "Beef Supply Response in North America." *Canadian Journal of Agricultural Economics 25* (3), 29–47.

Steger, D. (1987). Fraser and Beatty, Barristers and Solicitors. Personal Communication.

van Duren, Erna H.K. (1987). *The Impact of Subsidized Boneless Manufacturing Beef Imports from the European Economic Community on the Canadian Cattle Industry.* Unpublished Master's Thesis, University of Guelph, Guelph, Ontario.

CHAPTER 8

THE POTATO WAR AND U.S.-CANADA AGRICULTURAL TRADE

C. Carter, R. Stern and A. Schmitz

The bilateral trade relationship between the U.S. and Canada has always been an important component of each country's international trade policy. As a result of proximity and similar consumer tastes, the U.S. and Canada have been able to enjoy the benefits of comparative advantage by trading with each other. In agricultural products alone, the U.S. has accounted for more than 50 per cent of Canadian imports from 1949 to the present, and Canadian farm products constituted between 25-33 per cent of American agricultural imports over the same period (Agriculture Canada, 1987, pp. 28–29).

Yet despite strong political and economic ties, free trade between the U.S. and Canada has not been achieved; the production and exportation of close product substitutes has led to fierce competition and trade frictions. Agricultural trade, in particular, has been a difficult issue to resolve, due to the similarity of commodities produced and the highly political nature of the agricultural sector. Alleged incidents of dumping of agricultural commodities by producers in both countries have occurred.

In 1987 the U.S. and Canada entered into a free trade agreement in order to reduce barriers to trade as well as to establish guidelines for more acceptable trade behavior. This paper will focus on the "Potato War of 1982–1983," which involved two dumping cases leading up to the Free Trade Agreement. The history of the Potato War highlights the problem of close agricultural substitutes, produced at or around the frontier, being sold across the border. Specifically, eastern (Maine) U.S. potato growers brought a case before the U.S. Department of Commerce in February 1983, accusing Canadian producers in the Maritime provinces of subsidizing production, flooding and undercutting their U.S. market. Eight months later growers from British Columbia formally charged, before the Canadian Anti-Dumping Tribunal, that western U.S. farmers were dumping potatoes in their market.

The first section of this paper will briefly sketch the background statistics on U.S.-Canada trade in potatoes. The second section will analyze the USITC case using a simple model of dumping and its effect on the foreign market. Similarly, the third section will study the Canadian Anti-Dumping Tribunal case. Finally, the fourth section will analyze the implications of these symmetric cases for the Free Trade Agreement between Canada and the United States.

U.S.-Canada Potato Trade: A Brief Overview

Production and Trade

Potatoes in both the U.S. and Canada are produced in the east (Maine to Maryland in the U.S. and the Maritime provinces in Canada) and in the west (Washington, Idaho, California and Oregon in the U.S. and British Columbia in Canada). The principal variety of potatoes produced in both regions is fall-harvested round white potatoes (table variety).

Eastern U.S. In the eastern U.S., there are an estimated 2,000 growers, with 75 per cent of the production occurring in Maine. Total production in this region over the past eight years has averaged between 45,000,000 and 50,000,000 cwt (USDA, unpublished). Table 1 shows the production of American and Canadian potatoes from 1980–1986 by region. From the table it is evident that the eastern U.S., though it only produces about 5 per cent of American potatoes, produces significantly more potatoes than the eastern Canadian provinces. However, the eastern U.S. consumes over 95 per cent of what is produced in the region (USITC, 1983, p. A–17).

The eastern U.S. mainly imports, rather than exports, potatoes from Canada. Most of the imports from Canada into this region originate in Prince Edward Island and New Brunswick. Importing firms resell the Canadian potatoes for table use and seed. These U.S. importing firms successfully "broker" Canadian-produced potatoes first by capitalizing on favorable transportation cost spreads from producer to consumer and second by taking advantage of a favorable exchange rate by buying cheaper Canadian products and selling them at a profit on the U.S. market (USITC, 1983, p. A–11).

Western U.S. Production in the western U.S. is facilitated by large acreage, ideal soil and weather conditions, and sufficient water for irrigation, coupled with low land and labor costs (and thus low production costs). Thus, from 1980–1986, roughly 74 per cent of American potatoes were produced in the western U.S. (USDA, 1987, p. 164) and thus the U.S. mainly exports potatoes from the west. Most of the potatoes exported from the U.S. to Canada flow from the Pacific northwest (Washington,

TABLE 1
U.S. POTATO PRODUCTION 1980–1986 (x1000 cwt)

YEAR	EAST	WEST	TOTAL
1980	78237	188191	266428
1981	87270	208323	295593
1982	92242	215284	307526
1983	79749	214930	294679
1984	89116	223972	313088
1985	98866	254772	353638
1986	83110	234661	317771

CANADA POTATO PRODUCTION 1980-1986 (x1000 cwt)

YEAR	EAST	WEST	TOTAL
1980	41398	13071	54469
1981	46441	12713	59154
1982	49107	12601	61708
1983	43828	12524	56352
1984	48483	13213	61696
1985	51001	15737	66738
1986	44619	16257	60876

Source: *Potato Market Review*, various issues.

Oregon, Idaho, and California) into British Columbia, Alberta, and Saskatchewan. The peak in American exports occurs during the May-July period when Canadian domestic supplies are at their seasonal low. The western U.S. to Canada potato trade is illustrated in Table 2, which shows the flow of exports originating in the U.S. and their Canadian destinations (east or west) from 1980–1986.

Eastern Canada. Though Canada produces potatoes in both the eastern and western regions of the country, roughly two-thirds to three-quarters of all production occurs in the eastern six provinces (with the majority of potatoes grown in New Brunswick and Prince Edward Island) (USITC, 1983, p. A–20). There is a surplus of potatoes in eastern Canada both because Canada's eastern population is significantly less than that of the eastern U.S. and because transportation costs make it more economical for western Canada to import from the western U.S. than from the Canadian east. Total potato exports to the U.S. averaged about 5 per cent of the eastern Canadian crop from 1980–1986 (USITC, 1983; USDA, 1987).

TABLE 2
U.S. EXPORTS TO CANADA, 1980-1986 (x1000 lbs)

YEAR	EAST	WEST	TOTAL
1980	71105	82966	154071
1981	86386	83193	169579
1982	80700	123483	204183
1983	62780	87148	149928
1984	71497	112979	184476
1985	84958	117098	202056
1986	75777	95135	170912

East refers to ports of Canadian entry (Ontario east)

CANADIAN EXPORTS TO THE U.S. 1980-1986

YEAR	EAST	WEST	TOTAL
1980	235211	23433	258644
1981	193936	41211	235147
1982	280598	46440	327038
1983	98350	14773	113123
1984	168757	20904	189661
1985	227069	22736	249805
1986	351485	31518	383003

East refers to ports of Canadian exit

Source: *Potato Market Review*, various issues.

Potato exports from eastern Canada are facilitated by both federal and provincial assistance programs. Specifically, potato production is enhanced by income and price supports under the Agricultural Stabilization Act. Exports are encouraged by technical and marketing assistance from Potatoes Canada, an organization supported by federal and provincial governments (USITC, 1983, pp. A–23 and A–25).

Western Canada. The majority of western Canadian potatoes are grown in Alberta and British Columbia. Though both the climate and soil of British Columbia are suitable for growing potatoes, production costs are high relative to growers in the western United States. Thus the comparative advantage in potato growing enjoyed by the western U.S. producers has caused western Canadians to import from one-quarter to one-half of their potato supply (Carter, 1984).

Historical Trade Flows

From the early 1960s until the mid-1970s, Canada was a net exporter of potatoes. During the 1970s, however, Canada became a net importer of potatoes, reaching an import high in 1977, with a value of CAN$5 million exported versus CAN$36 million imported (Gifford, 1982, p. 2). By 1982, Canada was again a net potato exporter with a surplus of CAN$10 million in 1982 (Gifford). From 1982 to 1986, Canada's production of potatoes grew by about 10 per cent, but exports fluctuated from a low of 1,892,615 cwt in 1984 to a 1986 high of 3,829,868 cwt. Thus no definite trend in trade with the U.S. has been established.

These swings from net exporter to net importer in less than 20 years can largely be attributed to two factors: the exchange rate, and trade policies. In 1977 the Canadian dollar was almost equal in value to the American dollar. Then in 1978 it dropped to about .90 Canadian dollars to 1 U.S. dollar, falling to less than .80 by 1983. Thus relative to the 1977 par year, the price of exports to the U.S. in American currency decreased by 20 per cent in the early 1980s. Canadian potatoes therefore became more competitive in the U.S. market even with (in some instances) high transportation costs.

Secondly, until 1980 the U.S. placed a 37.5 cents/100 lbs (up to a certain limit) and then a $0.75/100 lbs import tariff (above the threshold) on potatoes from Canada. From 1980, a stepwise reduction in tariffs on potatoes to a reciprocal rate of $0.35/100 lbs by January, 1987, was negotiated during the Tokyo Round of General Agreement on Tarrifs and Trade (GATT). In addition, the U.S. and Canada agreed to harmonize their respective tariffs and to eliminate the U.S. tariff rate quota system. These two events have contributed to the change in bilateral potato trade flows.

Potato War Case Study I: USITC Case of Canadian Dumping

Background

On 9 February 1983, the Maine Potato Council filed a petition with the U.S. Department of Commerce alleging that fall-harvested round white potatoes from eastern Canada were being sold at a "less than fair value" (LTFV) price in the eastern United States. The USITC began a preliminary investigation in February 1983 which resulted in a non-binding ruling that the Canadian exports were being dumped on the U.S. market. In order to formally charge the Canadians with dumping, the USITC had to show first that the Canadian exports were being sold for LTFV with respect to a comparable substitute (in terms of weight, quality, and end usage) and second that the U.S. industry would suffer "material injury by reason of imports from Canada" in present and future markets (USITC, 1983, pp. 1–15). After six months of investigations, including a public hearing in November 1983, the USITC determined that the case of Canadian potato exports did not meet the two criteria that constitute dumping and thus no countervailing action was required.

Economic Determinants

Though export "dumping" generally implies that the foreign country's exports are dominating the home country market, causing material injury to domestic production, there are various methods of determining whether dumping is taking place. Schmitz, Firch, and Hillman (1981) describe a similar dumping case involving Mexican fresh vegetables flowing into the United States. They identify three tests which determine dumping. Dumping is said to occur when the exported good price is below the domestic price *and* when one of the following conditions are met:

1. The export price is below the exporting country's domestic price for2 the same commodity.

2. Sales are made below the exporting country's cost of production.

3. In absence of a viable home market, the export price is significantly lower than the export price to a third country.

Schmitz et al. explain that determining whether dumping occurs in cases involving fresh vegetables is difficult because the domestic and foreign products must be homogeneous. They conclude that exporters of perishable agricultural products will have a difficult time defending themselves in anti-dumping suits if the cost-of-production criterion is used to determine fair market value.

The ITC defined dumping as material injury caused by less than fair value pricing (LTFP) of an imported product. Specifically, the ITC required that the injured party prove, in addition to the LTFP, that 1) the volume of imports increased significantly over a specified period, or 2) the price of the import significantly changes the domestic price, or 3) the imports adversely affect domestic production decisions (USITC, 1983).

Figure 1 summarizes these two effects in a simple supply and demand diagram. The success of the foreign firm (Canada) in dumping its product in the home country (United States) relies on the assumption that the foreign firm can charge a price below the domestic price and still make a profit. The foreign firm, assumed here to be a monopolist, determines its at-home quantity, $Q1$, where the domestic marginal cost (MC) crosses domestic marginal revenue (MR_d), and then determines price where the level of quantity meets domestic demand (P_1). In the export market, the foreign firm sells at a point where foreign marginal revenue (MR_t) equals marginal cost which is below domestic price. At this quantity, Q_2, the corresponding price, P_2, is the world market price. The domestic quantity is $0Q_1$, and the exported quantity is $0Q_2$.

The effect of dumping on price depends upon the strength of the foreign firm to control the price and upon the price elasticity of demand for the product, in this case potatoes. If the foreign firm can exert a price leadership role in the market to which it

FIGURE 1
DETERMINATION OF DOMESTIC AND FOREIGN PRICES WHEN THE FOREIGN FIRM ACTS AS A MONOPOLIST

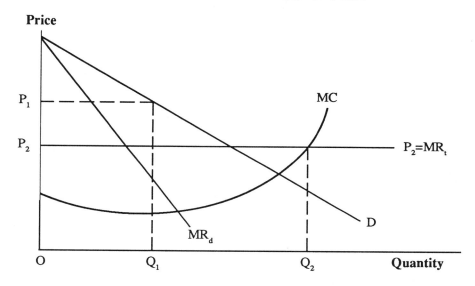

exports, the effects of dumping are more severe than in the case of a non-strategic price setter. Economic theory tells us that in the absence of economies of scale prices set by pure competition are necessarily lower than prices set by firms (either monopolistic or oligopolistic) with power over the market.

In the Canadian potato case, the USITC found that Canada had lacked price leadership power during the entire period under question, September 1979 to October, 1983. In fact, potatoes from Prince Edward Island sold in New York, Maine, and Boston at prices higher than U.S. market prices during the 42 month period (see Table 3). Thus the U.S. domestic price for round fall-harvested potatoes was not affected by the comparable Canadian imports.

The effect of dumping on price also depends on the price elasticity of the product. George and King (1971) estimate that the retail elasticity of demand for potatoes is 0.3, meaning that with a 1 per cent increase (decrease) in price, the quantity of potatoes demanded decreases (increases) by 0.3 per cent. Or, American demand for potatoes would not drastically change by any fluctation in price. Thus, even if Canada had been able to exert price setting power and undercut the U.S. domestic price, the change in American demand for potatoes would not have been significant enough to cause material injury to the U.S. market.

TABLE 3
AVERAGE PRICES OF CERTAIN ROUND WHITE TABLESTOCK
POTATOES FROM MAINE, CANADA, AND LONG ISLAND SOLD IN
NEW YORK CITY BY MONTHS, SEPTEMBER 1979 TO OCTOBER 1983

(Per 50 pound sack)

Period[1]	2 Inch Minimum[2] Maine	2-1/4 Inch Minimum[3] Prince Edward Island	2 Inch Minimum[4] Long Island
1979–1980			
September 1979	–	–	$2.77
October 1979	$2.93	$3.34	3.02
November 1979	2.95	3.20	2.94
December 1979	2.78	3.06	2.63
January 1980	2.92	3.78	2.89
February 1980	2.83	3.58	2.81
March 1980	2.64	3.34	2.67
April 1980	2.63	3.04	2.73
May 1980	3.48	3.66	3.38
June 1980	4.19	–	3.54
1980–1981			
September 1980	–	–	4.91
October 1980	5.50	5.53	5.48
November 1980	5.13	5.47	5.75
December 1980	5.31	5.50	5.75
January 1981	6.75	7.13	6.75
February 1981	6.72	7.00	6.75
March 1981	6.85	7.38	6.53
April 1981	7.22	7.88	6.88
May 1981	7.19	8.03	–
June 1981	8.04	8.75	–
1981–1982			
September 1981	–	5.00	–
October 1981	3.88	4.75	3.94
November 1981	4.03	4.38	4.03
December 1981	3.94	4.38	4.13
January 1982	4.16	4.50	4.25
February 1982	4.31	4.69	4.42
March 1982	4.10	4.60	4.31
April 1982	4.31	4.50	–
May 1982	4.66	4.75	–
June 1982	5.55	5.70	–

TABLE 3 (Continued)
AVERAGE PRICES OF CERTAIN ROUND WHITE TABLESTOCK POTATOES FROM MAINE, CANADA, AND LONG ISLAND SOLD IN NEW YORK CITY BY MONTHS, SEPTEMBER 1979 TO OCTOBER 1983

(Per 50 pound sack)

Period[1]	2 Inch Minimum[2] Maine	2-1/4 Inch Minimum[3] Prince Edward Island	2 Inch Mimimum[4] Long Island
1982–1983			
September 1982	–	4.38	3.19
October 1982	–	4.13	3.16
November 1982	3.13	3.83	3.08
December 1982	3.00	3.60	3.09
January 1983	2.95	4.00	3.25
February 1983	3.21	4.19	3.22
March 1983	3.15	4.06	3.00
April 1983	5.00	5.31	4.37
May 1983	4.84	5.62	–
June 1983	4.94	5.31	–
1983–1984			
September 1983	–	–	5.25
October 1983	5.50	5.83	5.42

[1] No quotations for July and August because supplies are minimal.
[2] U.S. No. 1 potatoes, size A. unwashed.
[3] Canada No. 1 potatoes, unwashed. Potatoes from Prince Edward Island are the only Canadian round whites for which the USDA regularly reports prices.
[4] U.S. No. 1 potatoes, size A, washed.

Source: USITC

As far as quantity effects are concerned, the USITC had to analyze:

1. The rate of increase of imports into the U.S. market.

2. The capacity of the exporting country to generate exports.

3. The availability of alternative but comparable (in terms of accessibility and expected profits) export markets to determine the quantity effects and extent of material injury.

During the period under question, the USITC found that import penetration actually had fallen. Canadian market share of the northeast U.S. dropped from 6.7 per cent in 1980 to 4 per cent in 1983. In quantity terms, the amount of exports fell from 2,076,000 to 1,253,000 cwt (USITC, 1983, p. 16).

This drop in Canadian potato exports to the U.S. coincided with an increase in Canadian production. The second USITC condition for quantity material injury was the capacity of the exporting country to generate exports. With a falling Canadian dollar and rising output, the Canadian *capacity* to export to the U.S. was actually increasing. However, despite the increased ability to export, the Canadians actually decreased potato exports to the United States.

And, finally, the Canadian producers did not possess a comparable alternative market to the United States. Thus the third condition for demonstrating quantity material injury could not be addressed.

In sum, the USITC found that the Canadian potato producers did not exert monopolistic price or quantity setting power over the eastern U.S. potato industry. Nor did the Canadian producers substantially increase their penetration of the U.S. market by price slashing due to export subsidy or to producer price reductions.

It is also important to note that the lack of Canadian strategic price and quantity setting power over the U.S. can be attributed to the absence of the ability to punish the U.S. (either by potato price depression or by countervailing trade barriers on other unrelated products) for limiting Canadian potato exports. Rotemberg (1986) demonstrates that the degree to which a firm can effectively penetrate a foreign market depends upon the degree to which that firm can inflict punishment on its competitors. In this situation, the U.S. unquestionably possesses more economic strength than Canada; hence, the Canadians did not possess the power to capture the U.S. potato market without incurring retaliatory measures.

Though the Canadian producers won the USITC case, it could be argued that the case brought before the Canadian Anti-Dumping Tribunal against western U.S. potato growers was to some extent a retaliatory move.

Potato War Case Study II: The Case Before the Canadian Anti-Dumping Tribunal

Background

On 30 September 1983, the British Columbia Vegetable Marketing Commission submitted a formal complaint to the Canadian Anti-Dumping Tribunal, charging that potatoes (russeted and netted skin but excluding seed potatoes) originating in or exported from the U.S. were causing material injury to the potato producers of British

Columbia. Subsequently the Canadian Deputy Minister of National Revenue for Customs and Excise began an investigation of U.S. potato exports into western Canada. The Ministry determined that potatoes originating from the US were being dumped on the Western Canadian market from 1981–1983.

The investigation began on 8 October 1983, and concentrated on shipments entering British Columbia from the U.S. between August, 1982 and September, 1983. As in the Maine potato growers' suit, the purpose of the inquiry was to determine whether imports from the U.S. were causing material injury to British Columbia producers in the form of price suppression, loss of market share, profit erosion, and the potential for future domestic market injury.

The British Columbia potato growers stressed that the American and Canadian potatoes under investigation were homogeneous products (perfect substitutes). In addition, the producers claimed that the supply of B.C.-grown potatoes would easily meet domestic demand, and that the only additional potato supplier in British Columbia was Alberta, and Alberta supplies less than 5 per cent of the total B.C. market (Canadian Anti-Dumping Tribunal, 1984, p. 6).

On 4 March 1984, the Canadian Anti-Dumping Tribunal determined that non-size A or "stripper" potatoes were being dumped from the State of Washington into British Columbia and that these potatoes "caused, would be causing and [are] likely to cause material injury to the production in the Province of British Columbia of like goods" (Canadian Anti-Dumping Tribunal, 1984, p. 2). However, the Tribunal also determined that no other variety of potatoes was causing material injury to the British Columbia potato industry.

Economic Determinants

In order to determine material injury, the Canadian Anti-Dumping Tribunal (CAT) had to analyze the quantity and price effects of U.S.-based exports into British Columbia. The average yield of British Columbia potatoes (1981–1983) was about 213 cwt per acre, compared to the 497 cwt received by Washington State producers over the same period. In addition, the average cost for potato production in British Columbia between 1981–1983 was CAN$9.68 per cwt, while the U.S. cost was about CAN$4.09 (Carter, 1984, p. 1). The absolute advantage in potato production of the western U.S. followed directly from better climatic conditions and from the benefits of economies of scale.

Thus, British Columbia producers believed that any amount of imported potatoes would necessarily undercut domestic production. The producers claimed that they had few alternative crops that could be produced that would be feasible given climate, market conditions, and transportation costs. Thus their absolute dependence on potato production meant that any competition for market share would necessarily cause them material injury.

The influx of foreign potatoes would immediately shift the supply curve outward; consequently, the first effect would be lower market prices. The second effect would be a gradual erosion of demand for domestically produced potatoes, thereby causing a severe drop in local profits. Specifically, since the cost of U.S. production was lower than it was in B.C., the U.S. could gain from exporting potatoes above U.S. market cost but still below B.C. market price.

Prior to the influx of U.S. potato exports, British Columbia producers had a *de facto* monopoly over supply of potatoes within the province. Figure 2 graphically depicts B.C., Washington State, and Alberta potato market shares from 1964 to 1983. Note that during that period, potato exports from Washington State into B.C. increased from 5 per cent to 27 per cent (Carter, 1984, p. 8). The only other alternative source came from Alberta, and as mentioned earlier, it controlled less than 5 per cent of the B.C. potato market share. British Columbia growers, however, maintained a powerful market position because they controlled over half of the market and maintained the greatest market share. The monopoly power of the British Columbia producers was enhanced by the relatively inelastic demand for potatoes.

But the monopolistic position of the domestic producers was threatened by U.S. potato exports into the B.C. market. Figure 3 shows the theoretical quantity and price effects due to the influx of potatoes from the United States. Assuming that the demand for potatoes remains unchanged (a valid assumption following directly from the low elasticity of demand for potatoes), the market supply curve for potatoes shifts out from S' to S as imports enter. The quantity supplied increases from Q' to Q^* and the corresponding price decreases from P'to P^* —both effects due to the breakdown of absolute monopoly control over the B.C. market. Thus, the increased supply of potatoes from the U.S. should theoretically have forced prices downward.

Consequently, the B.C. producers claimed, the retail price was lowered below their cost of production in order to compete with U.S. exports, thus rendering domestic production unprofitable. Figure 4 depicts a comparison of Washington State and British Columbia average farm prices. It is interesting to note that from 1978 to 1982 the B.C. price dropped, while concurrently Washington State's market share rose (see Figure 2). The B.C. producers testified that the loss of price control, quantity (market share), and thus production revenues were the bases for material injury.

It is unclear whether the introduction of U.S. potatoes did in fact materially injure the B.C. producers. The domestic production of potatoes was reduced between 1980 and 1983, and domestic prices were higher, a result consistent with the supply response in a monopoly setting. Thus, producer revenues were higher, and it is not clear that the

FIGURE 2
B.C. AND WASHINGTON POTATO MARKET SHARES
1964–1983 (PER CENT)

Source: Annual Unload Report - Agriculture Canada, 1974–1983.

FIGURE 3
ECONOMIC EFFECTS OF A REGULATED MARKET

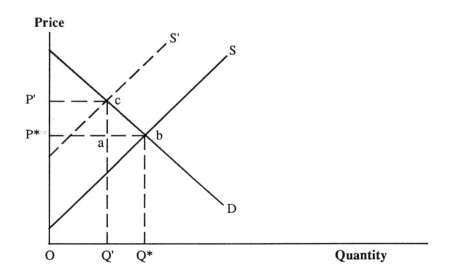

British Columbia potato industry suffered enormous financial hardship during the years in dispute.

FIGURE 4
B.C. AND CANADIAN POTATO AVERAGE FARM PRICES
1964-1982 (CENTS/LB)

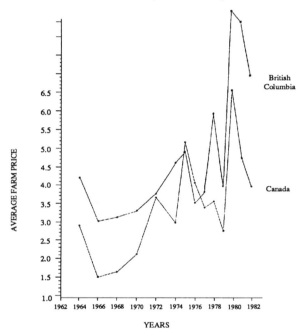

Source: Fruit and Vegetable Production Statistics Canada CAT 22–003.

Though the economic determinants of material injury were not "unambiguously satisfied," the Anti-Dumping Tribunal ruled favorably toward the B.C. producers on the grounds that the U.S. was entering and could potentially dominate the market. This decision was based on the classification of the B.C. potato market as a "regional market" as defined by Article VI Paragraph 4(a) of the GATT Code, signed in June 1967. In addition, the Tribunal determined that the B.C. potato growers had few crop alternatives to potatoes and therefore were extremely sensitive to any influx of potatoes.

In sum, the Tribunal ruled that:

1.   Given production costs in British Columbia are double those in Washington State;

2. Potatoes from Washington State could supply the entire British Columbia market;

3. British Columbia producers had to lower their prices in 1983 in order to compete with Washington State potato prices (plus transportation costs);

4. The British Columbia producers had few viable alternative crops to substitute for potato production;

there was sufficient evidence supporting the need for protection from Washington State potato exports. Thus the Tribunal found that dumping of "non-size A potatoes" solely exported from Washington State was causing material injury to the British Columbia potato producers.

Implications for the U.S.-Canada Free Trade Negotiations

Article XXIV of the GATT requires that "substantially all bilateral trade be covered by a free trade agreement" (Raworth, 1987, p. 352). However, no formal GATT provision has ever been made specifically concerning agricultural trade, due to the fact that most domestic agricultural sectors receive protection and/or subsidization, and most GATT members are unwilling to allow unrestricted agricultural imports which could undercut domestic production. The history of U.S.-Canada potato trade illustrates this problem, and underscores the need for a bilateral agreement on agricultural trade issues.

Given the geographical proximity and similarity of consumer tastes, the flow of products between the U.S. and Canada is inevitable. At the same time, given the similarities in climate (especially along the frontier) and factors of production, trade conflicts such as dumping are also inevitable. As each nation acts to maximize production revenue and exploit its comparative advantage, specific guidelines are necessary to minimize conflict.

The two potato cases point to the most controversial points in the Free Trade Agreement: whether or to what degree agricultural trade should be included. First from the U.S. standpoint, there is the question of production and export subsidies. Specifically as argued in the USITC case, the Canadian agriculture system is designed to encourage domestic production through effective production subsidies (price and income support programs) which reduce the cost to farmers. Thus the farmer can sell his or her product at a lower price and still earn a profit. In addition, export promotion, supported by the Federal Government, helps to make Canadian agricultural products more attractive to foreign buyers (U.S.ITC, 1983, pp. A–24, A–25). In the ITC case, the U.S. claimed that this use of subsidization is a direct violation of the GATT Code and warrants countervailing action. As the potato case demonstrates, a strict definition and subsequent prohibition of export subsidies would have to be accepted before a general free trade agreement could be reached (Raworth, 1987, p. 356).

It has been argued by some Canadians, on the other hand, that their domestic agricultural production is constantly threatened by American dumping of agricultural goods, without export subsidies but at lower than Canadian prices due to lower production costs. Thus, agreement must be made explicitly defining what constitutes material injury to non-substitutable crop production. This complicated process involves the question of whether to allow less-than-efficient domestic production (like the B.C. potato industry) to be protected and substituted for a more efficient and less expensive imported commodity. Implicit, then, is the need for fair price legislation and a means to settle disputes.

In conclusion, the two potato case studies present the problems associated with bilateral trade between the U.S. and Canada and the need for specific guidelines to be set in order to prevent trade disputes. As the Potato War illustrates, each side possesses some strategic leverage over the other but is unable or unwilling to exercize pure monopolistic power over the export market. The Canadian producers, as shown in this case, have the advantage of a favorable exchange rate (making their products cheaper to U.S. buyers) and a strong network of regional and federal production and export programs. The U.S., in contrast, has the advantage of lower production costs.

Development of the Free Trade Agreement for the prevention/resolution of trade disputes has both economic and political ramifications. The United States and Canada are *de facto* trading partners—neither country can replace the other as its most important (in terms of both value and quantity) export market. In addition, for geopolitical and cultural reasons, the U.S. and Canada must maintain a strong political alliance; such a strong tie is intensified by the resolution and prevention of trade disputes. Bromke and Nossal (1987) explain that:

A successfully concluded pact will be an important step forward in con-solidating cooperation between the two North American neigh-bors...conversely failure to reach a mutually satisfactory agreement will not only be a distinct setback in bilateral relations between Ottawa and Washingt-on, but will also encourage nationalist and protectionist trends. (p. 151)

As the potato cases suggest, economic and political disputes are inevitable without a formal agreement to codify acceptable trade behavior. Thus the importance of the Canada-U.S. Free Trade Agreement cannot be overestimated.

REFERENCES

Anti-Dumping Tribunal of Canada. (1984, June). *Finding of the Anti-Dumping Tribunal in Inquiry No. ADT–4–84 under Section 16 of the Anti-Dumping Act.* Ottawa.

Agriculture Canada. (1987). *Canada's Trade in Agricultural Products 1984, 1985, 1986.* Ottawa: Minister of Supply and Services.

Agriculture Canada. (1981–1986 issues). Potato Market Review. Ottawa.

Bromke, A. and K.R. Nossal. (1987). "A Turning Point in U.S.-Canadian Relations." *Foreign Affairs, Fall,* 151–165.

Carter, C.A. (1984, April). *Statement to the Canadian Anti-Dumping Tribunal.* Ottawa.

George, P.S. and G.A. King. (1971, March). "Consumer Demand for Food Commodities in the U.S. with Projections for 1980." (Giannini Foundation Monograph No. 26) University of California, Berkeley, California.

Gifford, M.N. (1983, February). *Canada-U.S. Trade in Potatoes and Potato Products.* (Staff Paper). Ottawa: Agriculture Canada.

Ingram, J.C. (1983). *International Economics.* New York: John Wiley and Sons.

Raworth, P. (1987). "Canada-U.S. Free Trade: A Legal Perspective." *Canada Public Policy, 13,* 350–365.

Rotenberg, J. and G. Solner. (1986, June). *Quotas and the Stability of Implicit Collusion.* (NBER Working Paper Series #1948). Washington: National Bureau of Economic Research.

Schmitz, A., R.S. Firch, and J.S. Hillman. (1981). "Agricultural Export Dumping: The Case of Mexican Winter Vegetables in the U.S. Market." In *American Journal of Agricultural Economics 63* (4), 645–653.

USITC. (1983, December). *Fall-Harvested White Potatoes From Canada.* (USITC Publication 1463). Washington, D.C.

United States Department of Agriculture (USDA). (1987). *Agricultural Statistics.* Washington: USGPO.

CHAPTER 9

DETERMINING ECONOMIC INJURY: THE CANADIAN CORN COUNTERVAIL CASE

G. Lermer

In Fall 1986, the Ontario Corn Producers' Association launched a countervail suit against the United States, alleging that U.S. subsidies for corn were causing material injury to Canadian producers. In March 1987 the Canadian Import Tribunal confirmed Revenue Canada's preliminary countervailing duty of \$33.35/tonne on U.S. corn exports to Canada, a sum which was later reduced by the Minister of Finance. The author of this paper was an active participant in the case, preparing reports for the Tribunal on the level of injury to Canadian producers and on the likely effect of the countervail duty on Canadian corn prices. The following is largely derived from the reports written for the Tribunal, and highlights some of the difficulties encountered in trying to determine the net economic impacts of U.S. agricultural policies on U.S. corn output, and consequently on both world corn prices and on the incomes of Canadian producers.

The story of the corn countervail is of particular interest since it was, in many respects, a precedent-setting case and may influence all future countervail suits. In particular:

1. The corn case was the first successful countervail duty case against the United States.

2. The corn case was the first instance in which relief was granted by way of countervailing duty although it could not be shown that there was an actual increased flow of subsidized imports into Canada.

3. The corn case was the first occasion on which the Canadian Import Tribunal, after upholding Revenue Canada's determination, initiated an inquiry pursuant to section 45 of the Special Import Measures Act. This section dates from 1984, and it allows the Tribunal to advise the Minister of Finance to eliminate or reduce a countervailing duty based on broad considerations of the public interest.

Background

Corn in Ontario's Agriculture

During the 1960s and 1970s, corn production in Ontario expanded noticeably; increased acreage was seeded in corn and yields rose rapidly. By 1985, corn had become a major crop in Ontario, accounting for 22.23 per cent of farm cash income from crops and 7.74 per cent of total farm cash income. Moreover, about 56% of the corn crop was not sold for cash, but instead was fed on farm to livestock (Statistics Canada). The scope of the expansion has been described by Deloitte, Haskins and Sells (1987) as follows:

> On the production front, the land area planted to grain corn has doubled, being 455,000 hectares in 1970 and a record 902,000 hectares in 1985. At the same time, average corn yields for the province have shown a 15 per cent improvement during this same time period. The cumulative effect is an industry that has exhibited a 5.6 per cent annual growth rate in production. (p. 2)

Acreage planted to corn in Ontario has increased faster than the total acreage planted to other crops. Between 1973 and 1983, the acreage planted in seven major crops increased by only one per cent per annum, but corn acreage expanded by 3.3 per cent. Corn acreage expanded at the expense of declining acreage in hay (-1.5 per cent), the addition of improved acreage (0.3 per cent), and the reduced number of improved acres not planted in one of the seven major crops (-1.5 per cent) (see Groenewegen and Kittle, 1985, p. 28). At the same time corn acreage and output expanded still more rapidly in Quebec.

Output increased faster than acreage, but relative prices had little impact. For the period 1961–82, yield increases due to technical improvements (excluding weather considerations and additions of nitrogen) averaged 2, 1, and 0.3 per cent per year in each of three Ontario growing zones (see Dumanski, Bootsma and Kirkwood, 1986, p. 481). Weather parameters explain between 21 and 64 per cent of observed yield variations; by adding a time trend to weather variables between 36 and 79 per cent of the yield variation can be explained. However, nitrogen applications data do not seem to explain any additional variation in the annual corn yield.

Meilke (1984) has reported that the rise of corn in Ontario is explained by plant breeding activities, improved chemical weed control, and the growing local demand for high energy livestock feed. Especially the first two factors suggest that corn acreage has expanded because technical change has made it more profitable to grow corn than to grow other crops in Ontario. In the past, changes in acreage responded largely to technical improvements that increased corn yields on land and in climatic zones that would not previously have supported the growth of corn. But Meilke concluded that the engine driving the corn expansion in Ontario is running slower today than yesterday.

Thus, over the period 1960 to 1985, corn supplies seem to have expanded strongly in response to changing technical conditions with little consideration being given to minor and possibly transitory changes in relative prices. Furthermore, over the same period agricultural stabilization payments would have reduced the impact of any variation in the corn to soybean price ratio on the farmer's planting decision; the corn to soybean price ratio is the price variable which Meilke (1984) uses to explain corn acreage decisions.

The Pricing Mechanism for Ontario Corn

Ontario corn production may have been insensitive to prices, but Ontario producer incomes do depend on corn prices that are sensitive to U.S. corn prices. Figure 1 shows the corn basis (the difference between the Chatham spot price and the Chicago near term future price) for the period 1982–87.

FIGURE 1
CORN BASIS: CHATHAM-CHICAGO

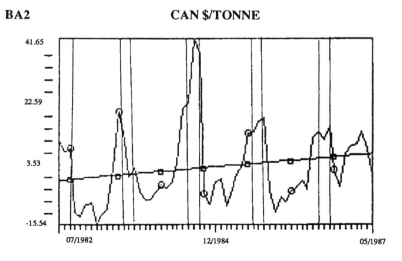

BA2   CAN $/TONNE

Over the past five years, the mean value of the Chatham-Chicago basis has been $2.24, with a standard deviation of almost $12, a high of $41.65, and a low of $15.54 (all values reported on a per tonne basis). Although there is a small upward trend, clearly the basis swings regularly and frequently rather widely around its mean value. The fluctuations are seasonal, as indicated by the fact that a simple pattern of seasonal weights over the crop year, together with the annual average corn basis, explains over 60 per cent of the variation in the monthly average corn basis (see Lermer, 1987b, p. 20).

Though the Chatham-Chicago basis is almost always high during the summer months, few Ontario farmers are able to profit from the rise. About half of Ontario corn is sold during the three months immediately following the start of the harvest. By summer, just between 9 and 15 per cent remains available for marketing (see Lermer, 1987b, p. 10.).

Like Martin et al., (1986), I conclude that the pricing of corn in Ontario has been reasonably efficient in the sense that it conforms to a traditional economic model. But the past efficiency of the corn market depended upon the close links between the American and Canadian markets. Canadians were able to acquire corn at any time of the year (with 1984 standing as a not fully explained exception) at a price that reflected the average cost of storing corn beyond the harvest period, and anticipations of the subsequent harvest. Corn users were easily able to avoid any inadequacies in Canada's storage system by importing corn at the time of year they needed it. In fact, up until the countervail duty was imposed, Ontario corn prices increasingly became tied to U.S. corn prices because the rate of increase of Ontario's corn production was faster than domestic consumption. Table 1 below indicates that Canada has been a net exporter of corn in many recent years. When exporting corn, the Canadian farmer must absorb the cost of handling and delivery into the U.S. market.

Given the close links between the Ontario and U.S. corn markets, U.S. agricultural policies that have the effect of depressing corn prices are transmitted quickly to Canada. Between the 1983–84 and 1986–87 crop years the average U.S. corn prices over each crop year tumbled from $3.25/bushel to $1.57/bushel. The declining market price forced the U.S. government to increase its deficiency payments to an average of $1.46/bushel in 1986–87 so that those American farmers covered by U.S. farm programs were fully protected from the decline, receiving instead the target price of $3.03/bushel. Evidently, U.S. farmers received in 1986–87 almost as much for their corn from the U.S. government as from the market.

But Ontario corn producers were not without support themselves. As U.S. prices fell, Canadian and Ontario grain corn stabilization programs combined to assure Ontario corn producers a return of 95 per cent of the five-year moving average price. This program provides an important cushion to Canadian producers. For example, as U.S. producer prices fell from $2.58/bushel in 1984–85 to $2.14 and then $1.57,

TABLE 1
APPARENT CANADIAN CORN MARKET
'000 TONNES

Crop Year	Production	Imports	Exports	Import Apparent	Share %
1976–77	3759.3	659.9	180.3	4238.9	15.57
1977–78	4249.5	386.1	322.7	4312.9	8.95
1978–79	4479.5	682.0	191.7	4969.8	13.72
1979–80	5276.1	993.9	344.0	5926.0	16.77
1980–81	5753.2	1363.5	1056.0	6060.7	22.50
1981–82	6673.4	822.2	1134.7	6360.9	12.93
1982–83	6512.9	758.9	510.8	6761.0	11.22
1983–84	5932.8	225.9	228.7	5930.0	3.81
1984–85	7023.5	612.4	554.5	7081.4	8.65
1985–86	7472.0	416.0	640.0	7248.0	5.74
1986–87	6694.0	515.0	127.0	7082.0	7.28

Source: Agriculture Canada (CIT Exhibit No. 7–86–4A) and Agriculture data from AgData on the IP Sharp Database.

Ontario producers' earnings per bushel expressed in Canadian dollars (after receiving stabilization payments) dropped from $3.51/bushel to $3.44 in 1985–86 and $3.26 in 1986–87. Evidently, Ontario corn producers suffered less from the price decline than did the treasuries of the Ontario and federal governments. But if U.S. prices were to remain low for a few more years, the five-year moving average for calculating the Canadian stabilization price would soon cause producer prices to track the declining U.S. market prices.

Launching the Corn Countervail Case

Facing dim prospects for the future market price of corn, in 1986 Ontario corn producers approached the federal government for assistance and subsequently filed a complaint against the U.S. pursuant to Section 31(1) of the Special Import Measures Act (SIMA). Acting on the complaint, Revenue Canada imposed (effective 10 November 1986) a preliminary countervailing duty of $41.33 a tonne (U.S. funds). This sum was reduced in January 1987 to $33.35 a tonne, still a sufficient amount to prohibit almost all imports. The Revenue Canada duty is collected when imposed, but it is preliminary in the sense that the duty would be refunded should the Canadian Import Tribunal fail to find that the U.S. subsidy caused Ontario corn producers material injury. The Tribunal sat during January 1987 and on March 6, 1987, it ruled, by a vote of two to one, that the U.S. subsidy program for corn producers "had caused, was causing and was likely to cause material injury to the producers in Canada of like goods."

On a finding of material injury by the Canadian Import Tribunal, Revenue Canada's provisional duties are confirmed and become binding. In the corn case the matter did not end with a finding of injury, however, because the Import Tribunal, pursuant to Section 43 of SIMA and after holding hearings, advised the Minister of Finance on October 20, 1987, to lower the countervail duty of $33.35/tonne to $12/tonne or $.30/bushel. On February 4 the Honourable Tom Hockin announced that the countervail duty would be lowered to $.46/bushel. Note that at this level the duty is still high enough to virtually exclude all imports of corn from the United States except those imports used for the further production of goods for export, which are eligible for duty drawback (refund).

The corn producers saw their case through to a successful conclusion, but at the outset some among them must have questioned the odds. The corn case charted new territory not only in the domain of Canada's contingency—trade law but also in the wider international arena, and was the first case of export subsidization initiated against the United States. In particular, certain features of the case might have suggested that a countervail suit would have difficulty succeeding. First, in recent years Canada has *not* been a significant importer of U.S. grain corn, and has in some years been a net exporter. Second, no allegation was made that U.S. subsidies were expressly export subsidies. Third, Canadian governments share the burden of the injury and cushion the impact on producers. Finally, the complexity of the U.S. stabilization program raised the possibility that high target prices merely transfer income to U.S. corn producers without creating an incentive for higher production, and, in fact, the program leads to *decreased* production by enforcing acreage restrictions on those producers who choose to become eligible for the subsidies.

Observing Injury

In traditional countervail duty cases, especially those involving manufactured products, a determination of injury is related to:

1.   The volume of imports and the increase of market shares.

2.   Their effect on domestic prices.

3.   Their effect on domestic producers' incomes.

(See Article 3 of the GATT Anti-Dumping Code and Article 6 of the GATT Code on Subsidies and Countervailing Duties.) The GATT Code emphasizes that authorities should look for a significant increase in imports at prices below domestic levels. The authors of the GATT code apparently believe that economic markets are less than perfectly efficient in an information sense. Their premise is that violators of the anti-dumping or the countervailing subsidy codes will leave their footprints. A stylized version of how the footsteps can be retraced by the authorities follows.

At first, the domestic market is in equilibrium. Tainted imports enter and expand their share of a stable domestic market by selling at below domestic prices. Domestic producers initially fail to notice the market entry, and simply lose market share; in due course, they may lower prices and try to regain their market share. In this scenario, if a product is well-defined and has few substitutes, the injury is easy to establish. The "cause" is the increased volume of imports and the "effect" is either reduced sales *or* reduced prices for domestic producers. When substitutes exist, the effect is more likely to be on prices than on production and injury will be shared by producers of substitute products who are probably not allowed any standing in an "import" case (because they are not producers of "like" goods).

Of course, the stylized version of economic reality that underpins the thinking of the GATT Codes on anti-dumping and subsidies is rarely an accurate reflection of reality when competitive markets prevail. In markets involving well-defined and roughly homogeneous products that are widely traded, the "law of one price" will tend to prevail every time. Such markets are said to be informationally efficient, and market prices for immediate and future delivery are established continuously on organized commodity exchanges like the Chicago Board of Trade. In such cases, dumped and subsidized imports will not leave a trace. Since most agricultural markets, like financial markets, are informationally efficient markets, searching for an actual increase of imports in order to determine the cause of domestic injury will usually be a fruitless task; this is certainly true of corn. Moreover, there has been no significant erosion recently in the Canadian corn producers' share of the domestic market.

A second problematic feature of the corn case is that most of the U.S. subsidies attacked by the Canadian complainants were not specifically "export" subsidies. In fact, the subsidies had the effect of raising the producer's price above the selling price to both U.S. consumers and export customers. The GATT anti-dumping and counter-vail duty codes are more readily understandable in cases where an exporter sells dumped or subsidized products at lower export prices than domestic prices. Under these circumstances, the mere observation of two distinct prices for like goods in two countries is an indication that something is amiss. In the corn case, no such "price" differentials existed.

The third feature of the corn case is relevant only to cases involving agricultural products. SIMA specifically directs the Tribunal to include in its measure of injury any extra costs imposed on Canadian governments (federal and provincial). Thus, only for agricultural products is it possible for the Tribunal to find injury even when producers themselves are largely or entirely sheltered from the effect of the dumped or subsidized products by government programs.

A final problematic feature of the corn case is the complexity of the U.S. stabilization program, and its actual effect on U.S. corn production. Because their complexity presents difficulties for an analysis of the net economic impacts of U.S. programs and policies, they will be considered in detail below in the section titled "Key Components of the U.S. Feed Grains Program." There is no doubt that U.S. agricultural programs lead, especially in years when market prices are low, to substantial subsidies for U.S. corn producers. And further, the U.S. industry is so large that if subsidies encourage increased production, they will influence the world market price for corn. If the United States were merely a price taker in corn markets, a subsidy might succeed in transferring wealth from U.S. taxpayers to U.S. corn producers without appreciably affecting the world corn market price. But this is not the case.

The Response of Corn Prices to Changed U.S. Corn Production

Should large U.S. subsidies lead to a significant net increase in the level of American corn production, it is incontrovertible that the U.S. corn program would influence world corn prices downwards substantially. One recent study using the Food and Agricultural Policy Research Institute Model (FAPRI), (see Meyers, Devadess and Helmar, 1986), reports the effects on the price level of a one year 5 per cent reduction in U.S. corn production. According to the FAPRI study, U.S. corn prices (and *parri passu* world market prices) would rise by 24.3 per cent in the same year that output falls by 5 per cent. Given the scenario used in the FAPRI model, price levels would return almost to normal by the following year. When the 5 per cent decline in corn yields continues, the price level rises permanently by about 23 per cent.

Based on the FAPRI study's measure of price response (which is assumed to be symmetric for output increases as well as for decreases), injury to Canadian corn producers follows if U.S. corn producers respond to the U.S. agricultural programs by increasing production by at least 5 per cent. By most reasonable standards, a price fall of 23 per cent is a material injury to those corn producers forced to rely upon the market price for all or a significant share of their income.

The FAPRI study measures the price response to an exogenous shift in the supply of output. In a simulation run on another large scale world agricultural sector model, Tyers and Anderson's (1986) Grain, Livestock and Sugar (GLS) model, I examined how the U.S. supply of coarse grains (of which corn is the largest constituent) increases in response to an exogenous increase of producer prices. In the GLS model simulation, a producer price increase of 25 per cent in 1985 leads American coarse grains production up by 8 per cent, 4 per cent and 1 per cent in 1986, 1987, and 1988, respectively.

It is safe to conclude that, at least in today's imperfect international grain markets, comparatively small changes in U.S. production levels lead the price level in the open market to swing widely. Based on the results from the two models just reported, it appears that an exogenous supply increase of 1 per cent causes the short term price level to decline by between 4 per cent and 5 per cent.

Key Components of the U.S. Feed Grains Program

There is potential for the U.S. Agricultural programs both to raise and to lower world corn prices. On the one hand, by guaranteeing participating U.S. producers a high target price, the programs elicit increased corn supplies and thereby weaken corn prices in world markets. On the other hand, the U.S. programs provide for corn to go into government storage when the market price falls below a predetermined level—the loan rate—which is a price and should not strictly speaking be called a rate. Furthermore, the programs force those producers who choose to become eligible to benefit from these government subsidies to set aside part of their acreage previously devoted to corn production.

The Ontario Corn Producers' Association, in their complaint against the U.S., recognizes the conflict among the three key components of the 1986 U.S. corn program. The Association's brief notes all three (target price, loan rate, acreage cut-backs) and comments that:

> The impact of the acreage reduction is tempered by the fact that participants will attempt to obtain maximum yield from seeded acres (because of the high target price) and will divert less productive acres from production. The net effect will be to encourage production above those which would occur in an open market situation, and to force prices down to the loan rate.

> The question which must be addressed is, "What would be the U.S. market price if the 1986 Farm Program did not exist?" Several answers can be given. It would seem reasonable to assume that the price would match the U.S. cost of production. We have chosen $3.83 per bushel ($151 per tonne) in Canadian funds which is the average 1985 cost of production for the states of Ohio, Illinois, Iowa, and Minnesota. Production cost in 1985 Ontario figure is lower $3.61 per bushel ($142 per tonne). (p. 31)

However, there were analytical weaknesses in the Association's brief which caused them to *underestimate* the size and impact of U.S. corn subsidy programs.

Using the Cost of Production as a Proxy for the Market Price in the Absence of the U.S. Farm Program

The Association's brief answers its own question by comparing the prevailing market price with an estimate of the average U.S. cost for producing a bushel of corn. This is a standard approach for determining a competitive market price in many industries, but it is not an appropriate assumption to make for the corn industry. This can be appreciated by observing that the variable cash cost of production per bushel swings widely from year to year, and that the total economic cost (including fixed costs and owner supplied labor) is largely dependent upon the price of land.

The variable cost of production per bushel in any given crop year is largely determined by yields, which in turn respond primarily to weather conditions (see Dumanski, Bootsma and Kirkwood, 1986). In the U.S. between 1975 and 1979 variable expenses totalled about $1 per bushel, and $1.51 per bushel in 1980 (Leath, Meyer and Hill, 1982, p. 84). Variable expenses skyrocketed in 1983 as a result of prevailing drought conditions, and were back to an estimate of $1.01 per bushel by 1986 (USDA, 1986, p. 201).

As mentioned, the total economic cost of producing corn depends significantly upon the valuation placed upon land. Total costs per bushel are reported to have averaged $2.11 between 1975 and 1979, $2.83 between 1980 and 1984, $2.42 in 1985 and $2.31 in 1986. The USDA has reported that since 1975 land costs have comprised about 20 per cent of the costs of production. It is notoriously difficult to use the average cost of production as the standard price for an agricultural product when land values swing widely. A large part of the return to land takes the form of economic rent that rises and falls with the price of the product produced on that land. In order to measure the average cost of production, the Association's suggested standard for measuring the price in the absence of a subsidy, it would first be necessary to measure the value of corn land in its next best alternative use. This task was not undertaken by the Ontario Corn Producers' Association, nor is it the methodology used here.

Data on movements of land prices serve better to indicate the shifting economic viability of the farm enterprise than to measure costs of production. Farm land values in the U.S. corn belt fell 15 per cent between April 1985 and April 1986, compared with a general decline in farm land values of 12 per cent throughout the United States, and a drop of 29 per cent since the peak in 1981 (Farm Credit Corporation, 1986). By contrast, Ontario farm land values dropped 4.8 per cent in 1985. If U.S. farm land values were to continue to fall at the rate of 15 per cent per year, the Ontario Corn Producers' Association, if they follow the same logic developed in their brief, would be forced to acknowledge that the U.S. cost of production is falling.

Evidently, the average cost of production of corn, including the cost of land, fluctuates widely from year to year, and an analysis of corn production should include all relevant factors. A critic might respond to the brief of the Ontario Corn Producers' Association by pointing out that U.S. land values are in fact falling, despite the subsidies, and by attributing the record corn crops of 1985–86 and 1986–87 to the unusually good weather conditions that prevailed in the corn belt during both crop years.

The U.S. Grain Storage Program

A critic might also point out that the brief of the Corn Producers' Association fails to take into account the way in which the U.S. government storage programs may support market prices.

This last oversight is a serious omission in light of the fact that the direct cause of corn prices dropping precipitously in 1986–87 was the reduced willingness of the U.S. government to store grain. This change in attitude towards storing grain is revealed by the drop in the loan rate (the price paid for grain to go into storage) and the large share of deficiency payments to farmers being made in the form of certificates redeemable in agricultural products. If the unwillingness to store grain drives prices down today, certainly the willingness to store grain yesterday supported market prices then.

By supporting market prices, the U.S. corn program subsidizes corn producers. Both the Association and Revenue Canada, by failing to assign a major subsidy value to the loan component of the corn program, seriously underestimated the overall amount by which the U.S. program subsidizes producers. Both parties probably chose to ignore the loan program because they use accounting and not economic concepts to measure subsidies. Revenue Canada goes so far as to reject explicitly such economic concepts as opportunity cost. An accounting measure has the virtue of being precise, but in all applied economic analysis accounting measures must be modified before the numbers can have any meaning. In the case of the U.S. loan program, Revenue Canada attributed a subsidy of just $0.1555/bushel in 1985, whereas the true subsidy is above $0.41. Revenue Canada erred also by overlooking the asymmetry between the situations faced by U.S. non-participating corn producers and Canadian producers. Unlike Canadian producers, American non-participating producers can choose to become eligible for program benefits in the subsequent crop year.

The Acreage Reduction Program

A third weakness in the Association's brief is that it declares the impact of U.S. acreage reduction programs to be insubstantial on total corn production. Yet this contention is far from self-evident in view of the fact that 13 million acres were set aside in 1986–87 and 69.1 million acres of corn harvested.

It is true that, despite acreage controls, the 1985–86 crop year saw 75.1 million acres of corn harvested. This was a record year, 0.6 million acres higher than in 1981–82, despite acreage restrictions causing 5.4 million acres to be set aside. The reason for this record output is that until 1985 relatively few corn producers joined the farm program because even small acreage restrictions (10 per cent in 1982 and 1984) dissuaded producers from joining a program that appeared to offer little if any subsidy. Deficiency payments were low, and market prices rarely fell below the loan rate. These non-participants were free to expand production. In 1984–85 just 50 per cent of acreage was covered by the program, expanding to 69 per cent and 83 per cent in 1985–86 and 1986-87 respectively. Therefore, harvested acreage declined by just 6 million acres in 1986–87 from the previous year despite the set-aside rising from 10 to 20 per cent. It is likely that those producers outside the program in 1984–85 and 1985–86 were motivated to increase production in order to acquire more base acreage upon entering the program in 1986–87.

Acreage set-asides were respectively 3.9, 5.4 and 13 million acres in 1984–85, 1985–86 and 1986–87. Producers reduced output below potential by 416, 637 and 1,556 million bushels, *if* national standard yields are applied to the foregone acres. However, many analysts disagree with using the standard yield and agree with the Ontario brief that if set-aside acres were brought into production, yields on these acres would fall well below average. Quite sensibly, they argue that only the poorest land is set aside, and that with less land available, a more intensive form of production is practiced on planted acres. Against this, others argue that farmers tend to have homogeneous land and that set-asides in high quality land areas involve good land, whereas set-asides in poor quality land areas will involve poor land. Until 1986–87 the yield on set-aside acres would certainly have been far below average because only those producers with poorer quality land available would have been induced into becoming eligible for the feedgrain program when a compulsory set-aside was in effect. But in 1986–87, 83 per cent of total acreage was placed under the program. At such high levels of participation it seems more likely than not that the yield from set-aside acres would have approached the national average yield.

Nor is it clear that the remaining land is farmed more intensively. One indicator of intensity is the amount of nitrogen fertilizer applied to the land. The number of pounds of nitrogen applied per acre varied in recent years as follows: 137, 135, 140 and 132 in 1981–82, 1982–83, 1984–85 and 1985–86 respectively (USDA, 1987). (Crop year 1983–84 is omitted because it is a special case; it was affected by a "payment in kind" program and a widespread drought).

No matter how much lower the hypothetical yield from set-aside acres may be, it remains true that the number of acres set aside is large and this component of the program should not be dismissed. Since as reported above a 5 per cent drop in production may cause a 23 per cent rise in corn prices, it is cavalier to dismiss the role of set-asides which took respectively 5 per cent, 7 per cent and 19 per cent of acreage out of production in the last three years.

Revised Estimates of the U.S. Subsidy to Corn Producers

The author prepared revised estimates of the subsidy for the Canadian Import Tribunal in order to correct for analytical weaknesses on the part of both Revenue Canada and the Ontario Corn Producers' Association. These estimates are presented in Tables 2 and 3 below. A serious omission from Revenue Canada's analysis is the risk reduction benefit enjoyed by the subsidized U.S. producers. I estimate that a typical risk averse farmer would value the risk reduction at $0.48 per bushel (see Lermer, 1987a, p. 36). Despite its importance, the risk reduction component of the subsidy was ignored when analyzing injury to Canadian producers because the methodology used to estimate the value of risk reduction is unfamiliar to many trade analysts and to members of the Tribunal. Nevertheless, eliminating the risk reduction component of the subsidy gives a conservative twist to the estimates of injury to Canadian producers described below.

TABLE 2
THE ECONOMIC SUBSIDY, 1*
(U.S. DOLLARS)

Component of Subsidy	1984–85	1985–86	1986–87
Deficiency Payment	.22	.281	.03
Loan Rate	.00	.28	.29
Acreage Restriction	-.22	-.24	-.42
All Other Programs Enumerated by Revenue Canada**	.11	.11	.11
Total Subsidy	**.11**	**.43**	**1.01**
Total Subsidy as a Per cent of Market Price	4	20	64

*Averaged over all output; non-participants are assumed not to benefit from the program.
**Assumed to equal .11 in 1984 and 1985.

TABLE 3
THE ECONOMIC SUBSIDY, 2*
(U.S. DOLLARS)

Component of Subsidy	1984–85	1985–86	1986–87
Deficiency Payment	.45	.48	1.11
Loan Rate	0	.41	.35
Acreage Restriction	-.22	-.24	-.42
All Other Programs Enumerated by Revenue Canada	.11	.11	.11
Total Subsidy	**.34**	**.76**	**1.15**
Total Subsidy as a Per cent of Market Price	13	36	73

*Not averaged over output; non-participants are assumed to benefit to the same extent as participating producers.

**The World Market Price of Corn in the Absence of the U.S. Subsidy
and the Level of Injury**

Considerations Regarding the Choice of Methodology

Modelling the price determination process is not different in principle for internationally than for domestically traded goods. In practice, however, the larger data requirements may preclude a complete analysis. Had we to measure demand and supply elasticities for each country individually we might be bogged down for some time; fortunately, the world's corn markets, like most agricultural markets, are dominated by a handful of giant producing and consuming countries. Various model builders have taken advantage of this to build economic models of the world agricultural sector, by capturing the aggregate behavior of producers and consumers only in each major country. Most large econometrically estimated models search for equilibrium prices, on the assumption that trade flows between, and production and consumption in the major countries will all respond to price differentials—until those price differentials not inherent in transportation and other transaction costs are fully eliminated. These models also recognize that government policies can permanently maintain barriers to trade, production and consumption through such instruments as tariffs, quotas, taxes and subsidies.

A common procedure is to capture these policy effects by distinguishing producer from consumer prices in the domestic market as well as domestic prices from border prices on imports and exports. The above distinctions reflect trade policy interference in the market clearing process. In order to capture policy interference that acts to slow market adjustment rather than to eliminate it, some models calculate price transmission lags which indicate how long it takes a price change in one country to be fully reflected in another country's prices. The price transmission lags will also pick up the lags usually built into demand functions related to technical requirements such as feeding livestock and poultry.

One such model recently developed with the support of the World Bank is the World Grain, Livestock Product and Sugar (GLS) model, which was used by Lermer to determine for the Canadian Import Tribunal the effect of U.S. subsidies on world grain prices. The GLS model was developed by Professors Rodney Tyers and Kym Anderson from the Australian National University and Adelaide University respectively (1986). (See Lermer, 1987a, Appendix E, p. 163.) Four scenarios were run using different producer to border price ratios for wheat, coarse grain and rice as described in Table 4. The price adjustments due to the U.S. subsidies are shown in Table 5 (Lermer, 1987a, pp. 61–62).

TABLE 4
PRODUCER TO BORDER PRICE RATIOS FOR REFERENCE LOW,
MEDIUM AND HIGH SUBSIDY SCENARIOS

	Wheat	Coarse Grain	Rice
Reference	1.15	1.00	1.30
Low	1.25	1.25	1.50
Medium	1.50	1.50	1.75
High	2.00	2.00	2.00

The "low" scenario sets the subsidy to U.S. producers at 25 per cent above the market price. This is a modest assumption in view of our finding in that the subsidy level was 18 per cent in 1984–85; 29 per cent in 1985–86 and 81 per cent in 1986–87 (Lermer, 1987a). One natural interpretation is to call the "low" scenario the short run subsidy, and the "medium" scenario the reaction to the "long run" persistence of the U.S. subsidy program.

TABLE 5
INTERNATIONAL PRICE LEVEL CHANGE (% DIFFERENCE) DUE TO
HIGHER GRAIN PRODUCER PRICES IN THE UNITED STATES
(FROM THE GLS MODEL SCENARIOS)

International Price Level (% difference from reference scenario):

		Coarse Grain
LOW	1986	-17
	1987	-10
	1988	-8
MEDIUM	1986	-28
	1987	-14
	1988	-19
HIGH	1986	-42
	1987	-22
	1988	-32

Relying upon an econometrically estimated forecasting or simulation model (a reduced form model) overcomes the appearance of arbitrariness that accompanies a simpler comparative static model of price determination. This is the virtue of a large model with sufficient freedom in its design to allow one to fix the relevant policy variables explicitly. This appearance of precision is of course bought at a price, if the results of the exercise are sensitive to different scenarios on future macro-economic variables. The question the Tribunal was asked to answer is whether or not Canadian corn producers have been materially injured by the U.S. program, not what cost is imposed in this, that, or another unknowable future state of the world. For such a determination, a structural model, even if an oversimplified partial equilibrium, comparative static one, may be a better tool than a large reduced form model. Moreover, most large models use price parameters to reflect policy variables. In this case, it is the analyst who sets the parameter value exogenously, based on a judgment of the effect of often complex policies.

The results from a partial equilibrium, comparative static model are also presented below. The comparative static framework focuses attention on the most relevant processes through which the U.S. subsidy is transmitted to world markets, allowing the interaction of the corn market with other agricultural and industrial markets to be subsumed in estimates of the demand and supply curves for corn. The model is comparative static in the sense that the interaction of demand and supply behavior determines an equilibrium price at which markets are cleared. After an external displacement occurs to either demand or supply, market adjustment over time is captured by comparing one equilibrium with another. Still longer term adjustments can be introduced by changing the demand and supply curves to better reflect lags in behavioral adjustment.

Table 6 reports the estimated equilibrium prices for a range of elasticities in the 1986–87 crop year. (For 1984–85 and 1985–86 see Lermer, 1987a, pp. 59–60.) In 1984–85, the equilibrium price in the absence of the program would have been about $2.80. This figure is below the target price of $3.03, but well above the market price and the loan rate, which were close together. In 1985–86, there is a pronounced effect of the loan rate on the market. The equilibrium prices are only modestly above the market price and are well below the loan rate. In that crop year acreage restrictions were low, but a high loan rate caused the U.S. farm program to support the market price of corn. Nevertheless, the equilibrium price is above the actual market price for every simulation except one. Canadian producers are clearly injured even in the year when the U.S. program does the most to remove excess production from the open market.

Despite lower output in 1986–87, equilibrium prices fell from the previous year's levels, reflecting in part the lower volume of government storage taking place. But actual market prices, driven down by U.S. certificate programs, fell much further. Consequently, equilibrium prices are between 33 per cent and 55 percent above the market level.

Except for stabilization programs, the incomes of Canadian corn producers would fall in direct relation to the price declines generated by the U.S. policies and described above. Detailed estimates of loss to producers and to Canadian governments respectively (reported in Lermer, 1987a, pp. 64–78) show that Ontario corn producers in 1986–87 lost about $40 million, and were protected from further loss by government payments of about $200 million. These imprecise estimates are sensitive to variations in the models and assumptions that underpin them, but these figures are mid-points and the interested reader is invited to consult Lermer (1987a) for detailed estimates and to judge the robustness of the estimates to alternative assumptions.

TABLE 6
EQUILIBRIUM PRICE; PER CENT ABOVE MARKET PRICE; PER CENT ABOVE LOAN RATE (1986–1987)
ADJUST
SIMULATION SUMMARY
YEAR: 1986–87

Deficiency: $0.92 (83% Weight)
Market Price: $1.57
Loan Price: $1.92

Simulation Number	Estimated Equilibrium Price	Percentage Above Market Price	Percentage Above Loan Price	US Domestic Demand Elasticity	US Domestic Supply Elasticity	Export Demand Elasticity
103	$2.17	38.1	12.9	-.40	.40	-.4
104	$2.14	36.5	11.6	-.40	.40	-.6
105	$2.13	35.4	10.7	-.40	.40	-.8
106	$2.11	34.5	10.0	-.40	.40	-1.0
107	$2.09	32.9	8.7	-.40	.40	-1.5
108	$2.34	49.0	21.8	-.40	.60	-.4
109	$2.30	46.8	20.0	-.40	.60	-.6
110	$2.28	45.2	18.8	-.40	.60	-.8
111	$2.26	44.0	17.7	-.40	.60	-1.0
112	$2.22	41.5	15.7	-.40	.60	-1.5
113	$2.44	55.1	26.8	-.45	.75	-.4
114	$2.40	52.8	24.9	-.45	.75	-.6
115	$2.37	51.1	23.6	-.45	.75	-.8
116	$2.31	47.0	20.2	-.45	.75	-1.5
117	$2.22	41.6	15.8	-.45	.75	-3.0
118	$2.16	37.3	12.3	-.45	.75	-5.0

Impact of a Countervailing Duty

Because Canada is sometimes a net exporter, and is largely self-sufficient in corn, the price effect of a countervailing duty will be minor. Other factors also act to diminish the effect of a countervail duty on Canadian corn prices. First, corn is available to Canadians by importing from sources other than the United States. Second, those industrial corn users who export all or part of their production will be able to avoid paying all or part of the duty because of duty drawback provisions of the relevant legislation. Most importantly, feed-wheat and barley are substitutes for corn in most livestock feeding uses. These characteristics of the Canadian corn market lead inexorably to the conclusion that the price effect of a corn countervail duty will provide little relief from the complained of injury. Canadian corn producers will remain dependent upon world market prices which the Canadian government is unable to influence.

It must also be recognized that a countervail duty imposes certain costs on Canadians. Efficient export and import opportunities will be prevented and next best arrangements will need to be made. Additional transportation and handling costs may be incurred. Risk management and storage become more complex.

Some may argue that Ontario Corn producers will benefit by selling more corn in the domestic market instead of into export markets. When selling into export markets, the Canadian seller must meet foreign competition by absorbing any differential in transport and handling costs. When selling at home, the Canadian seller enjoys some natural protection because foreign sellers must incur higher transport and handling costs in order to move corn into Ontario (see Martin, et al., 1986; Gilmour, 1986a and 1986b).

Before the countervail, two way trade of corn between Canada and the United States might have depended upon local transportation costs because for certain Canadian locations transporation costs from a U.S. source will be lower than from a Canadian source. Moreover, the relevant transportation cost will be affected by the opportunity to back haul other products on the return journey. In these circumstances, transportation efficiencies are achieved by free trade across the border. Unfortunately, both the United States and Canada levy tariffs on corn, so that the export-import pattern in place prior to the countervail cannot be said to have been optimal.

A countervail duty will cause more Canadian corn to be sold at home, but one should not jump to the conclusion that therefore there will be a net saving in transportation and handling costs accruing to Ontario corn producers. If this were the case, then without the countervail Ontario corn producers would have successfully displaced imports and pocketed the extra revenues for themselves. Canadian exports must have been sold at a price sufficiently high to more than offset the additional cost of delivery. Since the countervail duty will cause Canada to lose most of its export trade, any net benefit to local producers from increased domestic sales will be minimal.

Substitutes

Feed-wheat and barley are substitutes for corn in virtually all feed uses except for chicken and turkey. Even for chicken and turkey producers the share of corn in the feed mix can be reduced, but gain is sacrificed unless more feed is used. When the per cent of higher energy corn in the mix is reduced, the producer must acquire more total grain. But even if the demand for corn by chicken and turkey producers is hypothesized to be perfectly inelastic, the scope for substitution in other feed uses limits the rise in the price of corn.

Ontario broiler and turkey producers use about 128,000 tonnes of corn each year. This is about 2 per cent of Ontario corn production. For Canada, corn use for feeding broilers and turkeys may reach about 5 per cent. Since most other feed grain users have elastic demand curves, even a perfectly inelastic demand curve for chicken and turkey production will not cause the demand for corn to be inelastic.

Supplies of feed-wheat and barley on the prairies are both high. Moreover, the Great Lakes-St. Lawrence Seaway System could readily handle any additional movements east of feed grains that may replace corn. (See Leath, Meyer, and Hill, 1982). In view of this, it hardly seems to be belaboring the point to state that domestic corn prices cannot move permanently to a large premium over U.S. corn, or over the traditional differential between corn and other feed grains.

Duty Drawback—Imports

Industrial users of corn who re-export products made from corn under duty drawback provisions of the relevant legislation will shift purchases of corn to the United States as long as Canadian corn is sold at a premium. Industrial corn accounts for about 13 per cent of domestic consumption; of this amount, demand by producers of high fructose corn sugar accounts for .531 million tonnes of corn (about 8.1 per cent of Ontario corn production). Exports of high fructose corn sugar cause a derived demand for 0.42 million tonnes of corn. Therefore, at any price premium high fructose corn sugar producers alone could reduce domestic demand for corn by 0.42 million tonnes of corn.

Apart from the corn sugar producers, only distillers are likely to enjoy the advantage of the drawback to a significant degree. In 1985, distillers purchased $282 million tonnes, of which sum almost 50 per cent is eligible for duty drawback (Association of Canadian Distillers, 1986, p. F–1). But there will be some slippage in the use of drawback privileges because the application of the provision may discourage its use unless the price premium for Canadian corn is large. If the price spread increases, the drawback rules are likely to lead to the displacement of somewhat more than .5 million tonnes of demand for Canadian by U.S. corn.

Net Exports

Imports will decrease because of the duty, but so will exports as long as the Canadian price remains at a premium. What will happen to this component of corn demand (exports) and supply (imports) is difficult to determine. Imports will surely drop—apart from the drawback component, but imports have not been significant in recent years—.226, .612 and .416 million tonnes respectively in 1983–84, 1984–85 and 1985–86. Exports were .229, .555 and .640 million tonnes over the same three-year period. Given the year-to-year fluctuations, it seems reasonable to assume that there will be equal declines in the levels both of exports and imports. (In the 1986–87 crop year, exports fell to a level of .127 million tonnes from .640 the previous year.)

The Supply/Demand Balance

For a modest premium of just $2, excess supplies will exist largely because of the duty drawback. If at a $2 premium industrial users find the costs associated with applying for the duty drawback make importing corn unattractive, then the $2 premium on Canadian corn would certainly be sustainable. However, as the premium rises the duty drawback option for certain industrial users certainly becomes a low cost means of lowering input costs. Therefore if the premium rises, if only to $7.25, (see Lermer, 1987b, p. 40) the excess supply in both the short and long run reaches the one million tonne range. It seems unlikely that a price premium would survive excess supplies at this level unless government introduces a program of subsidized storage or of acreage control.

The Public Interest

The Tribunal's finding on 6 March 1987, in favor of the Ontario corn producers, did not end the matter. The Canadian users of corn sought relief from the countervailing duty pursuant to Section 45 of SIMA. Two user groups were exempted from the countervail study in the Tribunal's finding of March 16, 1987. One group was manufacturers of snack foods, who argued that the particular corn hybrids they used were not produced in Canada. The second group was the British Columbia feed industry, which argued that it rarely purchased Ontario or Manitoba corn. But other feed and industrial users were not granted relief.

Though much of the Canadian corn crop is used on the farm as a feed grain, each year over one million tonnes is sold to the commercial feed sector and a like amount to industrial corn users. In most feed uses, other feed grains may replace corn. Nevertheless, for some specific purposes a minimum ration of corn is required in the feed mix. At those points in Canada where U.S. corn can be delivered more cheaply than can Canadian corn, corn users will be forced to absorb additional freight costs or the countervail duty. The countervail duty, therefore, imposes a hardship on these groups even if Ontario corn prices fail to reflect any significant portion of the duty. In the main it is prairie poultry industries that are damaged by the corn duty, but the Tribunal noted that Manitoba's corn production was increasing rapidly and that Manitoba supplies would be sufficient to meet the limited demand for corn by prairie poultry producers.

Industrial users are not free to substitute other grains for corn and this group of producers argued that they cannot absorb the higher corn costs induced by the countervail duty because their products must sell at competitive prices with products produced from U.S. corn or from other non-countervailed agricultural inputs like sugar or wheat. They argued further that their costs of doing business would rise because prior to the countervail duty they were able to hedge against the risk of unforeseeable price increases of corn. Since the industrial users generally sell products under year long contracts, and at fixed prices, any upward fluctuation in the price of corn during the production period might prove disastrous.

The Tribunal recognized the validity of the lines of argument for both the industrial users. But their first claim was mitigated by the Tribunal's finding that on average the cost increase would be modest. One consideration is that almost half the industrial corn used would be eligible for duty drawback (refunds) because the output derived from the corn is exported. More importantly, the Tribunal recognized that only a modest amount of the countervail duty would be passed on in higher Canadian corn prices. Expert testimony on the precise amount that the Ontario corn price basis might increase due to the countervail duty ranged from as low as $1.60/tonne (about $.04/bushel), to a high of $20/tonne.

Moreover, if the Tribunal were to recommend that the industrial users' claim for relief be acted upon, the Tribunal would undermine the very purposes of the import contingency legislation, i.e., to provide relief to the producers. The Tribunal recognized this fact, but it saw no useful purpose in unnecessarily raising costs for users. This risk to industrial users could be reduced without disadvantaging corn producers by reducing the level of the countervail duty to the level of the average long—term price premium associated with it. The Tribunal determined the maximum price premium to be $12/tonne, or about $.30/bushel. Accordingly, on October 20, 1987, the Tribunal recommended to the Minister of Finance that the countervail duty be reduced from $.849/bushel U.S. (about $1.10 Canadian) to $0.30/bushel Canadian.

On 4 February 1988, the Honourable Tom Hockin announced that the duty would be reduced to $0.46 per bushel. The Department of Finance news release agreed with the Tribunal that "Market uncertainty will be greatly reduced and both users and producers will be better able to plan their activities." The $0.46 per bushel figure was justified by the simple observation that "After the countervailing duty was imposed, quarterly prices rose by as much as $0.46 per bushel above what they otherwise would have been."

Any economist reviewing the data would in my judgment conclude that a duty of $0.46 per bushel erects just as significant a trade barrier as a duty of $1.10 per bushel. At present what can be said for the Department of Finance's decision is that it provides some relief for users in the event that Canada suffers a failure in its corn crop while the U.S. corn growing region goes unscathed. But this possibility could be dealt with otherwise by executive action to eliminate the countervail duty. The Department of Finance's decision gives the corn producers all they wanted: a virtual ban on corn imports.

"Subsidized Goods" or "Subsidized Imports"

The Ontario corn producers succeeded before the Tribunal despite the many obstacles to their case. One hurdle is especially noteworthy because economists can only hope that the majority opinion in favor of the Ontario corn producers will prevail in subsequent countervailing duty cases. I refer to the objection that Canada, not being a significant importer of corn, cannot seek relief from U.S. subsidies under the Special Import Measures Act (SIMA). The Tribunal's three man panel divided on this question. Mr. A.L. Bisonnette, for the minority, believes that SIMA does not provide for relief to Ontario corn producers because Canadian corn prices were not depressed by actual subsidized imports from the United States. For the economist there is little to distinguish between a price decline due to potential imports and a price decline accompanied by an actual increase of imports. But the legal distinction is a real one. Article 6 of the GATT Code on Subsidies and Countervailing Duties uses the term "subsidized imports," (See in particular Article 4, Section 4 and Article 6, Sections 1, 2 and 4.) Section 42 in SIMA uses the term "subsidized goods" rather than "subsidized imports," but Mr. Bisonnette did not find this distinction compelling and concluded that the Tribunal must follow GATT language and must "be concerned with the harmful effects of subsidized imports, not simply the harmful effects of a subsidization program in a foreign land" (Canadian Import Tribunal, 1987, p. 31).

The majority view, representing the Chairman, Mr. Robert J. Bertrand and Mr. Howard J. Perrigoe, is one I think all economists will find persuasive and apt in the circumstances of the corn case. The relevant excerpt of their finding is as follows:

Both the Special Import Measures Act and the GATT Subsidies Code exist for the express purpose of dealing with unfairly traded goods which cause or threaten injury. Necessarily, their provisions must be interpreted, not in the abstract, but within the context of the environment within which they apply, namely, international trade. Since the economic and commercial realities of international trade dictate that price be met or market share lost, the majority of the panel is persuaded to adopt the broader interpretation of "subsidized imports," that is, that cognizance be taken of potential or likely imports in the determination of material injury. To do otherwise, in the view of the majority of the panel, would be to frustrate the purpose of the system.

In the case of grain corn, imports into Canada have existed in recent years, albeit at modest levels. The issue, therefore, is not whether imports have taken place, but whether they would have increased substantially in the absence of a price response by the domestic producers to the subsidized U.S. corn. Given the openness of the Canadian market, much higher levels of imports would have been a certainty. (Canadian Import Tribunal, 1987, p. 16.)

Economists may be less pleased with an important potential consequence of the victory of the Ontario corn producers. The Ontario victory might lead other countries to seek countervailing duties against American grain exports. In particular, Hathaway (1987, p. 31) reports that French corn growers might initiate a case in order to prevent corn gluten from the United States entering into Europe. Because grain substitutes are not exempt from GATT, as are grains themselves, and are not subject to tariffs on entry to Europe, these derivative products are in high demand by Europeans for livestock feed supplements. Should corn gluten be subjected to countervail on entry into Europe, more European grain would be diverted to livestock feeding thereby reducing European surpluses and partially shifting the burden of Europe's grain subsidies from the European Community's budget to its consumers. This potential outcome is certainly not in the interest of the Canadian corn producers.

Conclusion

One may surmise that the corn countervail case appeared to the Ontario corn producers to be an effective way of registering their plight with the Canadian government, with an eye to seeking more direct financial support in the event the countervail duty failed to strengthen corn prices. The government's motive for avoiding an offer of immediate subsidies to the corn producers, and directing their attention to the relief available to them under the Special Imports Measure Act, is unknown. It is possible that the government intended the countervail case to demonstrate to Canadians that Canada could retaliate against the several well-publicized U.S. initiated cases against alleged Canadian subsidies. The corn case allowed the Canadian government some leverage against the U.S., not because the U.S. feared losing corn sales in Canada, but because of the potential threat to U.S. exports of corn gluten into the European Common Market (see Hathaway, 1987, p. 31). At the same time, the corn countervail case had at most a moderately harmful impact on Canadian corn users, so the political cost of the duty to the Canadian government is modest. Moreover, the corn countervail duty case, if only by introducing a note of chaos in world markets, added fuel to the raging international agricultural subsidy wars, and might thereby have strengthened Canada's argument that it is time to begin moving towards unsubsidized world agriculture.

REFERENCES

Association of Canadian Distillers. (1986, 19 December). *Preliminary Submission.* (CIT–7–86). Ottawa.

Canadian Import Tribunal. (1987, 20 March). *Subsidized Grain Corn Originating in or Exported From the United States of America.* (Statement of Reasons). Ottawa.

Deloitte, Haskins and Sells. (1987, January). *The Positive Influence of High Fructose Corn Sugar on Ontario Corn Prices.* Guelph, Ontario.

Dumanski, J., A. Bootsma and V. Kirkwood. (1986). "A Geographic Analysis of Grain Corn Yield Trends in Ontario Using a Computerized Land Information Base." *Canadian Journal of Soil Science, 66,* 481–497.

Farm Credit Corporation. (1986, December). Economic Report: "Trends in Farm Land Values." Ottawa.

Gilmour, B. (1986a). *Analyzing the Market Impacts of a Countervailing Duty on Incoming American Corn.* Ottawa: Agriculture Canada Policy Branch, Commodity Coordination Directorate.

Gilmour, B. (1986b). *Potential Impact of a Corn/Ethanol Plant to be Located in Southern Ontario.* (Working Paper 8–86). Ottawa: Agriculture Canada, Marketing and Economics Branch.

Grennes, T., P.R. Johnson, and M. Thursky. (1978). *The Economics of World Grain Trade.* New York: Praeger Publishers.

Groenewegen, J.and S. Kittle. (1985, June). *Changing Cropping Patterns of Ontario's Agricultural Land.* Ottawa: Agriculture Canada.

Hathaway, D.E. (1987). *Agriculture and the GATT: Re-writing the Rules.* Washington, D.C.: Institute for International Economics.

Leath, M.N., L.H. Meyer and L.D. Hill. (1982, February). *U.S. Corn Industry.* Washington, D.C.: U.S. Department of Agriculture.

Lermer, G. (1987a, 13 January). *Determining Injury to Canadian Corn Producers Due to the U.S. Food Security Act of 1985.* (CIT–-7–86–7). Ottawa: Canadian Import Tribunal.

Lermer, G. (1987b, 15 June). *The Effect of the Corn Countervailing Duty on the Price of Canadian Corn.* (CIT–7–86; PL–1–87). Ottawa: Canadian Import Tribunal.

Martin, L., K.D. Meilke, J. Stevens and D. Rasmussen. (1986). *Basis for Corn in Ontario and the Adequacy of Market Information for the Ontario Corn Market.* (Report prepared for the Ontario Corn Producers' Association). Guelph, Ontario: University of Guelph.

Meilke, K.D. (1984). *An Economic Profile of the Ontario Grain Corn Industry.* (Report prepared for Agriculture Canada). Guelph, Ontario: University of Guelph, Ontario Agricultural College, School of Agricultural Economics and Extension Education.

Meyers, W.H., S. Devadess, and M. Helmar. (1986, January). *Baseline Projections, Yield Impacts and Trade Liberalization Impacts for Soybean, Wheat and Feed Grains: A FAPRI Trade Model Analysis.* (Working Paper 86–WP7). Ames, Iowa: Iowa State University, The Center for Agricultural and Rural Development.

Ontario Corn Producers' Association. (1986, 19 December). *Preliminary Submission.* (CIT–7–86). Ottawa.

Statistics Canada. (21–001), Ottawa.

Tyers, R. and K. Anderson. (1986, January). *Distortion in World Food Markets: A Quantitative Assessment.* The Australian National University, National Centre for Development Studies, Research School of Pacific Studies, Canberra.

United States Department of Agriculture (USDA). (1986, 10 November). *World Agricultural Supply and Demand Estimates.* (WASDE–199). Washington, D.C.: United States Department of Agriculture, Economic Research Service, Foreign Agricultural Service.

CHAPTER 10

REGIONAL IMPACTS OF REDUCED TRADE DISTORTIONS ON THE CANADIAN GRAINS AND RED MEATS SECTORS

R.J. MacGregor, C. Webber, J.D. Graham and K.K. Klein

World trade in agricultural products, and especially grains, is in disarray. Individual countries or groups of countries are pursuing domestic trade policies with little regard for economic reality or the impacts on other nations (Oleson, 1987). Often, policies are specifically enacted to counter the action of export competitors, even if the cost on the instigating country is high. This atmosphere is "poisoning political relations" between otherwise trading partners (Warley, 1987).

The current trade war between the United States (U.S.) and the European Community (EC) is but one example. At the heart of this confrontation is the fundamental issue of how countries are going to discipline their domestic policies and trade relationships with respect to other nations of the world. The issues between the U.S., the EC and other trading nations are complex and interwoven, and not solely restricted to agriculture. However, agriculture is the sector in which much of the battle over restructuring international trade relations will be fought. The hope for a successful resolution to the current situation lies in the Uruguay Round of the General Agreement on Tariffs and Trade (GATT) multilateral trade negotiations (MTN's) inaugurated in September, 1986. For the first time agriculture will be specifically addressed. The Punta del Este Ministerial Declaration states:

> Negotiations shall aim to achieve greater liberalization of trade in agriculture and bring all measures affecting import access and export competition under strengthened and more operationally effective GATT rules and disciplines (Warley, 1987).

There is no certainty that the issues separating the major trading nations can be bridged or a lasting solution found. Although reference is made to a fast track approach for agriculture and an early harvest, negotiations are expected to last until 1990, or longer, with implementation stretching into the next century. Yet within these agricultural discussions some commonality has been achieved for the first time (Hathaway, 1987). In the work undertaken by the Organization for Economic Co-operation and Development (OECD) Ministerial Trade Mandate Study, member countries have accepted that domestic policies and their associated supportive border measures are the root cause of structural surpluses and current distortions in world trade (OECD, 1987).

Public expenditures on domestic agricultural programs have increased significantly during the 1980s. Expenditure levels from 1979 to 1985, shown in Table 1, demonstrate this clearly. The magnitude of the cost of government involvement in agriculture, in total and on an individual basis, for the period 1979-81 is also shown in Table 2. Since government expenditures have continued to increase since the 1979-81 period, costs will have been higher for more recent years.

TABLE 1
PUBLIC EXPENDITURES RELATED TO NATIONAL
AGRICULTURAL POLICIES & PROGRAMS

	CURRENCY (million)	1979	1980	1981	1982	1983	1984	1985[c]
United States[a]	$US	22,000	25,900	27,300	37,200	47,600	39,100	57,000
Canada[a]	$CDN	1,600	1,800	2,100	2,300	2,800	2,900	3,000
Australia	$Aust.	165	192	218	329	301	306	398
New Zealand	$NZ	254	230	314	512	778	617	279
Japan	Yen(bill)	2,820	2,925	3,020	3,028	2,927	2,792	2,646
EC-FEDGA[b]	ECU	10,844	11,918	11,557	13,056	16,548	19,823	20,464

[a] Federal (excluding state or province).
[b] EC-FEDGA does not include national outlays.
[c] Estimate.

Source: OECD, 1987, pp. 52–53.

Acknowledgement that domestic support programs are the root cause of current problems in agricultural trade and that trade wars and international friction have resulted does not mean a solution will be easily found. Progress is being made by countries (and country alliances) that are submitting views on agricultural discussions of the MTN should proceed. Some commonality does exist, but so do significant differences.

TABLE 2
COST OF AGRICULTURAL POLICIES IN SELECTED COUNTRIES,
AVERAGE OVER 3 YEARS (1979–1981)

	Public Price[a] and Income Support	Total Public[a] Expenditure	Total Government[a] and Consumer Cost	ECU per Farm	ECU per Capita
United States	3,549	19,387	26,200	10,810	115
Canada	848	1,635	2,500	10,248	103
Australia	101	467	600	3,708	43
New Zealand	83	249	200	3,458	79
Japan	4,466	10,187	23,800	5,110	284
EC-FEDGA	10,378	11,432	56,508	11,437	208

[a] million ECU.

Source: OECD, 1987, pp. 128 and 134.

Negotiations imply that countries will have to put some of their domestic policies on the table if the basic problems outlined above are to be addressed. Past MTN negotiations have not called for this, but with specific domestic sector support policies now under consideration a great deal of uncertainty is created as to the eventual outcome of the negotiations. It also cannot be forgotten that agricultural trade is only one component of the overall negotiations and any solution reached in agriculture cannot be isolated from the whole.

One difficult problem that negotiators and policy makers have to face is that support programs often convey significant economic rents to specific commodity groups. In the past when negotiations on tariffs and border measures were discussed, the impacts on producers were less direct. The removal of programs that involve direct government transfers to farmers will not always be readily accepted by groups that benefit from existing programs and policies. In the U.S. and Canada direct government payments now constitute roughly half of the net farm income producers receive; for the U.S. in 1987 it was 48 per cent (FAPRI, 1987) and in Canada it was 52 per cent.[1] Other indirect transfers are also sizable. Reducing these transfers will not only affect incomes, it may also affect land and quota values.

The farm community is split over the MTN's; positions taken are largely determined by each sector's dependence on foreign markets. Commodity sectors that have isolated themselves inside domestic borders (e.g., Canadian dairy and poultry industries) see the MTN's as a threat to the security and wealth they have obtained under past policies. However, closed borders strike right at the issue of import access and raise the question of how trade liberalization will occur if every country excludes sensitive sectors. On the other hand, Canadian grain, oilseed, beef and pork producers see trade as indispensable to their sectors. Canada has suffered dramatically in the last few years as world prices for grains and oilseeds have been driven down by the U.S.-EC trade subsidy war.

Canada's most important agricultural trading partner for both imports and exports is the United States. The recently signed, but yet to be ratified, Free Trade Agreement (FTA) does address some conflicts and trade barriers that exist between these two countries and hopefully will allow for quick resolution of future problems. However, the FTA does not affect domestic support programs in either country in the way contemplated by the MTN's.

The MTN: Goals and Signatories' Positions

The goal of the MTN can be stated in a simple way: to bring order to world agricultural trade so that increased economic benefits can be obtained through the forces of comparative advantage, thus making better use of the world's resources. Associated with this is the development of an effective set of GATT rules designed to discipline policy interference with agricultural trade, to prevent confrontations, and to develop mechanisms for settling disputes that do arise. Three basic objectives are of the Punta del Este Ministerial Declaration (Warley, 1987) are:

1. Improving market access *inter alia* through the reduction in import barriers.

2. Improving the competitive environment by increasing discipline on the use of all direct and indirect subsidies and other measures affecting directly or indirectly agricultural trade, including the phased reduction of their negative effects and dealing with their causes.

3. Minimizing the adverse effects that sanitary and phytosanitary regulations and barriers can have on trade in agriculture.

Canada supports these goals and has stated in presenting its negotiating proposal to GATT that "fundamental agricultural trade reform can only occur if there is a parallel reform of domestic policies" (GATT Secretariat, 1987).

Even if an agreement is reached, its implementation will be slow. Countries need time to determine what reforms to domestic policy are required and the adjustment periods needed. Realizing this, Canada has stated its position for the midterm Ministerial GATT review (Gifford, 1987) as being that:

1. Agreement on the depth of cut (in distortionary policies) and time frame be reached.

2. Acommitment to universal application of the rule of law be made by participating countries.

3. Agreement on a contractual freeze, as put forward by the Cairns Group, come into force.

Canada therefore acknowledges that trade reform can only occur with a parallel reform of domestic policy and the elimination of subsidies that distort trade or restrict access. The Cairns Group proposal,[2] to which Canada subscribes, is to "prohibit the use of all subsidies and other government support measures, including consumer transfers, having an effect on agricultural trade" (Cairns Group, 1987). Government programs that do not distort trade can be maintained under this proposal.

The U.S. position, however, calls for the complete elimination of all agricultural subsidies which directly or indirectly affect trade. Only direct income support programs which can be "decoupled" and provide protection against natural disaster or other extraordinary circumstances can be maintained under the U.S. proposal. The EC position is less encompassing than that of other countries. While its members acknowledge the problem and its cause they see the solution as better control of production. The EC also insists on retention of its double-pricing system, fundamental to the operation of the Common Agricultural Policy. Japan's position is also narrower than that of other countries; it sees a need for importing countries to protect their domestic agriculture but recognizes the need to prohibit the use of export subsidies.

Implications of the MTN for Canadian Agricultural Policy

If the GATT process is to be successful, participating countries will need to reconsider and adjust their domestic policies in ways yet unknown at this time. For purposes of this analysis, the Cairns position will be adopted. Programs that involve direct or indirect transfer to producers and support income will be assumed to be eliminated and an attempt will be made to determine the impact of the removal of these programs on the agricultural economy. Programs of a structural, extension or research nature will be assumed to remain.

Canada's rich diversity has given rise to a complex policy mosaic, and there are many interrelated characteristics of Canadian agriculture that explain why our policy has developed the way it has. Firstly, Canada is a federal state in which both the provinces and the federal governments share jurisdiction. Two important areas in agriculture that are not shared are trade policy, which is a federal responsibility, and resource management, which is a provincial one. Otherwise, the two levels of governments can either cooperate or enact dissimilar types of programs. This shared jurisdiction and need to cooperate has been given prominence in the latest national policy statement (NAS, 1986).

TABLE 3
DISTRIBUTION OF FARM CASH RECEIPTS BY COMMODITY GROUP FOR EACH PROVINCE, 1986

PROVINCE	Wheat %	Feed Grain %	Oil-seeds %	Cattle %	Hogs %	Dairy %	Poultry & Eggs %	Other Cash Receipts[a] %	Gov't. Payments %	Total %	Total Cash Receipt
B.C.	1.0	0.6	0.3	15.8	5.5	23.1	16.0	32.0	5.7	100	1,003
Alberta	13.8	9.1	7.3	29.3	7.2	6.0	3.5	6.6	17.2	100	3,759
Saskatchewan	39.2	6.9	7.9	12.0	2.6	2.2	1.2	5.5	22.3	100	4,130
Manitoba	25.8	8.1	10.4	14.2	11.7	5.2	4.7	9.5	10.5	100	2,074
Ontario	2.2	5.9	4.4	21.2	12.5	17.7	9.8	23.8	2.5	100	5,458
Quebec	0.5	5.3	0.0	9.3	20.9	31.4	11.1	12.6	9.0	100	3,227
Maritimes	0.3	0.8	0.0	11.5	11.9	24.0	15.4	32.5	3.6	100	729
CANADA	**13.8**	**6.4**	**5.2**	**17.6**	**10.4**	**13.8**	**7.1**	**14.4**	**11.3**	**100**	**20,380**
Total Cash Receipts ($million)	2,822	1,303	1,060	3,594	2,118	2,805	1,445	2,934	2,301		

[a] Other cash receipts includes Canadian Wheat Board Advances plus net change in deferred grain receipts which totalled $250 million.

Source: Statistics Canada, 21–603.

A second important feature of Canadian agriculture is the regional diversity in commodities that results from a regional production capability related to soils, climate and historic development. The commodity production mix varies significantly between provinces (Table 3). Although all provinces produce some of each major commodity group, their relative importance is quite different. For example, production of grains and oilseeds is far more important to Saskatchewan than it is to Quebec, where the dairy sector accounts for more than 30 per cent of cash receipts. The importance of agriculture to each provincial economy also differs. Although Ontario cash receipts are greater than those of Saskatchewan, agriculture is more important to Saskatchewan's economy. A higher priority will most likely be given to agricultural issues in Saskatchewan than in Ontario.

A third aspect is the extent to which various commodities have benefited from both provincial and federal agricultural programs. Some programs involve direct government payments and others do not. An example of the latter is that of supply managed commodities, which receive most of their support via controlled domestic production and restrictive import policies. The beef and pork sectors receive payouts intermittently under their stabilization programs. Grain and oilseed producers in the prairies have benefited from CROW transport rates along with various stabilization programs.

This paper attempts to provide estimates of the impact of world trade liberalization on the Canadian agricultural economy. The analytical focus is on individual commodity effects, concentrating on the grains and red meat sectors, and on regional production and income changes that would result. It is critical that these regional and commodity trade-offs be identified to ensure that appropriate adjustment policies are developed.

Methodology

The Canadian Regional Agricultural Model (CRAM) is used to undertake a comparative static, partial equilibrium analysis. This is a multicommodity, multiregion linear programming model. It represents Canada's agricultural sector with 29 crop regions producing wheat (4 grades), barley (including other coarse grains), flax, canola, corn, soybeans, hay, pasture and other crops. Livestock production is modelled at the provincial level, with well-developed beef and pork blocks and single activities for poultry. The dairy herd component is also well developed to complement the beef block. Shipments of livestock, livestock products and grains occur to meet provincial demand levels, with excess domestic demand or supply being met by import or export activities. Demand for beef, pork and grains is endogenized using stepped functions. Opening inventories of cattle and sows are adjusted through incorporation of retention functions responding to own price and feed grain price effects. Trade in red meats and grains requires that export and import prices be established. Domestic floor and ceiling prices are specified. A small country stance is adopted, which means that Canadian trade will not affect world or North American price levels. For more information on the model see Webber et al. (1986).

As a first step a base solution is required from which comparisons can be made. The model is calibrated to 1986: livestock inventories, prices and government payments for various commodities are set at 1986 levels. The demand functions are calibrated to replicate prices and domestic consumptions for that year. Government programs are explicitly incorporated into the model by supplementing market returns with expected payouts under each of the various programs. Payments under the following programs are explicitly considered:

- Western Grain Stabilization Act (WGSA)
- Agricultural Stabilization Act (ASA)
- Crop Insurance
- Federal and provincial red meat stabilization programs
- Two Price Wheat Program
- Input subsidies
- Special Canadian Grains Program (SCGP).

In addition, the benefits of the Western Grains Transportation Act are captured as are the benefits of supply management for the dairy and poultry sectors. Actual payouts to grain producers under the various grains programs in 1986 are calculated on a per tonne benefit basis. These amount to $51/tonne of grain and oilseed in western Canada and $33/tonne in eastern Canada. The difference represents the amount paid out by WGSA in western Canada and by the ASA in eastern Canada (non-Canadian Wheat Board area). The payout of $1 billion under the SCGP is also included. For red meats net benefits to producers of stabilization programs and input subsidies averaged over the 1981–82 to 1985–86 period are used (Intercambio, 1987). This assumes that although producers do not know exactly how much governments will pay each year, they do expect some payments to protect their income position, with some payments nominally fixed. Their production decisions are then based on the total expected return from both the market and government payments. The assumption is that farmers view government payments as equivalent to market receipts.[3] Using CRAM, which models producer decisions, an estimate of changes that producers are expected to make when relative profits change is provided.

The Trade Liberalization Scenario

"Trade liberalization" in this experiment does not represent perfect free trade; rather, it reflects a movement toward freer trade prices brought about through an elimination of major subsidy and support programs and other price distorting programs by various national governments. In this analyis, two changes are introduced simultaneously. First, all direct government support payments to producers in Canada are eliminated, and, second, prices are set at levels that may be expected under a trade liberalization scenario. In addition, in the case of beef and pork a price adjustment to world prices is also required because higher feed grain prices impact upon red meat prices.

TABLE 4
COMPARISON OF 1986 OBSERVED VALUES WITH BASE RESULTS

	1986	Base
PRICES ($/T)		
Domestic Price Wheat[a]	257	257
Food Barley, West Canada	82	76
Domestic Canola	240	240
High Quality Beef, West	3,070	3,196
High Quality Beef, East	3,129	3,291
Pork, West	2,964	2,950
PRODUCTION (000 T)		
Wheat	31,400	25,960
Coarse Grains	24,400	26,400
Flax	1,026	450
Canola	3,800	1,500
Soybean	960	850
Beef	1,030	1,038
Pork	911	925
Milk (million L.)	7,305	7,219
Chicken	471	470
Eggs (million doz.)	409	500
EXPORT (IMPORTS) ('000T)		
Wheat	20,800	21,973
Coarse Grains	6,800	12,343
Canola	2,100	0
High Quality Beef	17	69
Low Quality Beef	(24)	(22)
Pork	200	270

[a] This reflects the Two-Price Wheat Program. The export price at Thunder Bay was set at $130/t.

Source: Actual data from Agriculture Canada (1987) and simulation results.

Data required to determine changing world price levels, exogenous to the CRAM model, are drawn from a number of sources and modified where necessary. For grain and oilseed prices, the trade liberalization results from Agriculture Canada's TASS model are adopted directly. These prices represent the impact of removing certain programs and border restrictions in Japan, Canada, the U.S. and the European Community. With serious distortions in this market at present, world prices are expected to increase with trade liberalization. The prices used, shown in Table 4, correspond fairly closely to price levels experienced in the early 1980s.

In the red meats sector, Canada operates in a fairly open North American market, and world beef and pork trade is relatively small compared to total production. A review of several recent studies (Parikh et al., 1986; Tyers and Anderson, 1987; Roningen, Sullivan and Wainio, 1987) did not clarify whether prices would rise or fall from their 1986 level if trade distorting policies were removed. This analysis assumes that Canadian (and American) beef and pork prices *ceteris paribus* will not change from their 1986 level through the removal of programs, thus implying that current distortions are not large. However, adjustments in herd sizes are needed to account for the impact of higher feed grain prices brought about by trade liberalization. Adjustments were made based on econometric estimates of changes in grain prices in the U.S. affecting cattle and hog stocks (FAPRI, 1987). Medium term elasticities are used, the assumption being that whatever price changes in feed grain occur in Canada will also affect U.S. feeders. The adjustments in opening stock numbers is exogenous and is made before solving the model. Another adjustment was made to reduce carcass weights to those experienced in 1984 (when feed grain prices were higher than 1986 levels).

For supply managed commodities production is assumed to remain constant, but Canadian prices are adjusted to correspond to American prices in 1986. If American prices in 1986 are distorted, Canadian prices will also reflect similar distortions. In the CRAM model, domestic demand levels for milk, eggs and chicken are set equal to production, and are not adjusted to own or cross-price effects. This is a limitation in the present analysis.

All government payments under the various programs are set to zero in the trade liberalization scenario. Only those programs mentioned earlier are affected; other government programs are assumed to continue at their historic level (e.g., research, extension, inspection). Grain transport rates are increased to compensatory rates for 1986, thereby resulting in a 370 per cent increase from 1986 WGTA rates paid by farmers. The net effect of the dairy subsidy and in-quota levy was incorporated into the 1986 milk price in the base case. In the trade liberalization scenario it is assumed that these are eliminated.[4]

The Impacts of Trade Liberalization

The Grain and Oilseed Sectors

Little change occurs in production of the various grains between the base and the liberalization scenario. Barley production declines in Alberta and Saskatchewan as production of canola expands. This is due to changing relative profits. Summerfallow acreage remains virtually the same. Exports increase as a result of lower domestic food and industrial use and lower feed demand. Wheat export supplies increase by 2 per cent and coarse grains by 8 per cent, even though barley production falls on the prairies. In the base run only sufficient canola is produced to meet domestic demand, but under liberalization 342,000 tonnes are available for export.

The impact of higher market prices for grains on the net farm value of production (market returns minus cash costs and transport costs to port) is significant. The three prairie provinces realize increases ranging from 119 per cent in Saskatchewan to 153 per cent in Alberta. In Quebec the impact is even more significant as the net farm value increases by 425 per cent. Nationally, the improvement averages out to 133 per cent and is worth some $2.95 billion. This improvement is noted despite a 370 per cent increase in prairie freight rates and elimination of the Two Price Wheat subsidy, which is worth an estimated $267 million in the base case. However, the picture changes significantly with the removal of all government programs and payments thereunder. In Table 5, government payments in the base case are added to net farm value as shown in column 2. With the removal of these benefits to the grain sector, higher market prices from trade liberalization are largely offset by the loss in government payments. The net effect at the national level is a 7 per cent increase in net farm value added, amounting to $323 million. In the prairies the change ranges between -3 per cent and 1 per cent. In Ontario and Quebec the net change is positive; however, most of this will not show up in added farm cash receipts as a large portion of this grain is fed on farm.

The Beef Sector

In the beef sector, higher feed grain prices affect production costs, reducing herd sizes and resulting in lower output levels. Lower output will, in turn, lead to higher market prices--which will limit the decline in production. Elimination of government support programs in this sector is also expected to have a negative impact as cow-calf producers look to calf sales and support payments for their receipts. The feeding industry buys calves at prices largely determined by feed grains prices, the price of slaughter cattle and support payments for finished animals. Government support payments across provinces are generally under $10 per head except in Quebec, where payments are four times as large. In the trade liberalization scenario grain prices are assumed to increase by 124 per cent in western Canada and by 100 per cent in the east,

TABLE 5

PROVINCIAL INCOME FROM CROP SECTOR AND TRADE SCENARIO INCLUDING GOVERNMENT PAYMENTS IN BASE

		BASE[a]	FREER TRADE[a]	ABSOLUTE CHANGE[a]	% CHANGE
B.C.	Cash Costs	50,358	49,967	-392	-1
	Total Farm Value	80,198	104,280	24,082	30
	Net Farm Value (excl. gov't payments)[b]	29,840	54,314	24,474	82
	Net Farm Value (incl. gov't payments)[b]	57,504	54,314	-3,190	-6
ALBERTA	Cash Costs	1,202,302	1,188,206	-14,096	-1
	Total Farm Value	1,713,165	2,485,218	772,053	45
	Net Farm Value (excl. gov't payments)[b]	510,863	1,297,012	786,149	153
	Net Farm Value (incl. gov't payments)[b]	1,339,696	1,297,012	-42,684	-3
SASK.	Cash Costs	1,685,629	1,679,707	-5,922	0
	Total Farm Value	2,538,606	3,554,409	1,015,803	40
	Net Farm Value (excl. gov't payments)[b]	852,977	1,874,701	1,021,724	119
	Net Farm Value (incl. gov't payments)[b]	1,926,146	1,874,701	-51,445	-3
MANITOBA	Cash Costs	763,317	760,536	-2,781	0
	Total Farm Value	1,222,668	1,358,194	135,526	11
	Net Farm Value (excl. gov't payments)[b]	245,676	597,659	351,983	143
	Net Farm Value (incl. gov't payments)[b]	592,620	597,659	5,039	1

TABLE 5 (Continued)
PROVINCIAL INCOME FROM CROP SECTOR AND TRADE SCENARIO INCLUDING GOVERNMENT PAYMENTS IN BASE

ONTARIO	Cash Costs	996,421	994,957	-1,464	0
	Total Farm Value	1,416,378	2,030,122	613,744	43
	Net Farm Value (excl. gov't payments)[b]	419,957	1,035,165	615,208	146
	Net Farm Value (incl. gov't payments)[b]	694,226	1,035,165	340,939	49
QUEBEC	Cash Costs	239,229	238,006	-1,223	-1
	Total Farm Value	273,138	416,122	142,984	52
	Net Farm Value (excl. gov't payments)	33,909	178,116	144,207	425
	Net Farm Value (incl. gov't payments)	99,384	178,116	78,732	79
MARITIMES	Cash Costs	163,404	163,210	-194	0
	Total Farm Value	276,082	281,572	5,490	2
	Net Farm Value (excl. gov't payments)	112,678	118,362	5,684	5
	Net Farm Value (incl. gov't payments)	122,526	118,362	-4,164	-3
CANADA	Cash Costs	5,100,659	5,074,588	-26,071	-1
	Total Farm Value	7,007,558	10,229,917	3,222,358	46
	Net Farm Value (excl. gov't payments)	2,205,900	5,155,328	2,949,428	133
	Net Farm Value (incl. gov't payments)	4,832,101	5,155,328	323,226	7

[a] $000's.
[b] Includes an estimated benefit for two-price wheat of $267 million allocated among British Columbia, Alberta, Saskatchewan, Manitoba and Ontario.

Source: Simulation results.

which in turn could increase beef prices by an estimated 14 per cent and 11 per cent, respectively.

The net impact on provincial herds of a small increase in beef prices, a large increase in grain prices, and a decrease in government payments for cow-calf and feedlot producers is shown in Table 6. In the west the cow herd declines by approximately 25 per cent and in Ontario by 12 per cent. In Quebec the decline is 23 per cent. The greater reduction in the west is partly due to the larger relative increase in feed grain prices, but the elasticity of cow numbers with respect to grain prices used in this analysis is also higher in the west (-0.22) than in the east (-0.14).

Nationally, slaughter declines by 17 per cent, with most of the decline occurring in Manitoba, Ontario and British Columbia. Surplus feeder cattle from Saskatchewan which in the base case were fed and slaughtered in Manitoba, are now shipped to Ontario. In the base run Manitoba fed cattle up to a maximum slaughter constraint but did not in the free trade scenario. This suggests that comparative advantage has shifted in favour of Ontario where government payments to feeders are currently $24 per head less than in Manitoba. When the decline in slaughter number is combined with lower carcass weights, national production falls by 20 per cent. With higher beef prices Canadian demand declines by 10 per cent (Table 7) and there are no exports of high quality beef (Table 8). With no imports, Canada is self-sufficient in high quality beef at an estimated price of $3,711 per tonne in western Canada (Table 9). Imports of low quality beef increase by 159 per cent.

Provincial beef sector earnings[5] (Table 10) are calculated taking into account feed and cash costs, changes in inventory within the year and the value of cattle shipped in or out of the province. Cull dairy cows and replacement heifers are excluded. Nationally, sector income declines by 27 per cent (Table 10). The increase in market prices of 16 per cent under the trade liberalization scenario does not offset the increase in the feed grain bill of some 38 per cent and the loss of $243 million in government support payments. In Manitoba and Quebec sector earnings fall by over 50 per cent while in Ontario earnings actually increase slightly.

The Pork Sector

Pork producers in Canada who under a free trade scenario face higher feed grain prices and the loss of government support payments will decrease their number of sows. Higher feed grain prices reduce; therefore an increase in market prices of 21 per cent in the west and 17 per cent in the east is anticipated (based on an estimated U.S. feed grain-market price elasticity). Provincial estimates of changes in sow numbers range from -6 per cent in Manitoba to -24 per cent in B.C. and Alberta (Table 6). Canadian production is estimated to fall by 14 per cent, and demand by 13 per cent (Table 7) as market prices increase by 17 per cent to 21 per cent (Table 9). Exports of

TABLE 6
CHANGE IN PROVINCIAL BEEF AND HOG SECTORS UNDER TRADE LIBERALIZATION

	B.C.[a]	ALBERTA[a]	SASK.[a]	MANITOBA[a]	ONTARIO[a]	QUEBEC[a]	MARITIMES[a]
BEEF SECTOR							
Opening Stock (Cows)	-26.85	-25.82	-23.84	-24.92	-11.82	-23.43	-13.49
Total Cattle Slaughter (HD)	-9.87	0.00	0.00	-50.42	-5.00	0.00	-1.96
Barley Feed to Beef (T)	-25.51	-24.00	-18.47	-52.79	-3.15	-11.60	-0.74
Production High Quality Beef (T)	-27.30	-25.60	-19.00	-56.45	-4.05	-15.60	-3.70
Low Quality (T)	16.64	-26.33	-31.25	-44.76	-13.58	-21.40	-9.93
HOG SECTOR							
Opening Sector (Sows)	-24.70	-24.98	-16.46	-5.84	-10.71	-11.82	-20.00
Total Slaughter (HD)	-15.38	-31.39	-16.43	-6.19	-12.37	-10.81	-20.94
Barley Feed to Hogs (T)	-24.70	-24.98	-16.46	-5.84	-10.71	-11.82	-20.00

[a] Percentage change.

Source: Simulation results.

pork fall 17 per cent, but at 224,000 tonnes they are still of significant value to the industry (Table 8).

TABLE 7
DOMESTIC DEMAND LEVELS INCLUDING INDUSTRIAL USE

	Units[d]	Base Run[d]	Freer Trade[d]	Absolute Change[d]	Percentage Change[d]
HQ Wheat: Western Canada[c]	tonne	0	0	0	5
HQ Wheat: Eastern Canada[c]	tonne	0	0	0	2
Barley: Western Canada	tonne	0	0	0	-18
Barley: Eastern Canada	tonne	0	0	0	-19
Canola: Canada	tonne	0	0	0	-14
Soybeans: Canada[a]	tonne	0	0	0	0
Other: Western Canada[b]	dollar	0	0	0	0
Other: Eastern Canada[b]	dollar	0	0	0	0
HQ Beef: Western Canada	tonne	0	0	0	-11
HQ Beef: Eastern Canada	tonne	0	0	0	-11
LQ Beef: Western Canada	tonne	0	0	0	-7
LQ Beef: Eastern Canada	tonne	0	0	0	-8
Pork: Western Canada	tonne	0	0	0	-14
Pork: Eastern Canada	tonne	0	0	0	-12
Milk: Canada[a]	liters	0	0	0	0
Veal: Canada[a]	tonne	0	0	0	0
Broilers: Canada[a]	tonne	0	0	0	0
Eggs: Canada[a]	dozen	0	0	0	0

[a] Demand set equal to domestic production.
[b] Demand set equal to production in terms of dollars rather than volume.
[c] For the base price is set by Two-Price Wheat program.
[d] 000's.

Source: Simulation results.

Provincial and national earnings for the pork sector are calculated in a manner similar to the beef sector (Table 10). Nationally, earnings fall by 15 per cent as the feed grain bill goes up 48 per cent and government support payments worth $152 million in the base run are eliminated. As with beef, significant provincial impacts are noted. In Manitoba earnings actually go up by 1 per cent and in Ontario and Quebec earnings fall by less than that in the other provinces, which experience declines in excess of 20 per cent. This is largely due to a higher market price elasticity on the breeding sow retention functions for Manitoba, Ontario and Quebec.

TABLE 8
CHANGE IN EXPORT (IMPORT) VOLUMES FROM BASE
TO TRADE LIBERALIZATION

	Base Run[a]	Freer Trade[a]	Per Cent Change
To And From World			
Wheat	21,973,066	22,340,386	2
Coarse Grains	12,343,069	13,310,787	8
Flax	450,107	442,980	-2
Canola	0	342,261	0
High Quality Beef	68,863	0	-100
Low Quality Beef	-22,886	-59,383	159
Pork	270,994	224,059	-17
From Western Canada to Eastern Canada			
Wheat	2,484,830	2,521,507	1
Coarse Grains	532,131	0	-100
Calves	120,459	103,500	-14
Feeder Cattle	137,080	186,698	36
High Quality Beef	179,733	144,260	-20
Low Quality Beef	99,237	51,756	-48

[a] Tonnes.

Source: Simulation results.

Dairy and Poultry

Less detail is available in the model for the dairy and poultry sectors; only changes in feed grain costs and revenue are reported for comparative purposes. Nationally, dairy revenue falls by 11 per cent ($341 million) as indicated in Table 11. The increase in the cost of grain is largely offset by the increase in the value of cull cows. Revenue less grain cost is 11 per cent below the base run. In the poultry sector the national feed grain bill increases by 72 per cent and revenue falls by 11 per cent, resulting in a decrease of 29 per cent in revenue less grain costs. Provincial changes range from minus 22 per cent in Quebec to minus 34 per cent in Manitoba.

TABLE 9
DOMESTIC PRICES AS DETERMINED FOR BASE AND
FREE TRADE SCENARIO

Commodity	Base Run	Freer Trade	Absolute Change	Percentage Change
HQ Wheat: Western Canada[a]	251	202	-49	-20
HQ Wheat: Eastern Canada[a]	251	228	-23	- 9
Barley: Western Canada	76	135	59	77
Barley: Eastern Canada	89	150	61	68
Canola: Canada	240	304	64	27
HQ Beef: Western Canada	3,196	3,711	516	16
HQ Beef: Eastern Canada	3,291	3,812	521	16
LQ Beef: Western Canada	2,458	2,865	407	17
LQ Beef: Eastern Canada	2,616	3,045	429	16
Pork: Western Canada	2,950	3,531	581	20
Pork: Eastern Canada	2,950	3,452	502	17

[a] For base run price set at $251/T under Two-Price Wheat Program.

Source: Simulation results.

Resource Values

Land values change very little on the prairies between the base and trade liberalization. However, the shadow value of beef cows in Alberta falls by 25 per cent. In Quebec the shadow value of land increases by 40 per cent, reflecting the substantial increase in earnings in the grain sector. However, the value of beef cows falls by 58 per cent. The decline in the shadow value of dairy cows, (7 per cent), providing an estimate of the impact on earnings from trade liberalization.

National Impacts

In the base case, the grain, red meat and supply management sectors accounted for roughly 85 per cent of farm cash receipts (including government payments) in 1986 (Table 3). Farm income for these sectors declines by 7 per cent with trade liberalization (Table 12). The higher market prices for grains are not sufficient to offset losses in direct government payments and other program benefits, lower prices for dairy and poultry products or higher red meat prices. All provinces except Ontario are worse off under trade liberalization. Income in Alberta falls by 12 per cent, more than in Saskatchewan (8 per cent) and more than the national average (7 per cent). This is partly explained by Alberta's relatively heavy dependence on both grains and red meat

TABLE 10

PROVINCIAL INCOME FROM BEEF AND HOG SECTORS IN BASE AND TRADE SCENARIOS

		BEEF				HOGS		
	Base[a]	Freer Trade[a]	Absolute Change[a]	Per Cent Change	Base[a]	Freer Trade[a]	Absolute Change[a]	Per Cent Change
B.C. Cost of Grain	10	13	3	32	11	15	4	33
Gov't Payments	18	0	-18	-100	4	0	-4	-100
Net Farm Value	55	50	-5	-9	49	37	-12	-24
ALBERTA Cost of Grain	115	155	40	35	63	83	21	33
Gov't Payments	74	0	-74	-100	25	0	-25	-100
Net Farm Value	558	405	-153	-27	287	218	-69	-24
SASKATCHEWAN Cost of Grain	33	47	14	42	28	41	13	48
Gov't Payments	46	0	-46	-100	14	0	-14	-100
Net Farm Value	217	135	-82	-38	108	85	-23	-21
MANITOBA Cost of Grain	30	28	-2	-6	48	80	32	67
Gov't Payments	19	0	-19	-100	12	0	-12	-100
Net Farm Value	146	70	-76	-52	260	262	2	1
ONTARIO Cost of Grain	67	107	40	60	194	292	98	50
Gov't Payments	24	0	-24	-100	29	0	-29	-100
Net Farm Value	261	268	7	3	527	459	-68	-13
QUEBEC Cost of Grain	12	17	5	44	171	254	83	48
Gov't Payments	58	0	-58	-100	55	0	-55	-100
Net Farm Value	117	54	-63	-54	590	504	-86	-15
MARITIMES Cost of Grain	5	8	3	61	20	27	7	35
Gov't Payments	5	0	-5	-100	13	0	-13	-100
Net Farm Value	29	26	-3	-10	90	66	-24	-27
CANADA Cost of Grain	271	375	103	38	535	793	257	48
Gov't Payments	243	0	-243	-100	152	0	-152	-100
Net Farm Value	1,383	1,008	-375	-27	1,911	1,631	-280	-15

[a] $ million.

Source: Simulation results.

TABLE 11
CHANGE IN DAIRY AND POULTRY SECTOR INCOMES BETWEEN BASE AND SCENARIO

	B.C.[a]	Alberta[a]	Sask.[a]	Manitoba[a]	Ontario[a]	Quebec[a]	Maritimes[a]	Canada[a]
Dairy Sector								
Base Net Income	221,826	270,689	103,636	134,511	1,096,459	1,376,975	195,871	3,399,967
Net Change in Income	-25,366	-27,778	-10,470	-13,894	-117,106	-146,623	-22,686	-363,924
Percentage Change	-11	-10	-10	-10	-11	-11	-12	-11
Poultry Sector								
Base Income	77,050	66,865	29,119	55,284	262,231	272,174	56,077	818,801
Change in Net Income	-24,183	-20,722	-8,504	-18,932	-86,564	-60,487	-18,108	-237,500
Per Cent Change	-31	-31	-29	-34	-33	-22	-32	-29

[a] 000's.

Source: Simulation results.

TABLE 12

CHANGE IN THE NET FARM VALUE EARNINGS (INCLUDING GOVERNMENT PAYMENTS) BETWEEN BASE AND TRADE LIBERALIZATION SCENARIO

| | Base Case[a] | | | Trade Liberalization | | | | |
PROVINCE	Crops[b]	Beef & Hogs[b]	Dairy & Poultry[b]	Crops[c]	Beef & Hogs[c]	Dairy & Poultry[c]	Absolute Change (All Sectors)[a]	Per Cent Change[c]
B.C.	58	104	299	-7	-16	-16	-69	-15
Alberta	1,340	845	338	-3	-26	-14	-307	-12
Sask.	1,926	325	133	-3	-32	-14	-180	-8
Manitoba	593	406	190	1	-18	-17	-99	-8
Ontario	694	788	1,359	49	-8	-15	73	3
Quebec	99	707	1,649	80	-21	-12	-267	-11
Maritimes	122	119	252	-3	-23	-16	-71	-14
Canada	4,832	3,294	4,219	7	-20	-14	-911	-7

[a] The base includes $3.02 billion in government payments to the grain, beef and hog sectors, Two-Price Wheat, WGTA and supply management.
[b] $ million.
[c] Per cent change.

Source: Simulation results.

production, whereas Saskatchewan receives over half its income from the crop sector (which helped balance the larger losses in the beef and hog sectors).

The benefit of trade liberalization to Ontario is estimated at 3 per cent. Ontario earnings decline in both the red meat and supply managed commodities, but this is more that offset by gains in the grains sector. Ontario is able to benefit from the full price increase for grains without incurring higher transportation costs to export points, as occurs in the prairies. (This benefit may be overestimated, as a large proportion of grains produced in Ontario are fed on farm and this will not affect cash receipts or net farm income as normally calculated.) In Quebec, the grain sector net farm value increases dramatically, but this sector is too small to offset losses in the red meats and supply managed sectors. Quebec suffers a 10% decline in earnings with trade liberalization.

Limitations

The limitations of these results and their interpretation need to be noted. The CRAM model attempts to capture important economic features of each of the markets discussed. Movement of resources among the various sectors is not well developed in the model, nor are cross-commodity demand effects. Historic constraints are also placed on certain production and shipment activities which may no longer be appropriate in a freer trade environment. Nor are all the structural adjustments that would occur in other countries accounted for; the opportunities that these may provide for increasing exports are ignored. The results also depend on the structural parameters incorporated in the model as well as on input-output coefficients and costs, all of which require updating and refinement. These coefficients have been drawn from a wide number of sources and different studies. The results must be viewed as tentative, providing an indication of the direction and magnitude of change based upon the assumptions made; they represent an initial attempt to measure some of the impacts for the scenario presented.

Concluding Remarks

Trade liberalization, as currently being discussed in the MTN's, could require signatory countries to alter significantly their domestic programs and related border measures. While most exporting countries, including Canada, are calling for "deep cuts" or the total elimination of programs that directly or indirectly affect trade, it is uncertain at this stage what will be achieved. However, it is important to understand what a comprehensive multilateral free trade agreement might mean to Canada, as well as to individual commodity sectors and provincial agricultural economies.

The grain sector in Canada is currently in serious financial difficulty due to trade distortions around the world. It is hoped that the MTN's will lead to a solution. Trade liberalization will result in an increase in market returns for the Canadian grain industry; grain producers in Ontario and Quebec are likely to benefit under trade liberalization. However, the net impact for the prairie provinces is slightly negative, although not significantly so. The improvement in world prices is insufficient to compensate for the loss of government programs that currently sustain producer incomes. These are not surprising results since improved market returns are simply replacing government payment. This liberalization experiment suggests that all livestock sectors would be worse off than under current prices and policies. In large measure this is due to the impact of higher feed grain prices. In the beef sector, the provincial variation is quite interesting as the comparative advantage of feeder location causes production to shift toward Ontario and away from Manitoba. Slaughter in Alberta and Saskatchewan is still constrained in the model and in follow-up analyses the implication of removing this constraint should be tested. In the dairy and poultry sectors, a movement to U.S. prices results in relatively similar negative impacts for all provinces. However, higher feed grain prices have differing effects on the supply managed commodities. Dairy and egg prices are set using cost of production formula, and the full impact would be passed on to consumers in the form of higher prices. For chicken, prices are set through negotiations, which means that producers may have to absorb at least some of the increase in grain prices, as may red meat producers.

Some provincial commodity sectors do benefit from trade liberalization, as shown in this analysis. However, most sectors either lose or show relatively little change. Total income, as defined in the model, declines by 8 per cent to 15 per cent in all provinces, except for Ontario. Nationally, income falls by 7 per cent. Based on these results, net income of the agricultural sector declines under the trade liberalization scenario. Furthermore, consumers face higher prices for most commodities. However, federal and provincial governments (and taxpayers) save as direct and indirect payments to these sectors decrease by some $4 billion.[6]

These results indicate that trade liberalization could lead to a significant down sizing of the beef and pork industries in response to much higher feed grain prices and a loss of government programs.

Resource shift questions are not addressed in the model. However, these results imply a major structural shift will be required to accommodate the reduced size of the industry, and that some resources will leave the industry. This will require adjustment policies tp ease the burden of such an adjustment on the red meat sector. The analysis assumes that national tripartite and provincial stabilization schemes are self-financed by producers alone. There may be a demand for alternative programs, but this largely depends on how trade liberalization is phased in and existing programs phased out. The dynamics of implementing trade liberalization are not addressed in a static model such as CRAM.

Although the grain sector faces improved world markets, these results indicate that it may want to keep some of its existing programs. Under this scenario prairie grain producers are slightly worse off than they are now, although they will be getting 100 per cent of their returns from the market. The opposite conclusion is reached for Ontario and Quebec, where grain producers may be more willing to eliminate programs they now have if trade liberalization leads to the world price increases assumed here.

Given these findings, why does considerable support for participating in the MTN's exist within Canadian agriculture? The first reason probably has to do with the desire of producers to be less dependent on government for their well-being. Government programs usually impose restrictions that affect investment and production decisions. Policies can also be changed, which entails uncertainty. A second reason is that there may be a realization that the current situation cannot be sustained indefinitely. Specifically, the WGSA and ASA support levels will adjust over several years to world price levels, and if prices remain at current levels, payouts will also fall. There is also the possibility that the current trade war could intensify if the MTN's fail. The U.S. and EC, with bigger budgets than Canada, continue to maintain their farm sectors regardless of market conditions. There are limits to how far other exporting countries can go in support of a specific export-oriented sector.

There is also an expectation that trade liberalization will lead to future growth opportunities for certain sectors of agriculture. This may lead to increased domestic opportunities as constraints are removed and new overseas markets are opened up. The problem is that these opportunities are largely unknown and may not materialize in the near future. Yet the opportunity to bring order to world trade in agricultural products makes economic sense from the point of view of resource allocation, especially if all that is preventing it are policies that can be changed to the mutual benefit of all countries concerned.

NOTES

1. Calculated from realized net farm income from Agriculture Canada, 1987 and net direct payments to producers from Statistics Canada 21–603.

2. The Cairns Group consists of Argentina, Australia, Brazil, Canada, Chile, Columbia, Hungary, Indonesia, Malaysia, New Zealand, Philippines, Thailand, and Uruguay.

3. The base case results are compared to actual 1986 values to validate the model (Table 4). Some differences are noted. For example, the use of five-year average yields in the case of wheat results in an underestimation of production since a larger than average crop was harvested in 1986. The serious underestimation of prairie oilseed production is a concern. Estimated livestock production is close to actual production except in the case of eggs. Trade is a residual in the model.

Overall the validation results are satisfactory, although high quality beef exports are overestimated. A more serious problem is the export level of coarse grains, double the actual level. This is partly attributable to an overestimate of production. Another possibility may be inappropriate specification of feed grain demand which is estimated on the basis of input-output coefficients used in the livestock production blocks.

4. The TASS model is currently being developed and tested at Agriculture Canada (McClatchy and Cahill, forthcoming).

5. Earnings do not take into account the cost of labor, depreciation of the cost of interest on debt capital and other overhead costs.

6. This includes $1 billion spent on WGTA and the dairy subsidy.

REFERENCES

Agriculture Canada. (1987). *Medium Term Outlook*. Ottawa: Agriculture Canada, Policy Branch.

Cairns Group. (1987). *Discussion Papers: Composite of Main Points*. Unpublished manuscript.

Canberra. National Agricultural Strategy (NAS). (1986, 20–21 November). *Report on Challenges Facing Agriculture*. Document submitted by the Ministers Responsible for Agriculture to the Annual Conference of First Ministers, Vancouver.

Food and Agricultural Policy Research Institute (FAPRI). (1987). *Managing the Food Security Act of 1985: The Current Strategy and Two Alternatives*. (FAPRI Staff Report #3-87). University of Missouri, Columbia and Iowa State University.

GATT Secretariat. (1987). *Proposal by Canada Regarding the Multilateral Trade Negotiations in Agriculture*. (MTN.GNG/NG5/W/19). Geneva: GATT.

Gifford, M. (1987). Personal Communication.

Hathaway, D.E. (1987). *Agriculture and the GATT: Rewriting the Rules*. Washington, D.C.: Institute for International Economics.

Intercambio Ltd. (1987). *Net Financial Benefits from Government Programs for Red Meat Producers in Canada, 1981–82 to 1985–86*. Prepared for Agriculture Canada, Ottawa.

Miller, G. (1987). *The Political Economy of International Agricultural Policy Reform.* Canberra, Australia: Australian Government Publishing Service.

Oleson, B.T. (1987). "World Grain Trade: An Economic Perspective of the Current Price War." *Canadian Journal of Agricultural Economics, 35*, 501–514.

Organization for Economic Co-operation and Development (OECD). (1987). *National Policies and Agricultural Trade.* Paris: OECD.

Parikh, K.S., G. Fischer, K. Frohberg and O. Gulbrandsen. (1986). *Towards Free Trade in Agriculture*, Laxenburg, Austria: International Institute for Applied Systems Analysis.

Roningen, V., J. Sullivan and J. Wainio. (1987). *The Impact of the Removal of Support to Agriculture in Developed Countries.* Paper presented at the AAEA annual meetings at East Lansing, Michigan.

Schmitz, A., A.F. McCalla, D.O. Mitchell and C. Cater. (1981). *Grain Export Cartels.* Cambridge, Massachusetts: Ballinger Publishing Company.

Tangermann, S., T. Josling and S. Pearson. (1987). *International Negotiations on Farm Support Levels: The Role of PSEs.* (Working paper # 87–3). International Agricultural Trade Research Consortium.

Tyers, R. and K. Anderson. (1987). *Liberalising OECD Agricultural Policies in the Uruguay Round: Effects on Trade and Welfare.* (Working Papers in Trade and Development No. 87/10). Australian National University, Canberra.

United States Department of Agriculture. (1986). *Embargoes, Surplus Disposal and U.S. Agriculture.* (Agricultural Economic Report Number 564 ERS). Washington, D.C.

Warley, T.K. (1987). "Issues Facing Agriculture in the GATT Negotiations." *Canadian Journal of Agricultural Economics, 35*, 515–534.

Webber, C.A., J.D. Graham and K.K. Klein. (1986). *The Structure of CRAM: A Canadian Regional Agricultural Model.* Report to Marketing and Economics Branch, Agriculture Canada, Ottawa, Canada.

CHAPTER 11

ASSESSING EXPORT PERFORMANCE FOR WHEAT: PAST PERFORMANCE AND FUTURE CHALLENGES

M. M. Veeman and T. S. Veeman

There is currently much soul-searching among government officials, academic researchers, and farmers themselves concerning future directions of the Canadian grains sector. Since assessment of past performance may provide insights as to future directions, we focus attention in this paper on past export performance in wheat, Canada's dominant grain export. World trade patterns in wheat over the past fifteen years are analyzed using a constant market share model of world trade flows from five major wheat exporting nations to major importing regions. We also examine briefly the recent grain trading environment, suggest ways in which that environment might be improved, and note potential impacts on the grain sector of the Canada-United States Free Trade Agreement.

Changing World Markets for Wheat

The market share figures in Tables 1 and 2 illustrate some of the structural changes that have occurred in world markets for wheat over the past two and a half decades. During this period the European Community (EC), once a major wheat importing region, has become a substantial net exporter of soft wheat, accounting for about 17 per cent of total world wheat exports in 1985–86. This change reflects not only the relatively high levels of support and protection for grains within the Common Agricultural Policy, but also results from changes in grain production technology involving substantial yield increases. Since the 1970s the USSR, once a net exporter, has become a major wheat importer due to changes in agricultural policy to encourage livestock production, a shift that has been aided by relatively low real prices for grains and the availability of foreign exchange stemming from the energy price increases of 1973 and

1979. The USSR accounted for 28 percent of world wheat imports in 1984–85, and 20 percent in 1985–86 (International Wheat Council, 1988). Other centrally planned countries have also increased wheat imports since the 1970s, with China becoming a major importer. Other striking changes in the structure of world markets for wheat that are reflected in Table 2 are the increasing proportion of world imports in aggregate by the many different national markets characterized as middle income developing countries and the dwindling markets in general for wheat in the higher income industrialized markets.

TABLE 1
AVERAGE EXPORT SHARES OF THE WORLD WHEAT MARKET[1] FOR MAJOR EXPORTERS, 1959–60 TO 1968–69, 1969–70 TO 1978–79, 1979–80 TO 1984–85, AND SUBSEQUENT ANNUAL AVERAGES

Exporters:	Argentina	Australia	Canada	EC	USA	Others
Time Period:			1959–60 to 1968–69			
Market Share	6.0	11.9	22.1	8.7	38.6	12.6
Time Period:			1969–70 to 1978–79			
Market Share	4.2	13.0	20.5	9.3	42.2	10.9
Time Period:			1979–80 to 1984–85			
Market Share	6.5	12.6	19.0	14.2	42.0	5.6

Subsequent Annual Averages, 1984–85 to 1987–88

1984-85	7.8	14.7	18.8	16.8	35.8	6.1
1985-86	7.6	19.5	20.5	17.4	28.7	6.3
1986-87[2]	4.7	17.0	23.5	17.2	30.7	6.8
1987-88[3]	5.1	12.9	21.7	13.8	40.5	5.9

[1] Expressed in percentage terms.
[2] Preliminary.
[3] IWC forecast as at 2/4/1988.

Source: Based on data from International Wheat Council, *World Wheat Statistics*, various issues, and International Wheat Council, Market Report, 4 February 1988.

TABLE 2
AVERAGE IMPORT SHARES OF THE WORLD WHEAT MARKET BY
SOCIO-ECONOMIC REGION,[1] 1959–60 TO 1968–69, 1969–70 TO 1978–79
AND 1979–80 TO 1984–85

Importing Regions:	Developed[2]	Eastern Europe[3]	C.P.Asia[4]	Middle Income[5]	Low Income[6]
Time Period:		1959–60 to 1968–69			
Market Share	33.0	15.2	8.4	28.6	14.7
Time Period:		1969–70 to 1978–79			
Market Share	22.3	16.9	9.9	39.3	11.6
Time Period:		1979–80 to 1984–85			
Market Share	12.6	25.7	12.2	42.3	7.1

[1] Expressed in percentage terms.
[2] Includes the countries of Western Europe, North America, Japan, Israel and South Africa.
[3] USSR and other centrally planned Eastern European countries.
[4] China and other centrally planned Asian countries.
[5] Includes, for example, Brazil, Chile, Iran, Iraq, Egypt, Turkey, and Nigeria.
[6] Includes countries whose GNP per capita was less than $410 U.S. in 1983—for example, India, Pakistan, Kenya, Malawi, and Sudan.

Source: Based on data from International Wheat Council, *World Wheat Statistics*, various issues.

Overall, these trends reflect changes in the domestic agricultural policies of many nations, changes in agricultural technology, and changing economic circumstances. Changes in agricultural technology have been particularly evident with respect to the development and widespread adoption of high yielding varieties of wheat and other grains. These varieties and associated intensive management of production techniques have been important in the increasing yields and production levels of wheat in countries as diverse as India and France. Changes in milling and baking technology have also contributed to the changes in the structure of world wheat markets (Veeman, 1987).

The nature of the international economic environment has also influenced the current structure of world trade in both wheat and coarse grains. This influence is likely to become of increasing importance in the future, in view of the declining importance in aggregate of industrialized importers and the increasing importance of the centrally planned and developing country importers. The changes in the structure of world wheat imports involving increasing importance of medium income developing nations are forecast to continue into the future. The International Wheat Council (IWC), in a recent update of its earlier forecasts of potential trade in wheat and coarse grains, suggests that the developing countries, including China, may account for over 80 per cent of world imports of grains by the year 2000 (IWC, 1987). Many of these countries now suffer from severe financial and balance of payment problems, curtailing their ability to import. Achievement of an international economic environment that is conducive to their growth is likely to be of considerable importance to the future volume and value of the world grain trade.

Assessing Export Performance in World Markets for Wheat

In this section we assess the export performance of major wheat exporters over the past fifteen years using a constant market share model. This model is based on the reasoning that the export growth of a country will reflect that country's competitiveness, relative to others, and will be affected by the structure of its exports. Competitiveness is normally considered to be based on the relative prices of the exports of different countries (Leamer and Stern, 1970) although, as Richardson (1971) points out, factors such as quality, reliability, related services, and institutional trading arrangements may also affect a country's competitiveness in export markets. The constant market share (CMS) approach does not delineate the source of a country's competitiveness. Rather, it accounts for changes in a country's exports that have arisen because of the structure of its exports and attributes export growth or decline, relative to a constant market share norm, to changes in competitiveness. The model is outlined below.

The Constant Market Share Model

Since a country's exports (q) are a function of its relative competitiveness (c), for any two countries, the relative level of exports and market shares of each (s) in total world exports (Q) can be attributed to their relative competitiveness. Thus:

$$q^a/q^b = s^a/s^b = f(c^a/c^b) \tag{1}$$

where the superscripts a and b denote two exporting regions.

Considering the market share of one exporting country alone, rearranging as:

$$q = sQ \tag{2}$$

and taking the derivative with respect to time yields:

$$q = sQ + Qs \tag{3}$$

The first right-hand side term indicates the world growth or market size effect. This is the change in exports of a country that would be achieved if it were to maintain its share of the world market. The second right-hand term is referred to as the competitiveness effect, and indicates the extent to which the actual change in exports by the country in question exceeds or falls below the level associated with maintenance of its share of the world market.

The structural composition of exports is also recognized to affect a country's export growth. Rewriting expression (3) to explicitly consider the regional orientation of this country's exports gives:

$$q = \Sigma_j \, s_j \, q_j \; + \Sigma_j \, q_j \, s_j \tag{4}$$

where q_j denotes the quantity of wheat exports from the country in question to region j for j=1, ...n importing regions; thus $q_j = q$ and s_j denotes q_j/Q. Manipulation of (4) gives:

$$q = sQ + [\Sigma_j \, s_j \, q_j \; - \; s \, Q] + \Sigma_j \, q_j \, s_j \tag{5}$$

The second right-hand side term (in square brackets) is viewed as the market distribution effect; the sign and magnitude of this term indicate whether the country's wheat exports are concentrated in markets that are growing more or less rapidly than is the world wheat market. As was the case previously, the first right-hand side term is the market growth effect and the last term is viewed as the competitive effect.

The effects must be calculated over a discrete time period, which gives:

$$\Delta q = s\Delta Q \; + [\Sigma_j \, s_j \, \Delta q_j \; - \; s\Delta Q] + \Sigma_j \, q_j \, \Delta s_j \tag{6}$$

Considering s and sj in terms of their initial period magnitudes and qj in terms of its second period level, and thus following the general computational procedures adopted by Stern (1970), this expression is restated as:

$$q^2 - q^1 = r \, q^1 + [\Sigma_j \, r_j \, q_j 1 \; - \; r \, q^1] + [q^2 - q^1 - \Sigma_j \, r_j \, q_j 1] \tag{7}$$

where: superscripts 1 and 2 indicate time periods 1 and 2, respectively; r denotes the percentage increase in world wheat exports from period 1 to period 2; rj denotes the percentage increase in world exports of wheat to region j from period 1 to 2 (j=1, ...5); and the other terms are as previously defined.

Following this approach, Equation 7 is applied to decompose changes in export levels for each of the world's five major wheat exporters into the effects of the growth in the aggregate market for wheat, the regional orientation of their exports to more or less rapidly growing markets for wheat, and changes in their relative competitiveness.

Since results from CMS models may be sensitive to the time period and end points chosen for the analysis, this application involves comparisons of averages calculated over several years of data. Three time periods were chosen to reflect different economic conditions in world markets for grains and apparent differences in the structure of world trade in grain. The three periods are 1969–70 to 1973–74; 1974–75 to 1978–79; and 1979–80 to 1984–85. The data on which the analysis is based are the annual volumes of trade in wheat and wheat flour reported by the International Wheat Council in *World Wheat Statistics*. Regional export markets are aggregated into five different socio-economic groupings: high income industrialized countries; the centrally-planned Eastern European countries, including the USSR; centrally-planned Asian countries, including China; and two groups of developing nations. The latter two groups are the middle-income developing nations and the low-income developing nations; the low-income developing nation group includes those countries in which gross national product per capita was less than U.S. $410 in 1983. The results of the analysis of wheat export growth and market shares over the selected periods are given in Table 3.

TABLE 3
RESULTS OF THE CONSTANT MARKET SHARE MODEL
ACCOUNTING FOR CHANGE IN GROWTH OF WHEAT EXPORTS BY
MAJOR EXPORTING NATIONS, COMPARISONS FOR THREE TIME
PERIODS FROM 1970 TO 1985

Exporting Regions:	Australia		EEF		Other
Argentina		Canada		USA	
Comparing 1974–75 to 1978–79 with 1969–70 to 1973–74					
Total Change					
('000 metric t.)1418.8	1263.8	783.4	734.2	6783.8	-1487.4
Market Size Effect					
('000 metric t.) 322.0	1206.2	2035.0	888.4	3837.1	1,207.9
(%) 22.6	95.4	259.8	121.0	56.6	81.2
Market Distribution Effect					
('000 metric t.) 112.1	165.8	-714.9	396.3	250.5	-203.4
(%) 7.9	13.1	-91.3	54.0	3.7	13.7
Competitive Effect					
('000 metric t.) 984.7	-108.2	-536.6	-550.5	2,696.2	-2,491.9
(%) 69.4	-8.6	-68.5	-75.0	39.8	167.5

TABLE 3 (Continued)
RESULTS OF THE CONSTANT MARKET SHARE MODEL ACCOUNTING FOR CHANGE IN GROWTH OF WHEAT EXPORTS BY MAJOR EXPORTING NATIONS, COMPARISONS FOR THREE TIME PERIODS FROM 1970 TO 1985

Exporting Regions:	Argentina	Australia	Canada	EEF	USA	Other
Comparing 1979-80 to 1984-85 with 1974-75 to 1978-79						
Total Change						
('000 metric t.)	2969.2	3598.6	5349.4	7765.5	10601.3	-402.8
Market Size Effect						
('000 metric t.)	1501.9	3821.0	5845.2	2726.7	13386.8	2599.5
(%)	50.6	106.2	109.3	35.1	126.3	645.4
Market Distribution Effect						
('000 metric t.)	492.2	-128.7	713.1	-796.0	-2300.4	2011.8
(%)	16.6	-3.6	13.3	-10.3	-21.7	499.5
Competitive Effect						
('000 metric t.)	975.1	-93.7	-1208.9	5834.8	-485.1	-5014.1
(%)	32.8	-2.6	-22.6	75.1	-4.6	1244.8

Source: Calculated from trade and market share data reported in Veeman and Veeman (1987).

Results of the Model

A comparison of export market performance from 1970 to 1974 with the performance from 1975 to 1979 illustrates that by far the largest increase in wheat exports was achieved by the United States. Although more than half of that increase can be attributed to the general growth in world exports of wheat (i.e., to the market size effect), an apparent increase in competitiveness accounted for much of the balance of this large growth in U.S. wheat exports. Argentina was the only other major exporter for which an appreciable competitive effect was apparent over the two comparison periods in the 1970s. In contrast, in the mid- to late 1970s, exports from Canada and the EC fell considerably below the levels that would have been required for these countries to maintain their earlier (1970 to 1974) market shares, suggesting an appreciable decline in the competitiveness of both these wheat exporters. A much smaller decline in apparent competitiveness was evident for Australia. For Canada, the inability to maintain wheat export market share in the mid- to late 1970s seems at least partly attributable to the deterioration in grain transport facilities and bottlenecks in grain handling and transportation that were evident at that time.

Canada was the only major exporter to exhibit an apparent negative impact on wheat exports from the regional distribution of export markets over the 1970s, indicating that Canadian wheat exports tended to be concentrated in relatively slowly growing export markets for wheat during the 1970s. As the growth rates given in Table 4 and the exporter market share data in Table 5 illustrate, this was evidently due to the feature that a relatively high proportion of Canadian wheat exports (one-third, higher than for any other exporter) were to shrinking developed country markets.

TABLE 4
PERCENTAGE GROWTH IN WHEAT IMPORTS, WORLD AND MAJOR IMPORTING REGIONS, UNDERLYING THE CONSTANT MARKET SHARE ANALYSIS

| | Rate of Growth in Wheat Imports | |
Region	Comparing 1974–75 to 1978–79 with 1969–70 to 1973–74 average percentage	Comparing 1979–80 to 1984–85 with 1974–75 to 1978–79 average percentage
World (r)	16.5	44.6
Developed Countries (r_1)	-12.9	-4.0
Eastern Europe (r_2)	10.5	123.2
C.P. Asia (r_3)	27.0	69.4
Middle Income (r_4)	35.8	44.8
Low Income (r_5)	20.7	-12.1

Turning to more recent time periods and considering the growth of wheat exports between 1975 and 1985 (based on a comparison of averages from 1974–75 to 1978–79 with those from 1979–80 to 1984–85), the results in Table 3 indicate some changes in the early to mid-1980s in the factors accounting for growth in wheat exports. Compared to the earlier periods, increased export volumes were achieved by all major exporters, although the extent of this increase was proportionately less for the U.S. than for other exporters. The regional distribution effects are quite different from those in the earlier period and indicate a positive effect only for Canada and Argentina. During the early to mid-1980s both of these countries reoriented wheat exports toward the segments of the wheat market that showed most rapid growth over this time period, the centrally-planned wheat importing countries of Eastern Europe and Asia. The most substantial negative distribution effect is for the United States, although negative effects for the EC and Australia indicate that these countries also tended to export to slower-growing import areas during the early to mid-1980s. However, only two major exporters, the EC and Argentina, exhibited market share increases in the early to mid-1980s, suggesting an increase in their competitiveness. Canada, the U.S., and

Australia appear to have suffered a decline in competitiveness; this decline was relatively modest for the U.S. and Australia and relatively larger for Canada.

TABLE 5
**EXPORTER PROFILES: THE PERCENTAGE OF MAJOR EXPORTERS'
WHEAT EXPORTS TO DIFFERENT IMPORTING GROUPS, 1959–60 TO
1968–69, 1969–70 TO 1978–79, AND 1979–80 TO 1984–85**

Importing Regions:	Developed	Eastern Europe	C.P. Asia	Middle Income	Low Income	Total Imports
Time Period:	**1959–60 to 1968–69**					
Exporting Region						
Market Share:						
Argentina	37.4	3.5	9.7	48.8	0.6	100.0
Australia	32.0	4.5	29.8	22.3	11.4	100.0
Canada	53.7	20.1	13.9	7.7	4.6	100.0
E.C.	33.5	15.4	8.5	37.4	5.3	100.0
U.S.A.	25.7	3.3	0.03	40.6	30.4	100.0
Time Period:	**1969–70 to 1978–79**					
Exporting Region						
Market Share:						
Argentina	20.4	13.6	6.4	53.9	5.5	100.0
Australia	20.0	6.2	19.9	43.7	10.1	100.0
Canada	33.3	22.8	19.7	17.6	6.6	100.0
E.C.	9.1	5.3	4.6	61.1	19.8	100.0
U.S.A.	23.7	10.6	2.6	47.8	15.3	100.0
Time Period:	**1979–80 to 1984–85**					
Exporting Region						
Market Share:						
Argentina	1.6	57.4	10.8	28.7	1.6	100.0
Australia	9.4	16.7	15.2	52.6	6.1	100.0
Canada	19.4	39.2	17.5	20.2	3.8	100.0
E.C.	3.3	33.7	5.2	46.1	11.8	100.0
U.S.A.	16.5	12.7	11.4	50.9	8.5	100.0

Source: Based on data from International Wheat Council, *World Wheat Statistics*, various issues.

The World Trading Environment for Wheat

The results reported in Table 3 only provide an accounting, within the framework of the constant market share model, of past patterns of export growth. Conclusions regarding the competitive effect must be treated with considerable caution; in a trading environment in which export subsidies have been extensively and increasingly used, these, rather than factors underlying comparative advantage, are likely to have been a source of market share gains. It is clear from the domestic and external grains policy pursued by the United States since 1985 that politicians in that country have perceived declines in U.S. export market shares for wheat and other grains as being primarily due to export subsidies and other unfair trading practices by its grain exporting competitors. Our analysis and other evidence shows that other factors, including the regional distribution of exports, may also have been associated with export performance in wheat markets in the early to mid-1980s. American policy and actions likely caused some of these changes; two factors that seem to be of importance in this context are the 1980 U.S. grain embargo on sales to the USSR and the domestic grains policy followed by the U.S. under the 1981 Farm Bill.

Scrutiny of Soviet import behavior since the 1980 embargo suggests increased diversification of the sources of grain import supplies since then (see Table 6), to the benefit of other suppliers during a period when Soviet import growth has been substantial. This factor likely contributed to the negative market distribution effect exhibited for U.S. wheat exports in the most recent time period considered in the analysis.

The 1981 Farm Bill was based on over-optimistic projections of future price and trade increases for grains. This feature, and the relatively strong U.S. dollar in the early 1980s, contributed to the situation wherein U.S. loan rates and associated price support operations were higher than market clearing levels of grain prices in world markets, leading to consequent loss of market share in export markets and the accumulation of large levels of U.S. grain stocks, setting the stage for the major reorientation of U.S. grain pricing policy under the 1985 Farm Bill and the subsequent and continuing world grain trade war.

The world grain market tends to display certain characteristics of an oligopolistic exporting sector, being dominated by a relatively small number of large exporters, each of which has some ability to influence market prices. In such markets, sellers tend to follow interdependent pricing policies and often emphasize non-price forms of competition, such as quality attributes, technical assistance to users, or favorable credit terms. Oligopolistic pricing behavior may involve various forms of price leadership and periods of relative price stability; intense price rivalry may be evident occasionally if sellers pursue an aggressive pricing strategy intended to restore or achieve the desired level of market share. The latter situation has characterized price behaviour in world markets for wheat and other grains since 1985 when the U.S. initiated its export

TABLE 6
IMPORT SOURCES OF MAJOR WHEAT MARKETS: THE PERCENT-
AGE OF IMPORTS BY MAJOR WHEAT MARKETS FROM MAJOR
WHEAT EXPORTERS, 1959–60 TO 1968–69, 1969–70 TO 1978–79, AND
1979–80 TO 1984–85

Exporting Region:	Argentina	Australia	Canada	EC	USA	Others	Total
Time Period: 1959–60 to 1968–69 Importing Region							
Market Share:							
Developed	6.3	11.2	35.1	8.6	30.5	8.2	100.0
East. Europe	1.8	2.8	27.5	8.5	8.3	51.1	100.0
C.P. Asia	7.4	39.7	32.5	7.4	10.0	3.3	100.0
Middle Income	9.6	9.1	5.9	11.2	55.1	9.0	100.0
Low Income	0.3	9.3	7.0	3.2	79.4	0.9	100.0
Time Period: 1969–70 to 1978–79 Importing Region							
Market Share:							
Developed	3.5	11.5	30.7	3.9	45.2	5.3	100.0
East. Europe	3.8	4.0	27.0	3.1	25.2	36.8	100.0
C.P. Asia	2.9	25.8	43.8	4.4	10.7	12.4	100.0
Middle Income	5.8	14.2	9.1	14.4	50.5	5.9	100.0
Low Income	2.0	10.8	12.0	15.6	54.5	5.2	100.0
Time Period: 1979–80 to 1984–85 Importing Region							
Market Share:							
Developed	0.8	9.6	29.1	3.7	54.8	2.0	100.0
East. Europe	13.7	8.7	29.0	18.7	21.0	8.9	100.0
C.P. Asia	6.7	17.4	28.6	5.2	38.4	3.6	100.0
Middle Income	4.5	15.3	9.1	15.3	50.4	5.5	100.0
Low Income	1.9	11.7	10.3	23.9	47.9	4.2	100.0

Source: Based on data from International Wheat Council, *World Wheat Statistics*, various issues.

enhancement program (EEP). The EEP, an export subsidy program involving bonuses of payments-in-kind from U.S. grain stocks, was initially targeted at markets in which the U.S. considered that it had lost market share due to EC export restitutions (cash subsidies paid to EC grain exporters, bridging the gap between the internal support prices and lower world market prices). Increasingly, however, the EEP has been applied more broadly to a wide range of markets and by 1988 this program was accounting for more than 60 per cent of all U.S. wheat export sales (USDA, 1988).

The most obvious end result of the intense price rivalry in world markets for grains in the mid- to late 1980s is that world prices have been driven to abnormally low levels. As Table 1 indicates, market share adjustment has been relatively minor until recently, reflecting the feature that all other grain exporters have followed the pricing lead of the U.S. in order to retain market share, as well as the lack of other production alternatives to grains in some exporting regions (particularly Argentina and western Canada), and increased levels of government-funded financial assistance to grain growers (as in Canada). Cessation of destructive price-warring strategies in world grain markets is of major importance to the achievement of a less distorted trading environment for grains.

Impact of the Canada-United States Free Trade Agreement on Grain Trade

Despite the fact that in the mid-1980s the United States was Canada's leading agricultural trading partner and despite recent increases in the export of Canadian grains to the United States, the majority by far of Canadian grain exports are to markets other than the U.S., in which Canada and the U.S. are major competitors. In 1986, Canadian exports of grains totalled $3.5 billion; only 3.7 percent of these were to the United States (Agriculture Canada, 1987). The provisions of the Canada-United States trade agreement are not likely to cause great changes in cross-border grain trade. Under the agreement, each nation's tariffs on grain and related products sold to each other will fall over a period of 10 years (although duties on animal feeds will be removed immediately after the agreement becomes effective). It is agreed that direct export subsidies will not be used on bilateral agricultural trade between the two countries. The agreement also encompasses elimination of Canadian import licenses for wheat, oats and barley when grain support levels are equivalent in both countries. Changes in the institutional procedures of marketing Canadian grain are not expected as a result of the agreement. The agreement also specifies a method of calculating producer support levels in both countries that is consistent with the proposals that each has made for use of producer subsidy equivalent measures in the current GATT negotiations on agricultural trade. One further change will remove rail transport subsidies on grain (and oilseed) products moving through West Coast ports into the United States. Overall, the provisions regarding bilateral trade in Canadian and American grains may be more significant as a precursor to multilateral negotiations on grain trade under GATT than in their effect on the bilateral grain trade of these two nations.

Conclusions and Implications for the Canadian Grains Sector

Despite the increasing importance of United States-Canada agricultural trade and the agreement relating to trade between these two countries, the most important issues in both nations regarding trade access to major markets for grains are with respect to other markets. The current (1986–1990) Uruguay Round of multilateral trade negotiations is, therefore, potentially of much greater importance to the grain exporting sectors of both Canada and the United States than is the Canada-United States trade agreement.

Substantial reductions in the extent of government intervention and protection in the grains sectors of many producing and trading nations may be extremely difficult to achieve but modest reductions in protection combined with a reduction in export subsidization and import restrictions is likely to yield gains to producers in Argentina, Australia and Canada. Even with liberalized world trade in grains, the real price levels for grains are likely to continue to follow a declining trend in the long run due to the driving force of technological change in agricultural production. It is apparent that factors other than protectionism alone have contributed to the changed structure of world markets in wheat over recent decades. Changes in technology and changing economic conditions have also contributed to these changes in structure. The importance of the GATT negotiations for world trade in both wheat and coarse grains is likely to depend not only on success in provisions that relate specifically to grains but also on whether the negotiations are successful in liberalizing general trading opportunities for medium and lower income countries and thus encouraging income growth in these countries. For many of these countries, which are forecast to be the major source of future demand increases for grains, the problems of debt levels and of debt-servicing costs are also likely to continue to be important influences on foreign exchange availability and the ability to import.

Overall, the major priorities in improving the international grain trading environment include the cessation of the grain trade war, reform of and effective application of GATT rules governing world trade in agricultural products, including grains, and intensified efforts to strengthen the economic performance of the global economy, in particular, the economic performance of middle-income developing countries.

NOTES

1. Support under the Farming for the Future program of the Agricultural Research Council of Alberta for the research on market shares in the world wheat market reported here is gratefully acknowledged as is the research assistance of Xaio Yuan Dong.

2. An analogous consideration of the effect of the commodity composition of a country's exports can be made but is not considered in this paper, since wheat is treated here as a single commodity.

REFERENCES

Agriculture Canada. (1987, August). *Canada's Trade in Agicultural Products, 1984, 1985, and 1986*. Ottawa: Minister of Supply and Services.

International Wheat Council. *World Wheat Statistics*. Various statistics. London, England.

International Wheat Council. (1987, 16 November). *Long-Term Outlook for Grains Imports by Developing Countries*, London, England.

International Wheat Council. (1988, 4 February). *Market Report*, London, England.

Leamer, E.E. and R.M. Stern. (1970). *Quantitative International Economics*. Boston: Allyn and Bacon.

Richardson, J. D. (1971). "Constant-Market-Shares Analysis of Export Growth." *Journal of International Economics, 1*, 227–239.

Stern, M. (1967). *Foreign Trade and Economic Growth in Italy*. New York: Frederick A. Praeger.

U.S. Department of Agriculture, Economic Research Service. (1988, May). *Agricultural Outlook*, Washington, D.C., 20.

Veeman, M.M. and T.S. Veeman. (1987, September). *Final Report to Farming for the Future Council on Export Markets for Western Canadian Wheat: Trends and Market Mix*. Mimeo, Edmonton, Alberta: Alberta Agriculture.

Veeman, M. M. (1987). "Hedonic Price Functions for Wheat in the WorldMarket: Implications for Canadian Wheat Export Strategy." *Canadian Journal of Agricultural Economics, 35*, 535–552.

CHAPTER 12

A MARKETING STRATEGY FOR CANADIAN BEEF EXPORTS TO JAPAN

W.A. Kerr and S.E. Cullen

The process of trade liberalization is often accompanied by the expectation that additional economic benefits will accrue to those sectors where barriers to exports are reduced. These expectations, however, are based on an implicit assumption that the domestic industry will be able to respond, in a significant fashion, to the opportunities created. In fact, the ability of firms in an industry to respond to a new trading environment may be constrained by a number of factors operating in the domestic economy. In particular, in an environment of constrained trade, domestic marketing systems may evolve in ways which are not sufficiently flexible to meet the needs of international markets. This is particularly important in agriculture, where there is a significant degree of intervention in the marketing process. As a result, either the market signals received by firms become distorted or regulations prevent the appropriate response. In addition, the institutions, whether public or private, required to expedite international transactions may not have developed. Hence, when trade liberalization has taken place and the expected domestic response is not forthcoming, a review of the existing marketing institutions is suggested. This review should be conducted with a view to developing a strategy which will facilitate the attainment of the benefits which the new trading environment provides.

It will be argued here that a significant liberalization of Japanese beef import restrictions has taken place over the last few years and that the Canadian industry has failed to respond to that liberalization. An even greater liberalization of the Japanese beef importing system will take place between 1988 and 1993. It is important that Canada take advantage of the opportunities which will arise as a result of this new phase of import liberalization. To facilitate an understanding of the complex issues involved in exporting beef to Japan, an in-depth review of the marketing systems, both in Canada and Japan, is presented. Based on this analysis the key elements of an appropriate marketing strategy are outlined.

Consumption of beef in Japan has been increasing throughout the entire period since the Second World War. This growth in consumption has been filled from expansion of domestic production and from increased imports. Although Japanese beef policy is extremely protectionist, import quotas have been increasing. For example, Japan agreed in 1984 to increase its total beef import quota by 9000 tonnes a year for the period 1984–87. This represented a 25 per cent increase over 1983. Largely as a result of political pressure from the United States, the majority of this increase (27,600 of the 36,000 tonnes) was in the high-quality-beef (H.Q.B.) portion of the quota (Mori and Gorman, 1985) and represents an increase of ninety percent for imports of this product. Further, as Table 1 illustrates, actual imports have significantly exceeded the official quotas in recent years.

TABLE 1
JAPANESE BEEF AND VEAL IMPORTS

	Total Import Quota[1]	Actual Imports[2]
	(tonnes)	
1983	141,000	211,000
1984	150,000	222,000
1985	159,000	226,000
1986	168,000	268,000
1987	177,000	308,000*

* Secretariat estimate.

Sources: 1) Mori, H. and W.D. Gorman (1985), "Issues, Facts and Opportunities for Exports of U.S. Beef to Japan," *Agribusiness, 1*, 211–218.
2) GATT (1987) *The International Market for Meat, 1986/87*, Geneva: General Agreement on Tariffs and Trade.

As a result of further negotiations between Japan and the United States, starting in 1988 Japan will increase its import quota for beef by 60,000 tonnes per year until 1990. At that point quotas will be abandoned and the *ad valorem* tariff on imported beef will be raised from its current 25 per cent to 70 per cent in 1991. The tariff will then be reduced over the next two years to 50 per cent. After 1993 the tariff will be part of General Agreement on Tariffs and Trade (GATT) negotiations. Beef exporting countries will be positioning themselves to take advantage of this major liberalization. It will be extremely important for Canadian exporters to establish import channels over the 1988–93 period so that a continued increase in market share can be assured. Hence, it will be necessary at the outset to work within the current quota and regulatory system and to be actively involved as the new import regime evolves.

Although the potential for the export of Canadian beef to Japan has been previously identified (Kerr, 1985; Kerr and Ulmer, 1984), the Canadian beef cattle industry has consistently failed to capture any significant portion of expanding Japanese imports. In the case of the H.Q.B. quota this failure is particularly disappointing for the Canadian industry and policy makers as Canadian production methods and standard are similar to those of the major H.Q.B. exporter, the United States. Between 1977 and 1983 the Canadian share of Japanese beef imports remained under 2 per cent while U.S. imports rose from less than 10 per cent to over 27 per cent, and as Figure 1 illustrates, by 1986 the U.S. share had increased to 32.6 per cent while Canada's share was only 1.4 per cent. Table 2 provides the total quantity of Canadian exports between 1975 and 1986.

FIGURE 1
SHARE OF JAPAN'S BEEF AND VEAL IMPORTS

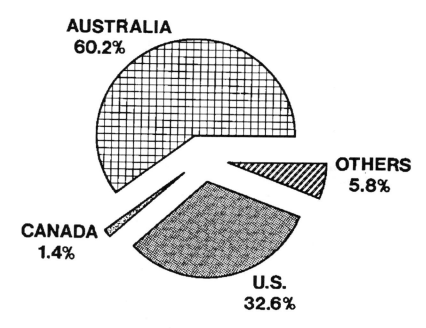

AUSTRALIA
60.2%

OTHERS
5.8%

CANADA
1.4%

U.S.
32.6%

While it is possible to contend that Japanese acquiescence to U.S. political pressure regarding beef has prevented Canada from accessing a larger portion of the H.Q.B. quota, there is little evidence that the Japanese beef quota allocation institutions discriminate against non-U.S. tenders (Longworth, 1983) and the explanation for Canada's poor export performance may lie elsewhere. It will be the basic contention of this paper that major changes will be required in the methods by which Canada markets beef before it can expect any success in penetrating the Japanese beef market. The horizontally segmented marketing mechanisms existing in Canada and the heavy degree of government involvement in both Canada and Japan suggest that a comprehensive Canadian strategy needs to be developed. It is the elements of such a strategy which constitute the subject of this paper.

TABLE 2
CANADIAN BEEF EXPORTS TO JAPAN
(BASIS DRESSED CARCASS)

	Metric Tonnes
1975	1,152
1976	1,984
1977	2,314
1978	2,757
1979	3,783
1980	4,616
1981	5,597
1982	3,746
1983	3,264
1984	3,308
1985	3,956
1986	3,846

Source: Statistics Canada, Catalogue 23–203.

Given that any major alteration in the marketing system for beef in Canada will require considerable commitment of resources, the market potential should be sufficiently large to justify this expenditure. Therefore the first part of the paper assesses the future potential for increased Japanese beef consumption. The relevant Japanese and Canadian marketing institutions are next discussed. A formal marketing strategy is outlined and some brief conclusions are then presented.

Japanese Market Potential

Although taste and cultural factors influence the consumption of meat, including beef, there is a consistent and strong relationship between income levels and per capita consumption (Cho, 1982). This relationship is illustrated in Table 3. The major and obvious exception is Japan. Annual per capita Japanese beef consumption increased from 1.2 kg in 1960 to 3.5 kg in 1980 and grew at an average of 3.2 per cent annually from 1972 to 1983 (Coyle, 1983). Of course consumption is also a function of price, and it is clear that the Japanese government has kept domestic beef prices 300 to 500 per cent higher than the landed import price (Coyle) so that consumption is considerably constrained. The motives which led to the implementation and maintenance of the "expensive" beef policy by the Japanese government are many. The primary motivations are concerns over food security, the pace of rural adjustment, political and sociological aspects of the meat trade, and conservation of foreign exchange.[1] Given the political sensitivity of the beef industry, any major move away from the "expensive" beef policy in the near future seems unlikely.

TABLE 3
TOTAL MEAT CONSUMPTION AND GDP/CAPITA
SELECTED COUNTRIES
(1981)

Country	GDP/Capita in U.S.$[1]	Per Capita Consumption (KG/YR)[2]
Turkey	1,262	24.5
Portugal	2,398	54.4
Greece	3,769	63.3
Ireland	4,855	95.3
Italy	6,123	76.5
New Zealand	7,957	101.9
United Kingdom	8,886	74.2
Japan	9,606	32.6
France	10,552	110.5
Australia	10,763	110.8
West Germany	11,076	98.0
Denmark	11,350	79.7
Canada	11,741	98.7
United States	12,647	114.3

Sources: 1) OECD Dept. of Economics and Statistics, National Accounts 1952–1981, Vol. 1. 2) Meat Balances in OECD Countries 1976–1981.

The means by which the Japanese government has maintained high domestic beef prices is complex, but its central element has been import quotas. Even at high beef prices, growth in demand can be met from increased imports if domestic production fails to grow apace with demand. There is considerable evidence that the domestic livestock supply is becoming very price inelastic and, therefore, no significant increases in output can be expected without major price increases. The crucial factors determining imports are then, the constraints on increased domestic production and expectations of demand growth.

Although there may be some potential for increased domestic Japanese beef production, as noted above, any major increases appear unlikely without substantial price increases. Japanese beef production has three major components: the traditional Waygu sector, the dairy beef sector, and cull animals from both these sources. The Waygu sector evolved, by careful breeding, from traditional draft animal stocks. These animals are used exclusively for beef production and supply that portion of the consumer market which prefers, by North American standards, overfat and extremely well-marbled beef. This product is, however, particularly suited to traditional Japanese cooking methods. Waygu production takes place on an extremely small scale (60 per cent of herds contain two or fewer cattle and 99 per cent of herds have less than 20 cattle) and is primarily a supplemental enterprise on small or part-time farms. Such operations can use available forage efficiently but growth is constrained by limitations on forage expansion, the opportunity cost of labor and the cost of purchased inputs. In addition, Waygu animals are not extensively used in feedlot production as their production efficiency is less than that of dairy steers. Even with a substantial increase in prices over the last decade, Waygu production has effectively stabilized with no apparent innovations available to increase production (Longworth, 1983).

Most of the growth in the Japanese beef industry over the last 25 years has come about as a result of expansion in the dairy sector. For dietary reasons the government encouraged the production of milk and the result, of course, was increased numbers of dairy steers available for the beef fattening industry. Milk production has reached self-sufficiency, if not surplus levels, over the last few years, and herd expansion has ceased. To stabilize cow numbers, over a short adjustment period additional heifers not needed for further herd expansion will be available for fattening, but subsequently the number of steers and heifers available for beef production will cease to grow. Although some improvements in management are possible—such as reductions in calf mortality and double suckling—no sustainable sources of additional animals are evident. Finally, as both the Waygu and dairy herds are stabilizing, no additional cull cows will be available for the low quality processed meat trade. Thus it would appear that significant increases in production are unlikely to be forthcoming.

Although the Japanese economy is not likely to sustain the rates of growth experienced in the past, continued economic expansion can be expected and, along with it, growth in income. Estimates of the Japanese income elasticity for beef range between 1.1 and 2.4 with 1.5 being approximately the mean (Longworth, 1983). Beef consumption in Japan is not homogeneous and is characterized generally by high and low quality products. Goddart (1983) estimated a disaggregated beef model for Japan and determined that there is relatively more potential for the import of high quality beef product, such as that produced in North America, than there is for low quality beef from Oceania. This suggests substitution within diets as incomes grow. Japanese consumption levels remain sufficiently low that there is little health concern associated with the increased fat content of such meat. All of this implies increasing market potential for beef produced in Canada.

Official Japanese projections (MAFF, 1980) suggest that imports would be 260,000 tonnes by 1990, an 84 per cent increase over the 1983 quota. These estimates are considered conservative (Longworth, 1983), and USDA projections for 1990 (Coyle, 1983) range between 601,000 and 680,000 tonnes. The evidence suggests that the Japanese import market should continue to grow and therefore may justify considerable effort to secure a portion of this market. As well, it is not necessary to secure a particularly large segment for it to have substantial effect on the Canadian industry. Given that import quotas are administered quantities, they may not reflect consumer preferences but rather the import quota holders' behavior. As Goddard (1983) has observed, "How closely import quota holders' behavior coincides with consumer preferences will depend to a large degree on the market structure in the importing retailing sector" (p. 27). It is to this problem that we now turn.

The Japanese Beef Importing System

The Japanese beef importing system is extremely complex and is characterized by a number of self-interest groups, both public and private, attempting to individually maximize their share of the margin which arises between the landed price of imported beef and the domestic wholesale price. The binding constraint on imports is the various quota allocations, but the Japanese government collects a 25 per cent *ad valorem* (c.i.f.) tariff on all beef imports. Although this tariff is neutral between importers it is important in Japanese decisions, as the amount of the tax increases with the per unit value of the imports (a function of quality) and, hence, affects the margin between the price at which imported beef is available and the wholesale price (also a function of quality). Clearly, in the period after quotas are removed and tariffs increase the determination of this margin will become of increased importance to importers. There are four major actors in the beef importing system: private firms which actually import beef, private end users of beef, and two public bodies with mandates to administer the import quota system to the best advantage of the domestic livestock industry.[2]

The number of firms which are allowed to import beef is strictly limited by the Ministry of International Trade and Industry (MITI), which is the powerful ministry responsible for developing and administering Japan's overall industrial and trade strategy. Although approved firms are added and deleted from the list from time to time, the number has remained fairly stable at around thirty-five. Once an intermediate or end user receives an allocation from the import quota it must contract with these importing firms to provide foreign beef of the correct specification. This applies to government agents as well as private firms. These importing firms attempt to maximize the difference between their landed price of beef and the price at which they release it to quota holders. Quota holders are allowed to freely choose among the importing firms with which they wish to deal. It is essential, however, that any exporter have a good working relationship with these importing firms. Without established reputations with such firms, access to the Japanese beef market is prohibited.

Although the actual end users of imported beef are individual firms,[3] quota allocations are made to groupings of users such as associations of meat canners, chain stores, consumer co-operatives, butchers or wholesalers. These associations are left to apportion their quota allotment among their members. Limiting quota allocations to such groups has the immediate effect of preventing foreign beef firms from entering the beef market directly as retailers or wholesalers and acquiring quota to import their own lines. There is both the problem of being allowed to join the association and, if successful, of ensuring that the association allocates quota in a non-discriminatory manner. Consequently, potential exporters must develop working relationships with the individual members of such user groups who have sufficient influence within their particular association to ensure that they receive allocations on a continuing basis.

About 90 per cent of the available quota is allocated only to exporters on the "preferred brand" list. Essentially, in order to be put on the preferred brand list, one must have provided trouble free imports by consistently conforming to Japan's strict set of health, safety and cutting specifications. Although it is relatively easy to have an end user nominate a new brand for a trial, if one does not meet the standards or is, for some reason, deleted from the preferred list it is extremely difficult to obtain a second chance. The constraints of "auditioning" are particularly inhibiting, as packing plant employees require a period of "learning by doing" to be fully competent at consistently satisfying the Japanese regulations. Brands may be determined on the basis of within-company lines, individual firm brands or a brand for an association of exporters. Clearly, product consistency is essential for widening the group of end users who will utilize a brand. End users are interested in maximizing their returns, which are determined by the difference between the price for which they can sell the product and the price which they can negotiate with importing firms minus the charges which the appropriate government agency levies on the imported product. These agencies are our next area of focus.

The more important of the two government agencies involved in the beef quota system is the Livestock Industry Promotion Corporation (LIPC), which allocates approximately 80 per cent of the import quotas. Global import quotas are established by the MITI for six month intervals, although the dates of their announcement is not standardized. Announced quotas can, however, be expanded or reduced, which increases the difficulty of export planning. Japanese beef quotas can be grouped into two categories—general quotas and special quotas. The general (and much larger) quotas can be further sub-divided into two portions—the private and the LIPC's, the latter's share being approximately 90 per cent. The LIPC is an administrative entity under the direction of the Livestock Bureau of the Japanese Ministry of Agriculture, Forestry and Fisheries (MAFF). It has the dual mandate of administering the beef quota to support and stabilize domestic beef prices and promoting the development of the domestic beef production industry. In essence, the LIPC attempts to manipulate flows of imports by the rate at which it allocates its portion of the quota and its apportionment among product types so as to keep domestic prices within pre-established bands. The LIPC is also charged with administering funds to restructure and modernize the beef industry. It is allowed to collect direct or indirect levies on imported beef as part of the means by which the large margins between the imported and wholesale prices of beef arising from the import quota system can be transferred from private to public hands. Hence, the LIPC has an institutional incentive to maximize its levies subject to the constraint that it keeps domestic beef prices within the acceptable bounds. A portion of the general quota is now designated H.Q.B. and, as will be argued later, this is the only portion with which Canada can realistically be concerned. The LIPC has a number of mechanisms in place to distribute its portion of the quota. These each have aspects which allow the LIPC to capture a significant portion of the import-wholesale margin.

For over 60 per cent of its quota the LIPC acts as the direct purchaser. In other words, it contracts directly with the importing firms, takes delivery of the product, and then auctions the stocks to end user groups. Part of these imports may be placed in storage to aid the LIPC in its short-run price stabilization efforts. The LIPC clearly has the ability to capture a large proportion of the import-wholesale margin via this mechanism and, thus, an incentive to import only that mix of products which will maximize this margin.

The second most important mechanism by which the LIPC allocates its quota is a system of "designated" stores. Designated stores participate in a program whereby they agree to sell quantities of beef at retail prices approximately 20 per cent below the market price. The rationale for this is to make some beef available at reduced prices so a wider segment of the public can acquire a taste for the product which, in the long run, will increase demand to the eventual benefit of the domestic beef industry. Participating stores are allocated quota and then contract with the authorised import firms for supplies. Once the contract is made the LIPC checks that the sale price meets the specified level and then adds a levy to the import price to capture the difference. These levies are fixed for certain periods and are not differentiated by quality, so that there is an incentive for firms to import higher quality product to reduce the proportion of the margin which is captured by the levy. The greatest benefit again arises from importing commodities which will produce the largest margin.

The final mechanism used by the LIPC is a tender system whereby the end users are informed of a quota allocation and then negotiate with importing firms. The contract is then awarded to the importing firm offering the lowest price. The LIPC purchases the product on behalf of the end user and subsequently resells the product to the end user at the specified price, hence capturing the margin. Again there is an incentive for the LIPC to maximize the difference in the two prices.

The portion of the general quota which is not allocated to the LIPC—the private quota—is administered by the second public body involved in the meat import trade, the Japanese Meat Conference (JMC). The JMC is one of the quasi-public "judicial person" organizations which are unique to the Japanese economy. It allocates quota among end users who then negotiate with the importing firms to fill their quota. The JMC then collects a levy on the imported beef but its levies are less flexible than those of the LIPC and, hence, less effective in capturing the import-wholesale margin. As with LIPC quotas there is an incentive for firms to import beef which maximizes the import-wholesale margin so as to reduce the proportion lost to the levy.

There is only one portion of the special quotas with which Canada should be concerned, the Hotel Quota.[4] This is administered by the JMC, which allocates it to one end use intermediary who negotiates with the Hotel Association; contracts are then let to importing firms. Again the JMC collects levies on this quota and there is, of course, an incentive to maximize the margin. The current Japanese importing system is summarized in Figure 2.

The effectiveness of the LIPC and the JMC in capturing the margin is in part constrained by a degree of administrative inflexibility and in part by lobbying and collusion among importing and end user groups (Longworth, 1983). The current importing system should be perceived as a dynamic process whereby the four groups maneuver to maximize their individual portions of the import-wholesale margin. According to the recent agreement negotiated between Japan and the U.S., the LIPC is to be phased out in 1991. This will allow more direct contact between importers and exporters. The demise of the LIPC will mean that the remaining three groups will vie for a share in the import-wholesale margin; how the shares will be apportioned is not yet clear. While the margin is likely to be reduced as a result of liberalization there is, however, an incentive for all groups to maximize that margin. The problem for any exporter is to provide the type of product which will maximize that margin. This problem, within the Canadian context, is addressed below.

The Canadian Beef Marketing System

To understand the constraints to satisfying Japanese requirements inherent in the current Canadian beef marketing system, one must first understand Japanese beef preferences and how they are subsequently reflected in prices. Beef quality in Japan is basically an increasing function of the fat content of the meat, specifically intra-muscular fat known as marbling. Increasing the degree of marbling in an animal is partially a function of the time an animal is fed a high energy finishing ration and partially a function of the components of the ration. The upper bound to the degree of marbling is determined by the biological limitations of the animals. Over their lifetime, the ability of cattle to add to intra-muscular fat declines and an increasing amount of weight gain arises from accumulations of surface or outside fat and, hence, waste.[5] The Japanese beef grading system reflects these preferences with the highest grade assigned to the most heavily marbled carcasses. The Japanese grading system and the approximate[6] period which cattle remain on feed to achieve these grades are presented in Table 4. Japanese beef prices increase as quality increases with the top grades receiving roughly three times the price of the lowest grade (see Table 5).[7] Thus, Japanese beef prices are an increasing function of time on feed, although the rate of increase declines given that the period an animal is within a grade range generally increases with the grade (see Table 4).

FIGURE 2
THE JAPANESE BEEF IMPORTING SYSTEM

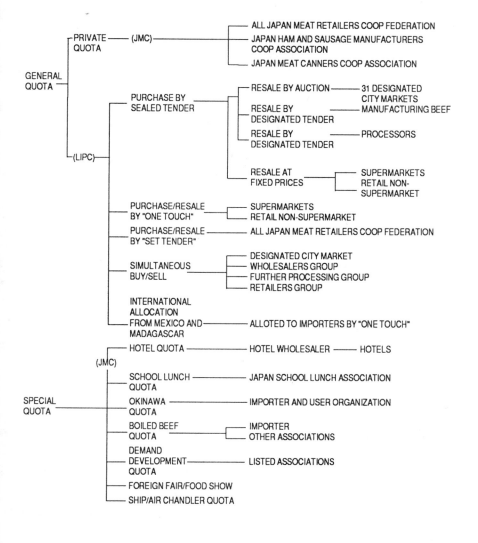

TABLE 4
THE JAPANESE AND CANADIAN BEEF GRADING SYSTEMS

Time on Feed	Japanese Grade	Canadian Grade
less than 100 days	Utility (togai)	B 2
115 - 125 days	3rd grade (nami)	A 1
120 - 130 days	3rd grade (nami)	A 2
130 - 140 days	3rd grade (nami)	A 3
140 - 180 days	3rd grade (nami)	A 4
180 - 280 days	2nd grade (chu)	A 4
280 - 440 days	1st grade (jo)	*
440 - 660 days	Superior (gokujo)	*
up to 900 days	Supreme (tokusen)	*

* No practical comparison can be made in these ranges as no Canadian cattle are fed for such periods and hence graded. As the Canadian system has an age component, animals fed this long would be discounted for their age and drop into the lower B or C grades.

TABLE 5
AVERAGE ANNUAL PRICES AT TOKYO BEEF CARCASS
AUCTION 1985 ($/KG.)*

Grade	Wagyu Steer	Wagyu Female	Dairy Steer	Dairy Female
Utility	$5.90	$5.61	$5.16	$5.02
Nami	8.57	8.09	6.73	6.23
Chu	10.32	10.10	7.53	7.69
Jo	12.33	12.57	9.04	9.29
Superior	14.54	15.23	–	–
Supreme	17.34	19.37	–	–

* Converted to Canadian dollars at a rate of 1 Can$ = 175 Yen.

Source: MAFF (1986) *Monthly Meat Marketing Statistics.*

Canadian taste in beef, in contrast to the Japanese, exhibits a preference for leanness, or a low degree of marbling. Tenderness is defined as an inverse function of age for Canadian beef, so that the beef production system in Canada strives to produce a mature carcass with a low fat content in the minimum amount of time. Canadian cattle grading A1, the highest grade, are usually on feed for approximately 120 days (see Table 4). Canadian cattle grading A2 receive approximately the same price as

A1 animals but usually are less profitable as the additional time on feed increases costs. Cattle grading A3 and A4 are considered overfat and are considerably discounted in the market. Such animals are genuine production mistakes in Canada and their numbers are small; typically less than one percent of all animals grade A4.[8] Generally then, Canadian beef exhibits an extremely low degree of marbling by Japanese standards and consequently falls within the lowest grades.

Beef with a low degree of marbling can be attained by two production methods. It can be achieved, as in Canada, by feeding animals a high energy, high cost, grain based ration over a short period. If one is not concerned with tenderness, a similar degree of marbling can be produced by grazing animals over a longer period of time. Grass-fed systems are considerably cheaper than grain-fed systems. The beef industry in Australia and New Zealand uses such grass-fed technology and can produce similarly marbled carcasses at a much lower cost than in Canada. However, Japanese cooking methods receive no advantage from the tenderness associated with the youth of Canadian beef. Hence, Canadian beef cannot compete with Oceanic product for the low quality portion of the general or special quotas.[9]

The so-called "high quality" (H.Q.B.) quota is largely filled by U.S. beef which is, by Japanese standards, still of relatively low quality. Tastes for beef in the United States exhibit a desire for slightly more fat than is required in Canada, and the U.S. grading system has a marbling component. Animals receiving the two highest U.S. grades, U.S. Prime and U.S. Choice, have usually been on feed for 130 to 150 days and thus are better marbled than Canadian carcasses but still within the lower Japanese grades. They are, however, by Japanese standards, of higher quality than Canadian carcasses and therefore U.S. beef fills a great proportion of the Japanese H.Q.B. import quota. Canadian firms that do ship to Japan do so by acquiring some of the few heavy carcasses available and processing them to Japanese specifications.

The essence of the Canadian problem in marketing beef to Japan is that the product does not competitively meet the requirements of the market. The situation can be summarized in Figure 3. Canadian domestic prices peak for product which has been on feed for approximately 120 days. Over 90 per cent of Canadian beef produced specifically for the high quality Canadian market falls close to this marketing specification. Any product shipped to Japan must have the transportation and insurance costs added to production coasts to determine the landed c.i.f. price in Japan. These are assumed invariant with output. To this must be added the tariff which increases with the value of the product as it is calculated on an *ad valorum* basis. This becomes the price at which imported product becomes available in Japan. For product on feed for 120 days the prices received in Japan are not sufficient to cover the import availability price. Mori and Gorman (1985) suggest that top grade U.S. beef in Texas was approximately competitive in the Japanese market. In other words, the Japanese price intersected the price at which imports were available in Japan for animals which had been on feed for approximately 150 days.

In terms of a marketing strategy, the way to increase Canadian exports seems clear:
beef must be tailored to Japanese tastes. In terms of marketing it is necessary to find
that output, defined according to time on feed, which maximizes the import-wholesale
margin. As suggested in the previous section, this is the type of beef that the various
actors in the Japanese importing system have the greatest incentive to import. It is also
the product for which there is the most latitude to exploit any imperfect information

FIGURE 3
THE STRUCTURE OF BEEF PRICES IN JAPAN AND NORTH AMERICA

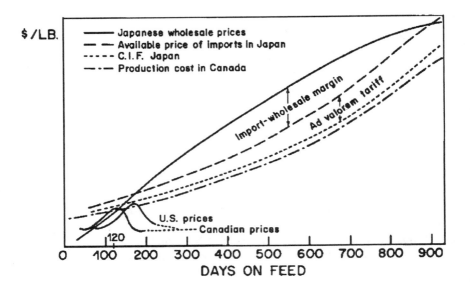

on the part of Japanese importers and, hence, increase Canadian profits.[10] Very little
is known, however, about either the biological parameters or cost relationships for
animals kept on feed under North American conditions in excess of 170 days. In the
only available economic study (Mori and Gorman, 1985), an estimate made for U.S.
cattle kept on feed for 250 days indicated that profits appeared to be above those
available from animals fed for 150 days. This tends to confirm our hypothesis. In a
strict cost sense, the costs of mixed grain rations in Canada tend to be about 50 per
cent of those in Japan. If Canadian cattle have a similar biological performance to
Japanese breeds over extended feeding periods, the maximum import-wholesale
margin should be found at some time on feed in excess of 150 days. Unfortunately,
no Canadian information exists on either the costs of production associated with the
entire range of feeding periods exceeding approximately 150 days or on the exact
relationship between Japanese beef prices and the time animals spend on feed in Japan.

These are the two vital pieces of information required before the maximum import-wholesale gap can be established. Before any progress can be made in penetrating the Japanese market, research needs to be conducted on these two topics. Although research using large animals is expensive, given sufficient resources good preliminary results could be attained in two to three years.

If these were the only constraints in the Canadian marketing system then a comprehensive strategy would hardly be required. However, there are other aspects of the current Canadian beef marketing system which, without considerable changes, will prevent any expansion into the Japanese market. It is to these problems that we now turn.

Although there appears to be considerable potential for growth in the Canadian beef cattle industry via the exploitation of export potential in Japan, successful exploitation will depend on the ability of the industry and its institutions to adapt to the requirements of international marketing. However, as there has been until recently, considerable and sustained growth in Canadian beef consumption (Kerr, 1985), the industry was able to concentrate its energies on refining a marketing system which could, in the most efficient manner, satisfy Canadian tastes. Although the industry has been adept at responding to changes in Canadian tastes, the very system which adapts itself so well to Canadian requirements may well be a straight-jacket when it comes to international marketing.

The domestic marketing system which has developed for beef is a simple, efficient marketing channel which minimizes the problems associated with geographically dispersed producers with somewhat heterogeneous products while allowing farmers and ranchers a choice of markets so as to ensure a degree of competition. Its efficiency is, however, dependent on a single standard for output. The rancher knows that if he produces an animal of a certain specification he will always receive a premium price. Hence, production planning lacks a time dimension. In other words, the producer can always be assured of the best price even though it may not always be one with which a profit can be made. The market is vertically segmented, and this is possible because all buyers and sellers at each level require the same product.

Product for the Japanese market will differ from Canadian specifications and be limited in quantity. Especially in the period of market development, sales will be on a lot by lot basis and, therefore, time becomes an important element in the production process. If beef to satisfy high quality Japanese standards is to be produced then the processor must inform the packing plant who must inform the feedlot operator as to what type of animal to produce *ex ante*, i.e. before feeding starts. If there are genetically controlled traits required then those with the breeding herds—cow-calf operators—must be informed. This process suggests a far greater degree of vertical integration or designated sales than have been required to date. Certainly such *ex ante* pre-production signals cannot be accomplished through the current marketing mechanism which has ranchers delivering to a general auction system which prices product *ex post* to the production process. There are three such markets between the cow-calf operator and the processor in most instances.

Basically, to be induced to produce beef to Japanese specifications, the feedlot operator must have a reasonably secure expectation of a price which will ensure him at least the same margin as is available for animals destined for the domestic market. This must occur, at a minimum, three months (an extra 100 days on feed) before the animal is ready for market. As most high quality beef is sold chilled in Japan it cannot be stored for later sale. If the rancher cannot sell to the Japanese market the beef must be sold in the domestic market where it will be heavily discounted as overfat, while the rancher has incurred considerable extra feed and other costs due to the extended feeding period (see Figure 3). Given the vagaries of the Japanese internal quota allocation system such risks as these are likely to be perceived as unacceptable by Canadian producers, most of whom tend to be small operators.

Problems might also arise from a system of designated sales. First, what happens if a foreign sale is cancelled or falls through? Again, the beef would have to be disposed of in the domestic market, and the question would arise as to which party (parties) in the vertical chain should bear the loss. Vertical integration, of course, internalizes the problem. Second, designated sales will remove the marketing choice from primary producers and as a result opportunities for monopsonistic profits or post-contractual-opportunistic-behavior[11] may be created. Formal vertical integration is probably unrealistic for much of the beef cattle industry given the diverse and often multi-enterprise nature of firms in the agriculture industry. Further, vertical integration has been resisted and discouraged in much of the agricultural community with its preferences for family operations. There is, however, some evidence that vertical integration can provide the means to success in the Japanese market. The "new" and vertically integrated hog industry in the province of Quebec has been raising heavier hogs specifically for the Japanese market and has had considerable success. In hogs, however, the duration of the extra feeding period is short and the overfat domestic discount small relative to those for beef.

Moreover, Canadian beef marketers have been able to concentrate almost exclusively on the domestic market, which requires understanding of only one set of specifications and regulations. As a result Canadians with the experience and expertise required to deal with foreign markets are few (Gillis et al., 1985). Individuals familiar with the intricacies of the Japanese beef system and other aspects of Japanese culture are almost non-existent. This is particularly true in the areas of trimming and cutting specifications, quality control, and packaging. Further, government exporting mechanisms are tailored to ensure that only product of the highest quality (by Canadian standards) is exported. This reduces the flexibility to tailor product to the Japanese market.

If the Japanese market can be penetrated it could become a significant outlet for Canadian beef and many of the problems associated with initial entry would disappear. Admittedly, the entry period will be particularly difficult and entail considerable risks, far greater risks than the industry has had to assume in the past. And the Japanese market will never be as certain and dependable as the domestic one—foreign markets will always be beyond direct political control and thus be riskier. Obviously the exploitation of the Japanese market will require a major effort by all those involved in the Canadian beef cattle industry, and a co-ordinated effort with both private and government participation.

A Marketing Strategy

Although any comprehensive strategy for market penetration would have to be developed in considerable detail and in consultation with all interests in the Canadian beef cattle industry, this inquiry suggests that such a strategy should have the following five elements: (1) research; (2) access to improved information; (3) risk-sharing provisions; (4) the opening of market channels, and; (5) institutional reform.

Research

The major research requirements have already been indicated. The crucial elements are: (1) the formal determination of the relationship between Japanese wholesale prices and grades at the point where Canadian product enters the Japanese marketing system, (2) the performance characteristics of Canadian beef cattle when kept on feed over the longer periods required to attain higher Japanese grades. Only when these relationships are established can a target animal be selected so as to maximize the import-wholesale margin. The first of these tasks is a fairly straightforward econometric task. It may require considerable primary data collection, especially as grade averages are not likely to be specific enough given the long within-grade feeding period. Hence, this will require major expenditures of resources and most probably the employment of Japanese personnel.

The research on beef cattle performance could be undertaken at government research establishments in Canada. It would seem advantageous, however, to have the work done under commercial feedlot production conditions over the widest possible number of operations. This would have the triple advantage of making available information over a range of production conditions, familiarizing a number of producers with handling animals in longer term production before formal market penetration, and providing the well-known advantages of the "demonstration effect." Of course, other research requirements will manifest themselves as the strategy evolves; but certainly no progress is possible without this basic research.

Improved Information

Improved information needs to be made available on a number of fronts. Of primary importance is price forecasting information for the Japanese market by grade. This must be provided for the planning period required between marketing opportunities in Canada and feeding cattle for the Japanese market. Although price forecasting models are never perfect, they can be reasonably accurate over the period of a few months. Such forecasts should be backed up by in depth qualitative assessment of the policy dimensions of the Japanese beef industry.

As the Japanese market will not, especially initially, be a major component of the Canadian market, an improved market information mechanism is required to ensure farmers a competitive marketing system. Some system of specified sale days or times should be designated for beef bound for Japan, and all auctions should be linked to a central clearing house for buyers.

Personnel, both production and inspection, at processing plants will require practical experience to become familiar with both the new carcasses and the specifications. If possible a group of individuals who have direct experience in the Japanese industry should be recruited and made available to train personnel and monitor operations in the learning-by-doing period and subsequently as problems arise. If possible such individuals should be hired on short-term contracts so that they are current with respect to the Japanese industry. A program should also be formally developed to share the limited number of heavy carcasses available plus carcasses from the feeding research program so as to give the widest exposure to potential exporters.

Risk Sharing

There are two aspects to risk sharing. The first relates to the inability to export product to Japan, which could arise for a number of reasons. In the period while quotas are still in place Japanese buyers with whom marketing channels have been developed might not receive quota allocations. Quota allocations might not be made for grades which have been produced. Announced quotas could be cancelled, as was the case in 1974, after a serious deterioration in the domestic beef prices in Japan. At such times product would have to be disposed of on the domestic market with substantial discounts. In the post-quota period the tariff rate could be raised 25 per cent if beef imports grow by more than 20 per cent in any year. A fund should be established which would make payments based on the difference between the planning price and the price realized in the market. Such a fund could be financed by a fee collected from all carcasses slaughtered similar to the automatic "checkoff"[12] used to finance current funds for beef marketing activities.

The second problem could arise when the planning price and the realized price for exported product diverge. As production decisions must be made on the basis of forecast planning prices (and such prices will have a component of inaccuracy), some incentive must be provided to encourage producers to retain their cattle for long feeding rather than selling them on the domestic market. If forecast prices are favorable, available supplies could exceed expected quota allocations. If all producers wishing to supply the Japanese market were required to inform the fund of their intentions then price guarantees could be based on statistical deviations from the planning price. Such guarantees could be auctioned to producers on the basis of their willingness to accept risk. In such a fashion, expected supplies could be equated to expected imports. The mechanism would be similar to that which the central bank uses to allocate securities so that the desired interest rate is achieved. In other words, producers unwilling to accept increasing degrees of price risk would not have their bid accepted and would receive no production guarantee. Hence, there would be a signal not to produce. Basically the expected export quantities would be allocated to the firms willing to accept the greatest price risk—those that would accept a price guarantee which deviated the most from the planning price. Firms could produce beef to Japanese standards without participating but would have no price guarantee and would not be eligible for payments from the fund. If the price deviated from the planning price more than the specified guarantee then the fund would pay the deficiency. Again, such a fund could be financed by a "checkoff" system.

Marketing Channels

Every effort should be made to open marketing channels between Japanese importing firms, Japanese end users and Canadian beef companies. It is particularly important that the number of preferred Japanese brands be expanded as far as possible. Only about half a dozen Canadian firms have branded status at present, as compared to thirty to forty each in the U.S. and Australia. The expansion would serve two purposes. First, until the abandonment of quotas it would provide more marketing channels and thus increase the probability that a Japanese importing firm with Canadian links will be one which receives a quota allocation. Second, it would reduce the general effect of brand cancellation if a particular lot of Canadian product fails to meet Japanese standards. Further, joint ventures with Japanese firms should be encouraged so that they have an incentive to maintain marketing channels.

Institutional Reform

Canadian exporting regulations should be reformed so that product can be graded and inspected to the standards of the importer. This would facilitate processing and allow tailoring of the product. For example, the Canadian system of inspection is undertaken at the 12th/13th rib section while the Japanese takes place at the 7th/8th rib section. Insisting that the carcasses be examined at the Canadian domestic position has ramifications for butchering and cutability. Similar problems are manifest for a host of packaging, labeling and health regulations. Clearly some accommodation could be reached to satisfy domestic health and image concerns while making it easier for exporters to satisfy Japanese requirements.

Conclusions

Up until now, Canadian beef producers have not responded to past Japanese beef import liberalization. Moving any industry from one which is primarily a domestic supplier to one which is a competitive exporter is likely to require considerable effort. When that industry is characterized by geographically dispersed, small unit production and a perishable product, as in the beef industry, that effort will require an added element of coordination. In the case of agricultural products, the higher up the biological food chain one moves the more likely international tastes are to differ. Unless one wishes to remain the producer of low value-added agricultural goods for export, one must find ways to satisfy different tastes. The only alternative, changing foreign tastes to conform to those in the exporting country, seems a forlorn exercise given the current price levels desired by Japanese policy makers.

Any marketing exercise will require some form of strategy. Given the particular structure of Canadian beef cattle production, such a strategy must have elements which encompass the industry. The particular structure to administer such a strategy and the degree of government involvement has deliberately been avoided in this discussion. Whatever the mechanism which evolves, it must establish a long-term marketing strategy. Such formal planning is particularly foreign to the beef cattle industry; however, it is just such a formal approach to the design of industrial strategy which leads to export success, as the Japanese so convincingly demonstrate. If a strategy can be successfully implemented for exports to Japan it may have considerable additional benefits in creating a more flexible marketing system and increased confidence so that other rapidly growing markets can be entered in the future.

Finally, perhaps the most important conclusion arising from this investigation is that changes in the trading environment do not automatically lead to firms being able to exploit the opportunities created. As Canadian agriculture faces a new Japanese beef trading environment this lesson should not be overlooked by economists or policy makers. The new trading environment is likely to require a commitment to a reformed domestic environment if the expected gains are to be realized.

NOTES

1. For an in-depth analysis of the politics of the Japanese meat- livestock industry the interested reader is referred to Longworth (1983).

2. In theory their mandate also includes protection of consumer interests but there is considerable evidence that this is consistently given little weight in the agencies decisions (Longworth, 1983).

3. Including such entities as co-operatives and institutions like colleges and hospitals.

4. The other special quotas, for Okinawa, School Lunches and Cooked Beef, are basically for low quality products and not relevant to Canadian production methods.

5. This outside fat is trimmed off in the butchering process and either discarded or rendered in the bi-product trade.

6. Unfortunately, as with much of the Japanese beef industry, no English language sources on the exact feeding performance of cattle appear to exist.

7. Further, Mori and Gorman (1985) reported that for the years 1975, 1980, and 1982, on average, 3rd grade Waygu steers prices were 32 per cent higher than the lowest grade, 2nd grade 60 per cent higher, 1st grade 87 per cent higher, superior 113 per cent higher and supreme 143 per cent higher.

8. For a more complete discussion of the percentages of animals in each grade and the grade discounts see Considine et al. (1986).

9. There is a market for low quality beef in Canada which is filled by cull cows from the dairy and beef industry. Canada is not self-sufficient in this product and imports low quality beef, largely from Oceania, to make up the deficit.

10. It is assumed here that the production costs include normal profit.

11. For a discussion of post-contractual-opportunistic-behavior the interested reader is referred to Klein et al. (1978).

12. An automatic checkoff means that a fee is levied each time a carcass is slaughtered and the amount deducted from the farmer's receipts.

REFERENCES

Cho, S. (1982). "Changing Consumption Patterns for Livestock Products: Korea and Japan." In J.C. Fine and R.G. Lattimore (Eds.), *Livestock in Asia: Issues and Policies* (84–112). Ottawa: International Development Research Centre.

Considine, J.I., W.A. Kerr, G.R. Smith and S.M. Ulmer. (1986). "The Impact of a New Grading System on the Beef Cattle Industry: The Case of Canada." *Western Journal of Agricultural Economics, 11* (2), 184–194.

Coyle, W.T. (1983). *Japan's Feed-Livestock Economy: Prospects for the 1980's.* (Foreign Agricultural Economics Report No. 177). Washington, D.C.: United States Department of Agriculture, Economic Research Service.

Gillis, K.G., C.D. White, S.M. Ulmer, W.A. Kerr, and A.S. Kwaczek. (1985). "The Prospects for Export of Primal Beef Cuts to California." *Canadian Journal of Agricultural Economics, 33,* 171–194.

Goddard, E.W. (1983). *Models of the Beef Markets in Japan and South Korea.* (Occasional Paper No. 3). LaTrobe University, School of Agriculture.

Kerr, W.A. (1985). "The Livestock Industry and Canadian Economic Development." *Canadian Journal of Agricultural Economics, 32,* 64–104.

Kerr, W.A. and S.M. Ulmer. (1984). *The Importance of the Livestock and Meat Processing Industries to Western Growth.* (Discussion Paper No. 255). Ottawa: Economic Council of Canada.

Klein, B., R.G. Crawford and A.A. Alchian. (1978). "Vertical Integration, Appropriable Rents, and the Competitive Contracting Process." *Journal of Law and Economics, 21,* 297–326.

Longworth, J.W. (1983). *Beef in Japan.* St. Lucia: University of Queensland Press.

Ministry of Agriculture, Forestry and Fisheries (MAFF). (1980). "Long-Term Prospects for the Demand and Production of Agricultural Products." *Japan's Agricultural Review, 80,* 1–26.

Mori, H. and W.D. Gorman. (1985). "Issues, Facts, and Opportunities for Exports of US Beef to Japan." *Agribusiness, 1,* 211–218.

CHAPTER 13

AGRICULTURE IN A MORE MARKET ORIENTED ENVIRONMENT: LESSONS FROM NEW ZEALAND'S EXPERIENCES IN THE 1980s

T. Rayner

As a result of George Orwell's novel, the year 1984 was faced with some trepidation by those of literary and superstitious bent. In the event, we Winston Smiths were not faced with any significant growth of Big Brotherhood; the world appeared to continue largely unchanged through into 1985. However in New Zealand an unexpected, but dramatic, shift in economic policy took place. The trading environment for the whole economy, and for agriculture in particular, was altered almost beyond recognition.

This paper, based on a report to the World Bank (Rayner and Lattimore 1987), tells the story of this policy change. It falls into five parts. The background to the 1984 policy change is given first. Then the events of that year and the evolution of economic policy since are described. The impacts of these changes on the economy and particularly on the agricultural sector are examined next. Then there follows an attempt to judge the necessity for and the successes and shortcomings of the 1984 changes, to allow inferences to be drawn for other similar countries contemplating liberalization. The paper ends with some brief conclusions.

The Background to the Events of 1984

In order to understand the events of 1984 it is necessary to first learn something about the economic background of New Zealand. At the turn of the century the country had by far the highest per capita income in the world, as a result of it being the farm of England. With large areas (relative to the population) of fertile, temperate land, New Zealand was able to export agricultural commodities obtained with very high productivity. Dairy goods, frozen sheep meat, and wool were exchanged for manufactured commodities. Eighty to ninety per cent of the country's trade was with what was described as "home." (See Tables 1 and 2 for export and import destination 1900–1985.)

This relative wealth continued well into this century, and even in 1950 per capita income was only just below that of the United States. The concentration of trade was not quite so great, but even in the early 1960s almost two-thirds of exports continued to be to England. Relatively little product diversification had taken place.

It is risky to be reliant on a single market, and when there is a concentration on so few products, the risk is that much higher. In 1972 the United Kingdom joined the European Community (EC) and was slowly drawn, admittedly with protests and some small safeguards for New Zealand, into the morass of the Common Agricultural Policy (CAP). New Zealand's trade with England died a slow and lingering death, and currently both exports and imports have fallen to around 8 to 9 per cent of the totals. Meanwhile world trade in agricultural products was increasingly being distorted by protectionism in the EC and elsewhere; prices for New Zealand's traditional exports fell and their markets became ever more artificial. On top of this pain for exporters came the oil shocks of the 1970s.

The policy responses in New Zealand were interventionist, as had been the norm since at least the 1930s. Up until the mid-1970s, the policy for traditional agriculture was to preserve and protect it from the price and market changes taking place overseas. The protection of domestic manufacturing was continued and indeed increased as it became more inefficient because of its isolation from world competition. In the late 1970s a start was made on a series of so-called "Think Big" industrial projects, designed to produce exports or save imports, and built with considerable subsidy and protection. (see Gould, 1985; Bollard and Buckle, 1987). As a result New Zealand has a steel industry and an oil refinery which have negative market capital values, unless their products continue to be protected from imports. Worse still is the gas to gasoline plant, which is a world leader in technology, but will only break even if world oil prices were to more than double.

The fall in product prices for our efficient agricultural industry and the protection of our inefficient manufacturing industry inevitably led to economic stagnation. By 1984 our world ranking in per capita income had fallen to the mid-twenties. Successive governments' attempts to stimulate the economy in Keynesian fashion in time with the three yearly electoral cycle had led to inflation at levels close to 20 per cent. Unemployment and the balance of payments deficit both continued to rise.

In the mid-1970s Robert Muldoon became Prime Minister and prime interventionist. As the external situation worsened, his solution was to resolve the problems by increasing governmental control and interference. By the early 1980s this had

TABLE 1
DESTINATION OF EXPORTS (PER CENT OF TOTAL EXPORTS)

Year	United States	Canada	United Kingdom	Australia	Japan	Other
1900	4	0	81	9	0	6
1920	15	3	75	5	0	2
1930	5	6	81	3	0	5
1940	3	2	89	1	0	5
1950	10	2	67	2	1	18
1960	13	1	53	4	3	26
1970	16	4	36	8	10	26
1980	14	2	14	13	13	44
1981	13	2	13	14	13	45
1982	13	2	14	15	13	43
1983	15	2	13	12	14	44
1984	13	2	11	15	16	43
1985	15	2	9	16	15	43

Source: Report and Analysis of External Trade. Department of Statistics, Wellington.

TABLE 2
ORIGIN OF IMPORTS (PER CENT OF TOTAL IMPORTS)

Year	United States	Canada	United Kingdom	Australia	Japan	Other
1900	10	0	63	14	0	13
1920	18	4	48	11	2	17
1930	17	9	49	8	1	16
1940	12	6	47	17	2	16
1950	7	2	61	12	0	18
1960	10	3	44	18	3	22
1970	13	4	32	23	8	20
1980	12	2	14	21	12	39
1981	17	2	10	21	14	36
1982	16	2	9	22	17	34
1983	15	2	9	23	16	35
1984	14	2	9	23	21	31
1985	14	3	9	23	20	31

Source: Report and Analysis of External Trade, Department of Statistics, Wellington.

inevitably exacerbated the difficulties. Muldoon's only perceived solution was in the form of controls on wages, prices and interest rates. The cost of the totality of his policies was such that the fiscal deficit reached around 9 per cent of GDP by the 1983–84 financial year. At the same time the macho image of "Muldoon the Fixer" prevented him from making any significant devaluation of the fixed exchange rate.

This interventionist policy had been pursued by a national government, New Zealand's Conservatives. It had been twice endorsed by the populace, which re-elected Muldoon. The left wing Opposition, the Labour Party, meantime had proposed more interventions rather than less, but had spent most of their efforts in leadership struggles. These culminated in the selection of David Lange, a substantially overweight Auckland lawyer, as leader shortly before 1984.

In 1984 it became clear to the Muldoon Administration that the economy was deteriorating quickly enough that an early election was preferable to holding out to its full term in October. Hence a poll was called at short notice for 14 July. The policy manifesto of the Nationals was essentially for more of the same, while the Labour Party was in favor of change. However, the change proposed was certainly vague and seemed likely to be continuing, but different, interventionism.

Before moving to the events of July 1984 and the policies that followed, we must first describe the state of agricultural policy and of agriculture itself at that time. As suggested earlier, the aim of succeeding governments had been to protect the industry from the impacts of falling world prices for traditional export products. In addition, there were in place a considerable variety of agricultural subsidies whose economic justification was to compensate for the increased costs resulting from the protection of manufacturing industry.

The number of these interventions was very great (see Table 3 for a list of programs). There were subsidies for inputs, such as fertilizers and irrigation. There were subsidized loans for farmers at rates well below market levels. There were subsidized interest rates for the various Producer Boards' stabilization schemes. (Indeed the Dairy Board achieved a certain notoriety by using its privileged borrowing position to obtain cheap loans which were then invested outside the industry at higher rates.) The attempt to counter falling world meat prices involved low interest or taxation incentive schemes for land development and increase of livestock numbers. Special provisions for tax write-offs were allowed. Services provided through the Ministry of Agriculture were largely free. Most visibly of all, for the last few years of the Muldoon Administration a system of Supplementary Minimum Prices (SMPs) was introduced as a direct production subsidy to traditional farming.

While it can be argued that there was a need to compensate farmers for the economic hardships their industry was undergoing, the methods of protection that were used were far from satisfactory. In particular, protection methods concentrated on

TABLE 3

MAJOR INTERVENTIONS IN NEW ZEALAND AGRICULTURE 1930–1981

Type	Name	When Introduced	Present Status and Date
CREDIT			
	Subsidized Purchase Credit	1930	Interest rates increased	1984
	Subsidized Development Credit	1960	Interest rates increased	1984
	Livestock Incentive Scheme	1976	Targets considered met	1985
	Land Development Encouragement	1978	Targets considered met	1985
	Vendor Finance Scheme	1979	Abolished	1984
	Rural Bank Loans Account	–	Privatized	1987
	Productive Development Loans	1984	Cancelled	1984
INPUTS			
	Subsidized Transport of Fertilizer	1965	Abolished	1984
	Subsidized Price of Fertilizer	1970	Abolished	1986
	Subsidized Weed Control	1975	Abolished	1984
	Subsidized Irrigation and Water Structures	1973	Reduced	1984
TAXATION			
	First Year Depreciation	–	Continues	1986
	Development Write-off	1965	Abolished	1986
	Standard Values Stock System	1965	Move to market values	1986
	Income Equalization	1965	Continues	1986
	Investment Allowance	1976	Abolished	1984
	Export Incentives	1963	Phased out	1985–1990
	$10,000 Spreading Restriction	1976	Abolished (not for horticulture)	
	10 Year Rule for Development Write-off	1976	Abolished	1985
SERVICES			
	Research	–	Cost recovery	1985
	Advisory	–	Cost recovery	1985
	Inspectorial	–	Cost recovery	1984

TABLE 3 (Continued)
MAJOR INTERVENTIONS IN NEW ZEALAND AGRICULTURE 1930–1981

Type	Name	When Introduced	Present Status and Date	
LAND TENURE				
	Land Aggregation	1952 legislation	Relaxed	1985
	Overseas Ownership	1952 legislation	Relaxed	1985
MARKETING				
	Price Smoothing Schemes			
	Wool	1976	Increased interest on deficits	1985
	Meat	1976	Increased interest on deficits	1985
	Dairy	1938	Increased interest on deficits	1985
	Trading Accounts			
	Wool	1976	Use of reserves and privatization	–
	Meat	1981	Use of reserves and privatization	–
	Dairy	1954	Use of reserves and privatization and subordinated loan	1983
	Supplementary Minimum Prices			
	Wool	1978	Abolished	1983
	Meat	1978	Abolished	1984
	Dairy	1978	Abolished	1983
	Wheat Board	1965	Deregulation	1983
	Milk Board	1967	Deregulation	1986
	Pork Board	1974	Reformed	1982
	Egg Board	1980	Deregulation	1986

Source: Johnson (1986).

traditional products and hence worked against the diversification of land use that was required. Moreover, the policies involved either considerably increased government expenditure or reduced revenue. Hence they led to a marked deterioration of the fiscal deficit. In addition, the policies were causing politico-economic reactions overseas. For example, in 1985 the United States imposed countervailing duties on the meat from New Zealand sheep. For this latter reason, the removal of the most visible of these policies, SMPs, was announced before the 1984 election.

Because of these policies, the economic situation of farmers was preserved, in the sense that their incomes generally stagnated, rather than suffering the substantial decline that would otherwise have resulted from the declining terms of trade for their products. Unfortunately this stagnation of incomes, or at best slow growth, was not reflected in land values. The combination of high rates of inflation, the perceived security of land as an investment, the tax breaks for farmers and the interest rate concessions, together caused land prices to increase at rates far faster than inflation and to a level that could not be justified by earnings (See Figure 1). In the early 1980s new entrants to farming were paying inflated prices for land to produce commodities that barely made interest payments possible, even though these were well below market rates and product prices were above world prices. The hope and expectation was that, as in the past, inflation would both ease the payments burden and lead to capital gains. With negative real interest rates of 10–15 per cent for farmers and tax breaks as well, it was not surprising that land prices were forced up.

FIGURE 1
SHEEP AND BEEF FARM INCOMES AND FARM LAND SALE PRICES

(Money Terms, 1975-76 = 1,000)

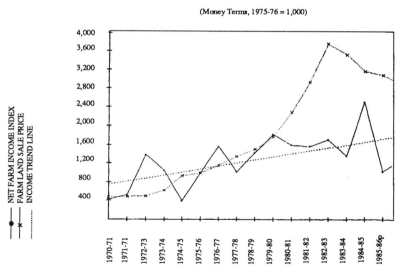

p = provisional net farm income

With the 1984 election approaching, the New Zealand Association of Farmers gave its policy prescription to the incoming government for a total and thorough freeing up of the whole economy, including agriculture. It is ironic that this policy prescription, which was certainly not echoed in the manifestos of either of the two main parties, turned out to be the one that was essentially followed by the new government after the election. The irony is made the more bitter because it was the farmers, particularly new entrants, that were to suffer the greatest adjustment costs arising from the new policy of liberalization.

The Policy Changes After July 1984

On 14 July 1984, the electorate rejected the policies of the Muldoon Administration and put the Lange Labour Government into power with a substantial majority; and the new Government was immediately thrown into a major financial crisis, as a result of a substantial run on the currency. The crisis was resolved over a period of three days by the decision to devalue the New Zealand dollar by 20 per cent. However, it was at this precise point that the normal New Zealand interventionist approach to problem solving suddenly disappeared. During these three days of crisis the new Finance Minister, Roger Douglas, was somehow able to gain ascendancy in the Cabinet and the support of Lange. Douglas had long been a market liberal and indeed had been chastised in the past, while his party was in opposition, for proposing market-oriented policies. In the situation of currency crisis and uncertainty he was the person who knew what he wanted to do, and he was able to seize the initiative. Within twelve months the economic policy rules of decades had been turned around.

Initially the financial sector was totally liberalized, both internally and externally. Controls on prices and wages were removed. Controls over interest rates were also removed; both individuals and firms were allowed to move as much money as they wanted in and out of the country. The exchange rate was floated in early 1985 and appears to have had a perfectly clean float ever since. The tax system was totally reorganized, with the introduction of a Value Added Tax, the dropping of the top marginal income tax rate from 66 per cent to 48 per cent and to 25 per cent by late 1980. Business perks were taxed at the same rate as income. The double taxation of companies' distributed profits was stopped. Company taxation was initially set at the same rate as income tax and is due to fall below 20 per cent. The fiscal deficit was reduced substantially and is supposed to move to a surplus in 1988, according to some measures. Privatization of government departments has progressed rapidly, while those remaining in the government have become more market oriented. Currently the aim is to apply these same more-market principles to the social services.

The agricultural sector received its own share of the new broom treatment in the budget of November 1984. Input subsidies were axed almost at once. Interest rate concessions on new loans were removed and on old loans phased out; the latter potentially meant increases from a 5 per cent level to 15 per cent over a few years.

Services such as research work and farm advice, which had been provided for free, were now to carry a charge. Interest rate concessions for the Producer Boards were removed. The removal of Supplementary Minimum Prices was confirmed. The various tax concessions were removed or reduced. The giving of incentives for development was stopped. (A more detailed list of the changes affecting agriculture is given in Table 3.) In short, the government moved out of all industry assistance, which had mainly been directed at agriculture. Farmers suddenly found themselves in a totally new and unexpected market environment, even though this was what their leaders had been requesting.

Before moving to a description of how agriculture and the whole economy responded to these changes it is necessary to mention two significant policy inconsistencies. First, the born-again belief in the virtues of the market was not applied to. Instead, the position of the unions was initially strengthened. However, major changes have since taken place that have improved the workings of the market, even though these changes were delayed when compared with what happened elsewhere in the economy. The second policy failure was the slowness in the reduction of protection for manufacturing. There was no instance here of a dramatically fast policy turnaround, as there had been with agriculture. Trade liberalization has taken place, however. Import quotas have been largely phased out through a tendering process. Tariffs on commodities produced in New Zealand have been reduced for each of the past two years by small amounts. (Although small, these decreases were the first in New Zealand's postwar history.) The plan is for a further 50 per cent reduction in these tariffs over the next five years. Tariffs on goods not produced in New Zealand have been eliminated.

The slowness of reform in trade liberalization and the labor markets has been important, the former being particularly significant for agriculture. The reasons for this will be explained after the responses of the New Zealand economy and agriculture in particular have been examined.

The Performance of the Economy and Agriculture Since 1984

Given the shocks administered to the New Zealand economy since 1984 it might be thought that it would by now be in severe trauma. Such is not the case. On the other hand there is no hard evidence that the country has embarked on a new and prosperous future. There are appearances of success and failure at both the macro and micro levels. The ease with which the economy has been able to adjust to these kinds of shocks has been a function of the mobility of factors of production and the entrepreneurial attitude of individuals.

Looking first at the usual measures of macro performance, real GDP has tended to stagnate, as it has for many years. However there has not been any massive downturn, as some were predicting, and indeed the expected minor cyclical downturn was delayed by one or two years (see Table 4 for short-term economic indicators 1983–1988). Because the labor supply has been growing stagnant GDP has meant growing unemployment, although this is still not high by world standards. Inflation has followed a checkered path, first bouncing up following the removal of price controls, then falling, only to rise again with imposition of the VAT. By 1988 it had fallen to single figures, which is the lowest inflation has been in New Zealand for a decade, apart from the period when price controls were in place. The trade balance has improved substantially, but more due to a fall in imports rather than to a rise in exports.

TABLE 4
SUMMARY OF SHORT-TERM ECONOMIC INDICATORS

	1983–84	1984–85	1985–86	1986–87	1987–88
% Change in Real GDP	+2.0	+7.0	+0.9	+2.0(e)	-1.0(e)
% Change in CPI	+3.5	+13.4	+13.0	+18.3	+9.0
Unemployment Rate*	N/A	3.8	4.2	4.1	5.0
Trade Balance as % of GDP	-3.8	-7.3	-7.1	-3.8(e)	-3.0(e)

(e) = Estimated
* As measured in the Household Labour Force Survey, which was only available from 1984–85.

Source: New Zealand Institute of Economic Research, Monthly Report to Executives, Various.

At the micro level the effects of the economic liberalization have yet to be quantified and analyzed. Hence all that can be reported are impressions of change. The initial major growth area was in the financial sector, which had been one of the most restricted before July 1984. However, there may have in fact been an over-expansion here, which was corrected following the stock market crash of October 1987. This was more severe than in almost any other country. There has been some growth in the manufacturing industries, although this has yet to be quantified. Undoubtedly, however, the main signs of adjustment in manufacturing have been the closures of firms in response to increased competition from imports. In a real sense this is a positive sign of the effects of the policy shifts, since these firms were typically very inefficient by world standards. Inevitably, however, the media and general public have focused on the resulting loss of employment, rather than the gains to the consumer.

What is clear is that there is as yet no obvious sign of the strong, export-led growth in the economy which was hoped would occur to pay for the growth in imports. Part of the reason for this is that traditional agriculture, which had dominated exports, received particularly harsh treatment under the reforms. More generally, the lack of export-led growth stemmed from changes in the real exchange rate.

The freeing of the capital market, coupled with initially high fiscal deficits, led to high real interest rates and an attraction of overseas capital. This attraction was strengthened by the good international press that the economic reforms were receiving. The result of these developments was that the nominal value of the New Zealand dollar rose following its float. In addition, the high relative rate of inflation meant that the real value of the currency rose even more. At present this real value is around 30 per cent above its post-devaluation level. The competitive position of the tradeable goods sector has been damaged as a result, leading to a lack of profitability of exports and an increase in the pressures placed on the domestic import competing industries.

It has been suggested (*Economist*, 1988) that New Zealand pursued its liberalization policies precisely the wrong way around—that the government should first have liberalized the labor markets and reduced the fiscal deficit; only then should the foreign capital markets have been liberalized. However, such a policy prescription ignores political reality. Labor markets are the most difficult ones to liberalize, and to achieve this end it is necessary first to put pressure on them. One way of doing this is through trade liberalization. Again, perhaps the fiscal deficit should have been reduced faster, but here too it is difficult to see politically how the seven percent could have had a faster reduction to its current low level. In any case, since the electorate was sufficiently supportive of the policy package, despite any extra adjustment costs, that they re-elected the Labour Government for another three year term in August 1987, there will be time enough for the benefits of the policies to emerge.

The situation of agriculture in this new environment is of particular interest. The removal of the various subsidies outlined earlier was initially compensated for by the 20 per cent devaluation of July 1984. Hence farmers were not too disturbed in the first year about the new policies. However as the subsidies were stripped away, as costs increased with inflation, and as the exchange rate floated up, the pressures on traditional agriculture mounted. Average farm incomes fell and for some classes became negative for a period. While these changes were only serious for marginal or inefficient farmers, the effect of the substantial increases in interest rates was particularly devastating for the group that had bought new property, or financed capital expenditures through loans, during the land price boom years of the early 1980s.

While these farmers had just been able to make ends meet in the climate of the early 1980s, they simply could not survive the various impacts of the new economic environment. Matters were made worse by the fact that the speculative bubble in land prices burst following the 1984 changes. Increasing numbers of farmers, who had borrowed heavily to finance land or improvement expenditures, reached a situation of not only holding negative equity in their property, but with interest payments that they could not hope to meet from farm income. There were fears of large scale mortgagee sales causing land prices to plummet.

As the pressure on farmers rose, their protests increased. The media put particular emphasis on the undoubted plight of the young entrants to the industry who had borrowed heavily in the early 1980s to buy their first farm. They typically had young families and were in danger of losing their savings, their home and their job. The government stood firm against these protests and did not reinstate subsidies or supports; their one major action was to set up creditors' meetings which had the power to jointly decrease the value of loans, although not the annual payments due, if a farmer was seen as being viable.

But as time has passed the protests have decreased. New Zealand farmers demonstrated their entrepreneurial ability to react to the new environment by altering their input and output plans. Record prices for wool, despite the overvalued dollar, also eased some of the stress. The refinancing meetings were able to reduce the intolerable pressures on some farmers. While there have been reductions in farm output and major falls in farm income, there has not been the mass exodus from the industry that was initially predicted, nor has there been the expected flood of mortgagee sales.

There has also been some increase in the size of holdings and there is no doubt that the changes have increased the speed of exit from the industry of the inefficient marginal farmers. There has certainly been a decrease in the overuse of subsidized fertilizer and irrigation, and a reduction in the over-capitalization of properties through excessive holdings of machinery and buildings. In addition, there has been a significant increase in the diversification of land use in many directions. (These alternative uses had not previously been subsidized to the same extent as traditional pastoral agriculture.)

In short, while some individuals did suffer severely, the industry as a whole demonstrated its ability to adjust to change in ways that were economically desirable. Interestingly, throughout the period since 1984, the farmers' leaders have continued to support the basic policy thrust that has been implemented rather than seeking a return to subsidization. Their complaint has been chiefly that the more-market approach was not followed far enough in the labor market or in freeing imports.

The high real value of the dollar discussed above has clearly caused the costs of adjustment for farmers to be greater than would otherwise have been the case.

Moreover, the continued protection of manufacturing caused a double dose of pain through the increased costs of inputs and the higher value of the currency to which it led. In addition, the imperfections in the labor markets saw wage and salary earners gaining significant nominal increases in their remuneration, despite high unemployment, at times when farmers were having to put up with substantial nominal decreases in their incomes.

An Evaluation of the Reforms, with Inferences for Others

There is a surprising degree of unanimity amongst economic analysts that the economic reforms instituted from 1984 onwards were undertaken very rapidly, yet at the same time thoroughly and largely in a consistent fashion. This combination of speed and economic soundness is a marked contrast to previous experience of economic policy in New Zealand, where ad hoc macro-and micro-meddling has been much more the pattern. These kinds of reactive interventionist policies have been the past norm in many countries including Canada, and continue to be used heavily, despite the efforts of Mrs. Thatcher in Britain to establish an alternative proactive approach.

The New Zealand experiment is in sufficiently strong contrast with what occurs in other countries as to ask whether it serves as a useful guide to policy from which inferences can be drawn. The following raises some of the issues that might be considered.

The Speed of Reform

Given that a consistent reform strategy is going to be undertaken, the question then becomes one of how rapidly to implement it. This question needs to be addressed from both an economic and a political standpoint. It would appear likely that the longer the period of time allowed for adjustment the more it is possible for those involved to plan in advance and so minimize adjustment costs. However, any delay also means that the benefits of the new policy are put off further into the future. In addition, it is not clear that adjustment costs will necessarily be lower over a longer time horizon. If the New Zealand climate is inappropriate to grow hard grained wheats, there is little advantage in continuing to protect domestic wheat growers from competition from those countries with better growing conditions, and so putting off the inevitable diversification that the New Zealand growers will have to make in the long run. Similarly, Canadian grape growers may not take action to pull out their inappropriate varieties and replant until they are forced to by the market.

In any case the costs of adjustment to a new policy are almost certain to be lower than expected. A recent study by the World Bank (Papageorgiou et al., 1986) on the experiences of trade liberalization in nineteen countries found that adjustment costs appeared to be very low and indeed often impossible to discover, while the advance expectations about trade liberalization were that they would be high. The same study concluded that in the case of every country in the study, whatever the pace of reform, it could and should have been even faster.

The second question concerning the speed of reform is political. Regardless of the speed of implementation, it is necessary for a policy to be in place long enough for the benefits to be perceived to exceed any adjustment costs. Moreover, it has to be remembered that the latter loom larger in anticipation than in actuality. Thus New Zealand introduced a Value Added Tax amidst great concern about its complexity and costs. Yet within a year the Opposition was the subject of widespread derision among farmers, as well as the rest of the business community, for saying that they would replace it with a simpler expenditure tax. In New Zealand the three-year electoral cycle really necessitated rapid action, with little lead in time before new policies were introduced; speed was the only way to get a consistent package fully implemented.

The Balance of Reform

Another of the lessons from the New Zealand experience is the desirability of ensuring that reforms across the various sectors of the economy are kept in balance. As has been explained here, the removal of assistance to agriculture has gone faster than the removal of protection from the manufacturing industry. As a result agriculture has had to bear increased adjustment costs. No sector of the economy, even agriculture, has the right to be preserved by the rest of the population if it is not economically viable, yet at the same time it is inefficient for any sector to bear greater adjustment costs than are required. Due to the imbalance of reforms in New Zealand, agriculture has, since 1984, been under financial pressure, and have adjusted by shrinking relative to the import competing sector. Once imports have been fully liberalized, the effects on farmers costs and on the exchange rate will mean that the farming sector can be expected to expand again relative to the import competing industries. This double adjustment is wasteful.

The Order of Reform

The question of the optimal order of reforms is only of relevance when an across-the-whole-economy policy is being implemented. New Zealand has been criticized on its ordering of reforms; the suggestion is that those markets where prices take longer to adjust, such as the labor market, should be liberalized first, while markets where prices can adjust rapidly, such as finance markets, should be liberalized last. New Zealand adopted the reverse ordering, and so is supposedly suffering higher adjustment costs as a result of an overvalued exchange rate.

The immediate response to this criticism is that it ignores political realities. The markets where prices take longer to adjust are often precisely those, like the labor market, where it is most difficult to institute a market dominated system. As a result it is necessary to exert greater pressure in these areas to obtain reform. Hence it may be politically necessary to move first on the easier markets in order to build up the economic pressures to force change in the difficult markets.

There are also some economic points to be made. In the first place, an overvalued currency conveys advantages to the economy, in terms of lower domestic prices, as well as disadvantages. Moreover the influx of capital which causes any overvaluation is presumably of benefit. Finally, we do not really know enough about the behavior of floating exchange rates to be certain when a currency actually is overvalued. One possible scenario is that the inflow of capital and the new economic climate have caused a sufficient change in the New Zealand economy that the current exchange rate is at a long-term equilibrium level. If so, farmers will have to permanently adjust to their new situation, which would be possible for the larger and more efficient units.

Part of what is at issue here is the specific question of whether the New Zealand dollar is currently overvalued. However, the more general question concerns the efficiency of international capital markets. How likely is it that overseas investors will continue to put money into another country, without covering against exchange risk, when that currency is believed to be overvalued? The answer must be that in the long run it is not possible for the currency to remain over-, or under-, valued. However it is clear from experience in a number of countries that such disequilibrium values can continue for a number of years. They can make the short run costs of economic reform substantially greater.

Should The Losers Be Compensated Or Their Adjustment Costs Be Met?

A common cry in New Zealand during the policy reversal has been that those groups who have lost from the reforms should be compensated for their losses, or that their costs of adjustment should be met. For example, farmers suddenly facing big increases in interest charges demanded compensation. There may seem to be some justification for such requests; however, there are two problems involved. In the first place, whenever the government takes any policy initiative there will usually be both losers and winners. Should the government previously have compensated the non-farming population whose interest charges were increased because of the diversion of low interest funds to farmers? Secondly, if equity suggests that losers from a policy change should be compensated, then presumably the same principle would suggest that winners should be taxed—an unpopular suggestion.

In any event, the New Zealand Government has been fairly hard-headed in its refusal to compensate losers. There have been two exceptions though, inconsistent with the general policy stance. First, following reduction in protection against Australian wines, New Zealand grape growers were given a subsidy to replace their inappropriate varieties with ones that the market wanted. The second exception was the willingness of the government to write down loans to farmers in order to prevent them having to leave the land. (This might have been justified financially, in that a series of mortgagee sales would in fact have prevented the government from getting the full value of its loans back in any case.) But the general difficulty with this kind of ad hoc compensation is the danger that it will set precedents.

How Long Can We Wait for Reform of World Agricultural Trade?

One of the problems that New Zealand has faced over the period since the 1970s is one that Canada faces today. This is the question of how long a government should continue to support its farmers in the expectation that the current low world prices for agriculture goods will rise, following the reform of world agricultural policies. New Zealand was hit very hard by England's entry into the EC and the subsequent effects of the CAP on world trade. For many years we have attempted to preserve our agricultural sector for the day when freer trade in temperate agricultural goods is restored. The reforms of 1984 essentially marked the end of that policy. The implicit decision was made that the economy had to respond to the market of the day and to its own predictions about the future. At the same time, the move towards bilateral free trade with Australia has been pursued as a second best option to the overall freeing of world trade.

Certainly New Zealand has been working hard with Canada through the Cairns Group to try to achieve as great a liberalization as possible for agriculture in the current Uruguay Round of the GATT. It would be very much to both our advantages, given the resources of our countries, if real progress were made. However, while New Zealand's fingers are crossed, the government is taking no other more concrete action taken to preserve those industries that will become highly competitive again in the unlikely event that the CAP is demolished. How long should Canada wait for trade reform while continuing to subsidize its agriculture?

Conclusion

For New Zealand, 1984 marked a dramatic turning point in the trading environment for the whole economy, and in particular for agriculture. The industry was thrown from a highly interventionist situation into what has been termed a "more-market" environment. There is no question in anybody's mind that there have been very substantial adjustment costs for farmers as a result. There have certainly been protests. Yet there is also little doubt that the industry has gained in terms of long-term efficiency, and farming leaders have steadfastly approved the general policy thrust. Their complaint has been that the full market philosophy has not yet been applied equally across all sectors. They are impatient, as are many economists, to see the completion of every aspect of the policy transformation, even though so much has been achieved in the past four years. A transformation in such a short period would have seemed quite unbelievable in the New Zealand of the 1970s and early 1980s.

What can be concluded from the New Zealand example? Admittedly the country is in a much healthier economic position than it was in 1984. This certainly decreases the pressures for radical reform, but does not necessarily decrease the potential benefits to be made. Enough can be concluded about the interventions in a good part of the land use and other sectors to believe that the policy of this economy is closer to the pre-1984 New Zealand than the market-led post-1984 model. Hence it would appear that there is still plenty of room for reform. Some of that reform will be forced by the GATT and Canada's Free Trade Agreement with the United States. Yet there are many "safeguards" left in place under the latter agreement, and a better approach might be a faster one. At the very least it provides an exciting environment for the participants; it turns out that they are more resilient and adaptable than they claim in advance.

REFERENCES

Bollard, Alan and Robert Buckle (Eds.). (1987). *Economic Liberalization in New Zealand*. Wellington, N.Z.: Allen and Unwin.

"Free markets: out of order." (1988, February 27). *Economist*.

Gould, John. (1982). *The Rake's progress? The New Zealand Economy Since 1945*. Auckland, N.Z.: Hodder and Stoughton.

Hawke, B.R. (1985). *The Making of New Zealand: An Economic History*. London, England: Cambridge University Press.

Johnson, R.W.M. (1986, July). *Livestock and Feed Policy in New Zealand: 1975 to the Present*. Paper presented at the Workshop on Livestock and Feed Grain Policies in the Pacific Basin.

Papageorgiou, D., M. Michaely and A.M. Choksi. (1986). *The Phasing of a Trade Liberalization Policy: Preliminary Evidence*. Paper presented at the Annual Meetings of the American Economic Association, New Orleans, Louisiana.

Rayner, A.C. and R.G. Lattimore. (1987). *The Timing and Phasing of a Trade Liberalization Policy: The Case of New Zealand*. Report to the World Bank.

A WORD ABOUT THE AUTHORS

Carter, Colin
Dr. Carter is an Associate Professor in the Department of Agricultural Economics at the University of California, Davis, California.

Chase Wilde, Linda
Dr. Chase Wilde is an Assistant Professor in the Department of Rural Economy at the University of Alberta, Edmonton, Alberta.

Cullen, Susan
Ms. Cullen is a recent graduate of the Department of Economics, Queen's University, Kingston, Ontario, and is currently employed as an economist with the Government of Canada.

Graham, John
Dr. Graham is an Associate Professor in the Department of Agricultural Economics at the University of British Columbia, Vancouver, British Columbia.

Kerr, William
Dr. Kerr is a Professor in the Department of Economics at the University of Calgary, Calgary, Alberta.

Klein, Kurt
Dr. Klein is a Professor in the Department of Economics at the University of Lethbridge, Lethbridge, Alberta.

Lermer, George
Dr. Lermer is a Professor and the Dean of the Faculty of Management at the University of Lethbridge, Lethbridge, Alberta.

MacGregor, Robert
Mr. MacGregor is a research economist, Policy Branch, Agriculture Canada, Ottawa, Ontario.

Martin, Larry
Dr. Martin is a Professor and the Head of the Department of Agricultural Economics and Extension Education at the University of Guelph, Guelph, Ontario. He is also a consultant on agricultural marketing and policy.

McGivern, Dennis
Mr. McGivern is a recent graduate of the Department of Economics, University of Calgary, Calgary, Alberta, and is currently employed as a economist with XL Food Systems, Calgary, Alberta.

Meilke, Karl	Dr. Meilke is a Professor in the Department of Agricultural Economics and Extension Education at the University of Guelph, Guelph, Ontario.
Rayner, Tony	The late Professor Rayner was a Professor in the Department of Agricultural Economics and Marketing at Lincoln College, University College of Agriculture, Canterbury, New Zealand.
Richter, Joseph	Dr. Richter is a Professor Emeritus in the Department of Rural Economy at the University of Alberta, Edmonton, Alberta.
Schmitz, Andrew	Dr. Schmitz is a Professor in the Department of Agricultural Economics at the University of California, Berkeley, California. He was the Van Vliet Professor of Agricultural Economics, University of Saskatchewan, Saskatoon, Saskatchewan, 1986–88.
Sigurdson, Dale	Mr. Sigurdson is a Policy Economist with Saskatchewan Agriculture, Regina, Saskatchewan.
Stern, Robert	Mr. Stern is in the Department of Agricultural Economics at the University of California, Berkeley, California.
van Duren, Erna	Ms. van Duren is a Graduate Research Assistant in the Department of Agricultural Economics and Extension Education at the Univesity of Guelph, Guelph, Ontario. She specializes in international trade and policy.
Veeman, Michelle	Dr. Veeman is a Professor in the Department of Rural Economy at the University of Alberta, Edmonton, Alberta.
Veeman, Terry	Dr. Veeman is a Joint Professor in the Departments of Rural Economy and Economics at the University of Alberta, Edmonton, Alberta.
Webber, Christopher	Mr. Webber is a Research Economist, Research Branch, Agriculture Canada, Lethbridge, Alberta.